UNIVERSITY OF LONDON
INSTITUTE OF COMMONWEALTH STUDIES

*

COMMONWEALTH PAPERS

General Editor
PROFESSOR W. H. MORRIS-JONES

22

THE COLONIAL OFFICE, WAR,
AND DEVELOPMENT POLICY:

*Organisation and the Planning of A
Metropolitan Initiative, 1939-1945*

THE COLONIAL OFFICE, WAR, AND DEVELOPMENT POLICY

*

Organisation and the Planning of A Metropolitan Initiative, 1939-1945

BY

J. M. LEE

University of Bristol

AND

MARTIN PETTER

McGill University

PUBLISHED FOR THE
INSTITUTE OF COMMONWEALTH STUDIES
BY MAURICE TEMPLE SMITH

First published in Great Britain 1982
by Maurice Temple Smith Limited
Gloucester Mansions, Cambridge Circus,
London WC2H 8HD

Copyright © University of London 1982

ISBN 0 85117 221 0

Typeset by Tata Press Ltd, India

Reproduced from copy supplied,
printed and bound in Great Britain
by Billing and Sons Limited,
Guildford, London, Oxford, Worcester

CONTENTS

CONCLUSION

FIGURES AND TABLE

FOREWORD

THE Institute of Commonwealth Studies endeavours to stimulate research within a Commonwealth framework in the fields of modern history, politics, and international relations. To this end it not only requires that its own academic staff engage in research, but also seek to facilitate and encourage work by other scholars — through the services of its Library, provision of working accommodation, sponsorship of research grant applications, and so on. In order that research findings may be presented and critically discussed, it organises scholarly conferences and maintains a series of regular seminar programmes. Finally, the results of research have to be made available and for that reason the Institute has sustained a series of publications under the title, *Commonwealth Papers*, as well as a more modestly presented series of *Collected Seminar Papers*.

The present volume in the *Commonwealth Papers* series is the result of work undertaken, with the help of a grant from the Nuffield Foundation, by Professor J. M. Lee during his period on the Institute staff in collaboration with Dr Martin Petter, now of McGill University. Their examination of the role of the Colonial Office during the war years is of particular interest to Commonwealth studies; it deals with a period of exceptional change in the scope of colonial administration and prepares the way for the paradoxical final period of colonial rule in which increased activity and decolonisation went side by side. At the same time the book can claim even wider significance by virtue of its exploration of both the compulsions of Britain's wartime difficulties and the roots of what was to become development administration. Based on the most careful study of official materials, the book offers an original interpretation which is a contribution to administrative as well as colonial history.

W. H. MORRIS-JONES

AUTHORS' PREFACE

WE would like to thank the Trustees of the Nuffield Foundation for financing our partnership. Two people can get through the hundreds of files at the Public Records Office which the subject demands much more easily than a single worker, and can spur each other on. We are particularly grateful to the Foundation for showing their confidence in us when we were obliged to change our plans. It had originally been intended to concentrate on the process of policy-making in a specific subject — education — now largely relegated to references in Chapter 5. When we discovered that the Education Adviser's archives were unlikely to be available in the time we had anticipated we transferred from a subject which has a large market — the teacher-training institutes of the Commonwealth — to one which has a narrower appeal — the appreciation of a department of state. Parkinson's *The Colonial Office from Within* (1947) provided the 'human background'; Shuckburgh's official history (1949), although never published, gave 'the facts' on the Second World War. What was missing was any attempt to show the interplay of personalities, ideas, and institutions.

We are particularly grateful to those who read our first draft and gave us the benefit of their advice: Sir Sydney Caine, Dr Stephen Constantine, Professor W. H. Morris-Jones, Dr K. E. Robinson, and the late Professor Eric Stokes. We have done our best to meet their criticisms. We are also grateful to McGill University for financing Martin Petter's visit to London in 1979. We would like to thank Mrs Caroline Cotterrell and Miss Sonja Jansen for their skill as typists in reading and reproducing our text.

JML
MEP

THE COLONIAL OFFICE: ORGANISATION CHARTS, 1928-1958

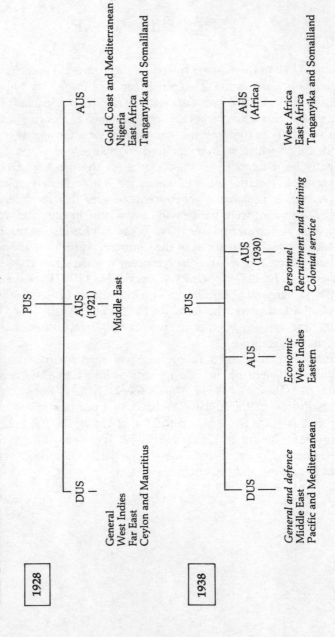

1928

PUS

DUS — AUS (1921) — AUS

Under DUS:
General
West Indies
Far East
Ceylon and Mauritius

Under AUS (1921):
Middle East

Under AUS:
Gold Coast and Mediterranean
Nigeria
East Africa
Tanganyika and Somaliland

1938

PUS

DUS — AUS — AUS (1930) — AUS (Africa)

Under DUS:
General and defence
Middle East
Pacific and Mediterranean

Under AUS:
Economic
West Indies
Eastern

Under AUS (1930):
Personnel
Recruitment and training
Colonial service

Under AUS (Africa):
West Africa
East Africa
Tanganyika and Somaliland

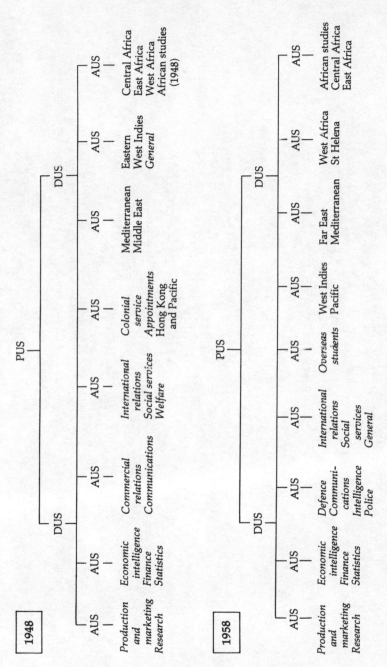

1948

PUS

DUS

AUS — Production and marketing / Research

AUS — Economic intelligence / Finance / Statistics

AUS — Commercial relations / Communications

AUS — *International relations* / *Social services* / *Welfare*

AUS — *Colonial service Appointments* / Hong Kong and Pacific

AUS — Mediterranean / Middle East

DUS

AUS — Eastern / West Indies / *General*

AUS — Central Africa / East Africa / West Africa / African studies (1948)

1958

PUS

DUS

AUS — *Production and marketing* / *Research*

AUS — *Economic intelligence* / *Finance* / *Statistics*

AUS — Defence / Communications / Intelligence / Police

AUS — *International relations* / *Social services* / *General*

AUS — *Overseas students*

AUS — West Indies / Pacific

DUS

AUS — Far East / Mediterranean

AUS — West Africa / St Helena

AUS — African studies / Central Africa / East Africa

In 1948 and 1958 there were also Information and Establishments Divisions reporting directly to the PUS. 'Subject Departments' are shown in italics.

INTRODUCTION

WHAT effects did the experience of war administration have on the organisation of the Colonial Office and the formulation of colonial policy? How far were metropolitan assumptions modified about what could be done in London for the colonies, after the resources of the whole Empire had been mobilised to support the Allies against the Axis powers? In the minds of the ministers and senior officials concerned, what kind of cross-fertilisation took place between their conceptions of the administrative machinery and their reflections on war management?

Such questions call for a special understanding of the way in which policies can change their meaning according to the context in which they are promulgated. Any policy is always something more than a declaration of interest or a programme of objectives because it can only be translated into practice if it has been conceived in relation to the means available. Assumptions about the forms of implementation have to be built into any definition of what can be pursued. These assumptions are often much more important in determining the outcome than the formal procedures employed. A great deal of driving force in government comes from the preconceptions of appropriate action which fill the minds of those responsible. To account for changes in the way they think is to make some contribution towards explaining the lessons of experience.

The administration of the British Empire was profoundly affected by the Allied war effort, particularly in the organisation of production and supply which brought a large proportion of trade and manufacture under defence regulations. The Allies discussed 'war aims' in a manner which altered the climate of opinion among the colonial peoples. Nothing in 1945 could quite be the same as in 1939 in a whole range of subjects coming under the general rubric of British colonial policy. Commodity agreements and bulk purchases of food supplies affected trade; defence agreements and strategic reserves influenced the disposition of resources; support for the armed services changed conceptions of social welfare.

But the war did not compel the British government to make any

13

formal changes in the constitutional structure of the Empire. The authority of the Secretary of State for the Colonies continued to be based on the sovereignty of the Crown and the conventions of Cabinet government in the British Parliament. This Minister was held responsible to the House of Commons, and at the same time advised the Crown on relationships between the British government and more than fifty territorial governments at different stages of constitutional development. The Empire was a complicated system of central-local relations. Unlike the system of local government in the United Kingdom, there was no common body of statute law which applied to all authorities. Each colony had its own constitution and its own means of making law. The Secretary of State legitimised the action of colonial governments by signifying the Crown's approval. All the powers of the Colonial Office stemmed from the basic constitutional fact that the colonies were subject to the Crown, not to the British Parliament. The relationships between the Crown and the colonies lay largely within the scope of the royal prerogative. The reference of business to the House of Commons was often a matter of courtesy.

The management of war in the context of a fairly immutable constitutional structure is therefore an interesting field for the study of changing preconceptions among the policy-makers. The Colonial Office — the body of official advisers to the Secretary of State on how the Crown's authority should be deployed — was *par excellence* a department in which changes of policy could be effected by giving fresh meanings to established machinery. The centre's conception of central-local relationships was a major element in determining what was done.

All the questions that can be asked about metropolitan assumptions about colonial policy under the impact of war are both technically difficult to answer and dangerously emotive to handle. But they cannot be ignored. The Second World War manifestly transformed the context of Colonial Office work.[1] Even if it seems easier to gather evidence of changes in the colonies themselves, it is still important to explore what happened in London. The task of exploration raises difficult questions precisely because the evidence of changes in assumptions is elusive. They have to be deduced from both what the principal participants wrote and how they acted. Ministers and civil servants do not normally write down the principles on which they are acting. The files they leave behind can never be allowed 'to speak for themselves' because they need to be read in the

14

context of contemporary opinion. Nor is it satisfactory to try to divide the evidence into questions of formulation, questions of application, and the consequences of action taken. It is rare to be able to abstract the evidence of a single problem — how it was conceived — and to set the conception against the implementation and its consequences. Each set of formulations takes on different meanings as action taken by others impinges on a department's line of thinking; each apparent implementation of a decision acquires the connotations applied by those putting it into practice; the consequences of any policy are not always immediately obvious and may be the subject of dispute. For much of the time the policy-makers are not consciously drawing lessons from an analysis of a particular diagnosis, its implementation, and its results; they are instead compelled to modify their formulations by what has failed to happen.

It is only too easy to expunge from memory all the intentions which were never realised. When what was not intended seems to dominate policy discussions — the awkward facts of the case — original hopes are often forgotten. The very organisation of the records of a government department such as the Colonial Office means that the accounts of abortive enterprises are not automatically linked with papers on subsequent and similar projects. It does not look as if such an organisation can learn from a self-conscious analysis of the differences between what was intended and what happened. The main forms of 'organisational learning' are all indirect.

The questions raised about metropolitan assumptions in the field of colonial policy during the war are emotive because to ask them is to challenge some established folklore. The Colonial Office after the Second World War had an interest in emphasising how the war had merely delayed taking action on behalf of the colonies and primarily diverted resources which might otherwise have been devoted to colonial investment. The department was inclined to claim that the 'centre' had worked out a philosophy of development for the 'localities' before 1940 which could not be implemented until there was a prospect of returning to peace-time conditions. The Colonial Development and Welfare (CDW) Act was a monument to the validity of this claim. Officials implied that the war effort had just postponed the application of policies for colonial improvement, just as the depression of the 1930s had hampered the schemes devised in the 1920s for a developmental approach. The more criticism was levelled against Britain in terms which accused the authorities of bribing the colonial peoples with promises of aid in return for mobilisation against Germany and Japan, the more those responsible were inclined to believe that war had been an important diversion from the true purposes of colonial administration.

The main thesis of this book is that the management of the war effort by the Colonial Office on behalf of the colonies had a distinct effect on metropolitan conceptions of what could be done from the 'centre', and that this positive experience of the 'lessons of war' was a key element in all subsequent handling of the traditional constitutional patterns in central-local relations. Whitehall's experience of war management from the 'centre' deserves to be recorded. It explains a curious paradox in the promulgation of British post-war plans for the Empire. The Colonial Office became both more vulnerable and more confident. It was more sensitive to attacks against its alleged failure to meet the expectations of the colonial peoples and at the same time it was better equipped to apply a more constructive set of policies to the whole range of colonial territories, whatever their stage of development.

The effects of war can be seen largely in the mode of operations being devised for the Secretary of State's management of central-local relations in the Empire. The administrative system was not naturally conducive to developmental planning from the 'centre'. What the experience of war administration achieved was to provide the methods and the rationale of a more centralised approach to colonial policy without compelling any permanent redefinition of the Secretary of State's responsibilities. The achievements of this switch of emphasis in colonial policy can be read in the exercise of discretionary power within the department to transform the functions of civil servants and to give expression to the range of research activities which planning required. Only a knowledge of the organisation at the 'centre' can be used to identify the effects of war on metropolitan opinion. What happened in the Colonial Office is as much part of the adjustments made for the post-war peace settlement as the claims made by representatives of the colonial peoples for the promotion of colonial prosperity. Indeed, the excitement and confidence of immediate post-war planning can only be appreciated with some reference to the deliberate cultivation by Colonial Office officials of the mood in Britain for post-war reconstruction. There was a sense in which the British people and the colonial peoples were thought to be in need of rewards for wartime sacrifice.

16

Contemporaries disputed the very existence of a 'central' endeavour. Many continued to believe that the conception of a unified colonial empire and a common colonial policy was purely fictional. These differences of opinion were apparent in the writing of the official history of the Colonial Empire at war. Could it be more than a mere aggregation of individual territories' histories? Was there a set of common experiences at the centre? Sir Keith Hancock, who was in charge of the Cabinet Office official histories, referred in 1942 to the strengthening of the will and the enlargement of the brain of the Colonial Office. He then tried to characterise the effects of war on the will to implement the Colonial Development and Welfare Act:

It was suggested to me that the existence of a sum of money available for spending on constructive purposes was having a marked effect within the Colonial Office. It was creating a new sense of power, a new disposition to take positive action. It was suggested similarly that the Research Committee was likely to have the effect of speeding up the comparative study not only of technical problems but of social and political ones. If these suggestions are well grounded, the development which has taken place during the war will have done a good deal to strengthen the will and enlarge the brain of the Colonial Office itself. I do not suggest that that kind of subject matter is easy to handle in a history, yet it is far more important than many more tangible matters which are easily handled, and all the history should at least not suggest unawareness of the issue.[2]

Hancock saw the difference between believers in central action and traditionalists as something akin to philosophical disputes between Nominalists and Realists.

However intangible was the historians' awareness of changing attitudes at the 'centre', the transformation of the Colonial Office can at least be made more concrete if the evidence of departmental activity is used to spell out modifications in the language of intention and in the determination of the most appropriate means to bring colonies into line with central plans. First, conceptions entertained by contemporaries about the intentions of British authority are not easily portrayed in terms of 'the response to the challenge' of external criticisms. Whatever may have been said or written about British official intentions, officials developed their views in the day-to-day context of running a large routine administration, often working excessively long hours under great pressure. Second, the design of appropriate action within the framework of central-local relations is not easily extracted from the daily round of decision-making. The application of familiar procedures often disguises the extent to which they are being re-appraised. The search for the qualities to be found in new approaches to a central endeavour can only be undertaken by showing how contemporaries changed their practice almost without realising the extent of their own adaptations.

The evidence of transformation at the 'centre' is best marshalled in relation to the special features of the Secretary of State's authority. The assumptions of ministers and officials can be seen in those aspects of the system of central-local relations which reflect adjustments between central supervision and local control. The Secretary of State had the doubtful privilege of being held responsible to Parliament for what ultimately happened in the colonies without always having adequate power to effect his wishes. Throughout most of the dependent Empire the principal authority in each territory was its Governor. He was constrained in the exercise of his duties by prerogative instruments. Governors were enpowered by letters patent which, although they had the force of statute, were normally supplemented by Royal Instructions in order to establish that the form of laws to be administered in each territory might include some expression of local custom. The constitution of a colony, which determined how local laws were made, was only amended by Order-in-Council. The technical standing of the Secretary of State rested on his entitlement to intervene in any matter of administration which fell within the Governor's authority, and to consider all forms of legislation passed by the territorial legislature, if such existed. It was the prime function of the Colonial Office to advise the Secretary of State on all matters that pertained to this jurisdiction, which enabled him to warn all officers serving in the field and to tender advice to the sovereign about using the sanctions of a prerogative instrument or withholding the royal assent to legislation.

In practice the Secretary of State's powers of advice and approval were largely delegated to his permanent officials. The balance between central supervision and local control for any territory and at any time depended upon their assessment of appropriate action. Civil servants at the 'centre' were caught up in trying to find what they considered was the right combination of central responsibility, approval, and advice for the circumstances which they envisaged. The key variables in imperial administration were judgments made at the centre about an individual territory's capacity to handle its own affairs, and claims made by officials in the field in order to argue a convincing case for greater territorial autonomy. The system offered plenty of opportunity for minor adjustments in the mixture of central approval and advice.

The management of the Secretary of State's formal jurisdiction entailed two sets of obligations which might easily come into conflict. First, the Colonial Office was obliged to generalise across the different experiences of governments within the Empire in order to defend the Secretary of State against charges of inconsistency, and to provide a minimum set of rules in central supervision. This obligation was normally expressed as a tradition of upholding the principles of 'good government', and was enshrined in Colonial Regulations — the only embodiment of central doctrine and the touchstone of established procedure — which provided 'directions for general guidance' issued on behalf of the Crown by the Secretary of State to all Governors and other officers administering territorial governments. The essence of these regulations was to approach the task of government in terms of the principles necessary for 'sound finance' and for 'the maintenance of law and order', not in terms of policy. It was assumed that territories' governments would themselves handle the policy questions affecting their own political, social, and economic life.

The obligation to generalise was nevertheless subject to what Sir Charles Jeffries, writing about the Colonial Service, used to call 'the two-way pull'.[3] This tension arose from the very process of building up a territory's capacity to handle its own affairs. The greater the pressure for local autonomy, the more necessary it became to particularise and discriminate in favour of a single colony. One set of forces pulled in the direction of decentralisation in order to give to the administration in the field the single-minded devotion which it required to manage its own affairs in ways commensurate with local interests. Another set of forces pulled in the direction of centralisation in order to give the Colonial Office a chance to create economies of scale and to pool resources so that the smaller territorial units could enjoy some special services which they would be unlikely to afford from their own finances. The 'two-way pull' was an inevitable hazard of imperial administration as soon as the Colonial Office moved away from the forms of generalisation embodied in Colonial Regulations and tried to consider questions of 'development'.

Second, the Colonial Office was obliged to represent both British and colonial interests within the same set of institutions. This

19

obligation was normally seen as the Secretary of State's 'dual role' at both ends of the central-local system. He had to be both the advocate who represented the interests of the colonies within the British government and at the same time the voice which carried the latter's wishes into the colonial territories themselves. As a member of the British government, each Secretary of State had to present to the Crown's ministers in Britain any claim made by a territory's government for United Kingdom consideration; he also had to instruct representatives in the field whenever the British government insisted on using the Crown's sovereignty over the colonies in pursuit of British strategic or trading interests. This meant that Colonial Office officials who advised the Secretary of State in this role-playing were always having to consider representations made outside the formal channels of communication. People living in colonies had the right to petition the Crown through the Secretary of State. A large number of special groups in London — City traders' committees, commodity and trade associations, native rights associations, church missions — had regular contacts with their opposite numbers in the colonies. There was nothing to prevent white settlers in the colonies raising their own sources of capital investment independently of government.

The obligation to represent both ends of the central-local system was a natural consequence of the constitutional structure of the Empire, which placed all territories in a direct relationship with the Crown. Power to legislate on imperial matters at Westminster was deliberately separated from power to legislate on territorial matters in each unit of the system. Although many reformers toyed with the idea of setting up in London some form of consultative assembly for the whole Empire, if only a select committee of the House of Commons, there was no method of avoiding a situation in which the central-local relationship had also to carry representative functions. No such assembly could have been given legislative powers; no appropriate Commons committee could have scrutinised both ends of the administrative system. Indeed, all proposals for a kind of representative system other than the Secretary of State's 'dual role' constituted an insult to the capacity of central officials to manage his departmental jurisdiction.

Thinking about representation was regularly confused by proposals which were tantamount to requests for sharing with Parliament the executive powers of the Secretary of State. Parliament was the most important source of pressure upon the latter, in spite of his largely prerogative powers, and any attempt to associate him with a consultative council tended to be cast in parliamentary terms, if only because his accountability to Parliament for the Colonial Office vote provided a formal opportunity for MPs to have access to the work of his officials. Anyone in London who made a speciality of representing colonial interests had to latch on to this ministerial responsibility. Members of both the Commons and the Lords said that they wished to join either 'a Colonial Council' which might also include missionaries and commercial interests, or a joint select committee of both Houses. Not surprisingly, however, some of them hoped to steer such a body towards policy advice functions, or even executive functions as a 'colonial development board'. A debate on these ideas was conducted intermittently throughout the Second World War, and particularly intensely in 1944-45 at Lord Samuel's instigation.[4]

The obligations to generalise and to represent conflicted if the Colonial Office failed to find the most appropriate level at which to handle a specific problem. The traditional central point at which to undertake both obligations was what was called in the Colonial Office a 'geographical department' — the collection of responsibilities under an assistant secretary who dealt with the affairs of contiguous or similar territories. Each Assistant Secretary in such a department was required to keep common standards of generality in his area and to satisfy the demands he received for political representation. He usually found it necessary to reconsider procedures if the subject matter in hand did not tally with his allocation of responsibility. A change in the price of sugar, an international agreement limiting production, or a defence treaty affecting colonial harbours were subjects which did not fit easily into the administrative format of the geographical department. The invention and development of the role of a 'subject department' after 1930 were the principal features of organisational adaptation to fresh policy demands. The Assistant Secretary of a subject department, such as economics or social services, had to generalise and represent interests across geographical regions.

It was always difficult to retain a set of uniform general principles and yet make recommendations which took local circumstances into account. The problems of different regions seemed to call for different tactics, and a rearrangement of the administration which was intended to promote more progressive policies could sometimes have the unexpected consequence of strengthening the forces of reaction. The same prescription could not be universally applied, but whatever was decided had to be in accord with the imperial system as a whole. Before the outbreak of war the centre was anxious to encourage cooperation between adjacent colonies in all matters of common interest. 'Closer union' was a watchword in East and Central Africa as well as in the West Indies, where there were no indigenous rulers. In the Far East, however, the corresponding slogan was 'decentralisation', because in Malaya it seemed important to lessen the differences between the unfederated states and the federated states, where local Sultans still exercised power, if there was to be any progress towards cooperation or amalgamation. The Colonial Office had to reconcile its generalising and representative functions in a manner which brought local configurations of power and influence into line with some general standards, if it was to secure respect both at home and abroad.

It was also questionable whether some colonial territories could ever be treated as entities which deserved a degree of local autonomy. Islands and small enclaves of territory which began as trading stations might well be suitable for a permanent association with the Secretary of State's representative functions without any plans for constitutional change; small colonies seemed unsuitable for developing a form of local representative government without some kind of link to a larger whole. The idea that territories should be encouraged to handle their own affairs entailed some notion of the most appropriate conjunction of peoples and land to form the basis of a state.

The Colonial Office always had to pay attention to the status of each colony within its administrative system and to the structure of law and procedure through which the Secretary of State's responsibility was expressed. Other departments of the British government handled the affairs of colonial territories with fewer inhibitions and less consistency. The Foreign Office thought primarily in terms of the areas in which colonial territories could affect diplomatic relations; the Board of Trade considered the flow of commodities and was less concerned than the Colonial Office with the uneven impact of the Ottawa Agreements on imperial preference; the armed services departments made arrangements according to their own estimates of Britain's requirements.

The nature of the Palestine Mandate underlined how much those at the centre always had to set their sense of obligation to generalise and to represent against the current interpretation of a territory's constitutional position. Almost by accident the Office had been made administratively responsible for an area which was crucial in British considerations of foreign and defence policy, and therefore not easily subsumed into the general framework of colonial administration. This responsibility became progressively more onerous and time-consuming during the 1930s, as the immigration of Jews from Europe was increased and Arab nationalism inflamed, and brought constant exposure to criticism in the newspapers and in Parliament. The Royal Commission which recommended the partition of territories between Arab and Jew in 1937 brought the Office into a running and often bitter debate with the Foreign Office, and the local campaign of sabotage and terrorism had important repercussions on its relations with the armed services departments. By 1939 the Deputy Under-Secretary in charge confessed that the Office would be ready and eager to hand over responsibility for the Mandate[5], but the British government never transferred these functions to another Secretary of State or created an office which dealt with the Palestine Mandate alone.

The administrative system of the Empire was particularly vulnerable to the impact of war. The traditional distinctions between territories seemed much less significant when the imperatives of mobilisation required quick responses and a reliable uniformity of support. The Colonial Office had to adopt the major elements in other departments' approaches which emphasised the production capacity, the raw materials and the strategic potential of territories scattered over the world. It is precisely the experience of learning about one's own organisation by being compelled to work with unanticipated assumptions that this book is designed to explore.

By setting out the position in 1939, the first chapter provides a base against which to judge what the war transformed. It concentrates on the context of imperial administration just before war was declared. The Colonial Office, although deeply involved in the preparations for war, was at that stage also committed to a reappraisal of its conception of what the centre might do. The reorganisation of the office, which was initiated by Leopold Amery as Secretary of State about 1925, was again scrutinised in terms of the proposals made in 1938 for 'colonial development and welfare'. The coincidence of a dispute on the future of Palestine and a concern about labour unrest in the West Indies brought to a head the department's disquiet about its ability to promote the social and economic development of the colonial peoples.

The two major parts of the book, each of three chapters, examine the impact of war. Chapters 2, 3, and 4 deal with the immediate experience of managing the war effort in order to mobilise colonial resources on behalf of the Allies. They show the increasing effectiveness of the centre in marshalling the territories behind the war effort. The second part — chapters 5, 6, and 7 — deals with the period after 1943 when the centre was able to turn its attention to planning for the peace settlement and thus to reflect upon the consequences of war. The abortive plans of post-war reconstruction were more important in giving an opportunity for reconsidering the central functions of the Colonial Office than the more concrete and direct commandeering of colonial work for war purposes.

The final chapter sets out the 'lessons of war'. The assumptions made at the centre reflected very clearly the experience of Colonial Office officials in reinterpreting the system of central-local relations for both mobilisation and reconstruction. Although the first step in preparing for peace was to reintroduce 'colonial development and welfare', the meaning of central supervision had been changed from an emphasis on defining local needs to a method of developing local capacities.

1

PRE-WAR EXPERIENCE AND ASSUMPTIONS

THE dominant assumptions of Colonial Office officials during the period between the Munich crisis in 1938 and the fall of France in 1940 were part of a contemporary preoccupation with the instability of world trade and manufacture. Civil servants at the centre of imperial administration were obliged to work out their approach to the costs of economic progress in the colonies while their colleagues in Whitehall were planning for rearmament and defence against air attack. Their attitudes reflected metropolitan thinking about economic development. They were acutely conscious, on the one hand, of the poor standard of life enjoyed by many colonies during the depression of trade, and, on the other hand, of the major disruptions in the customs of native peoples which almost any kind of industrial investment seemed to bring. Colonial Office assumptions were an expression of the discovery of the 'externalities' of economic activity, the price that had to be paid for progress, and the cost in terms of social relationships in those parts of the Empire which provided support for European industry without apparently receiving any corresponding benefits. The British Empire had been brought into the economic system of Europe and the United States, but in a very haphazard way with uneven effects. By 1937 the keynote in central discussions was the level of what was called social expenditure, how much the colonies could afford to spend on the social services, particularly health, education, and various forms of welfare.

Hancock, writing in 1941 for the *Survey of British Commonwealth Affairs,* used the concepts developed in Australia by A. G. B. Fisher in order to characterise the tensions which the centre had identified.[1] Fisher's book, *The Clash between Progress and Security,* published in 1937, examined the difficulty of maintaining continuity in social tradition in the midst of economic change. There seemed to be a dearth of serious economic studies which set out to measure the social effects of commercialisation, particularly in those colonies where the structure of society followed a system of tenure in which

25

the land belonged to the whole community. Both Colonial Office officials and economic historians began to interest themselves in the forms of industrialisation which seemed more appropriate to existing societies. They thought that world depression had taught all investors in the colonies that they could no longer rely on the traditional profit motive. The slump in world prices had removed the basic stimulus for development. Hancock declared that 'Adam Smith seems to be deserting West Africa when he has only scratched the surface of his ... task'.[2] The 'invisible hand' of classical economic theory had somehow been withdrawn.

The Colonial Office found itself in the centre of a dispute not about the need for progress but about the method. The conceptions of senior civil servants belonged to a widely held view that the hitherto normal sequence of economic development which had been experienced in Europe could no longer be expected to run in other parts of the world. It had been assumed that development was a by-product of profit and that social welfare was a natural consequence of the government's share in collective prosperity. But it seemed no longer possible in the late 1930s to assume that a progressive economy would in some sense be self-adjusting and supply resources for investment in health and education. At least for the dependent Empire government intervention seemed necessary. But what kind? What degree? What was the best means of rectifying the social damage which had already been inflicted and at the same time of providing the basis for a happy and prosperous set of social changes? The methods of government and the assumptions of officials seemed crucial factors in anticipating the answer to such questions.

From the point of view of officials at the centre of the Empire, these questions had two sets of embarrassing implications. First, any increase in the volume of social expenditure by colonial governments meant a shift in the balance between public and private employment. Many colonies had experienced paid employment largely in the form of public service, or, if in the private sector, in the form of attachment to large plantation-type companies. There were many questions about the structure of employment to which the Colonial Office could not give straightforward answers. Above all, the level of remuneration in the higher ranks of both the Colonial Service and private management was fixed in order to meet the expectations of European expatriate staff. Any expansion in public sector employment which kept the same rates of pay and at the same time encouraged the local community to be trained for the highest levels might well endanger the social betterment which more jobs were intended to create. The colonial economy might not be able to sustain an inappropriate level of civil service remuneration. Second, any direct intervention by the British government in colonial markets, either with fiscal measures or with international agreements on production and supply, could only be made in relation to what could be achieved in each territory by the established form of government. The system of administration in many colonies was just not geared to tackling economic problems. The tradition of 'indirect rule' — working through the native rulers and other authorities — was not conducive to a series of technical improvements in marketing and production. As soon as Governors began to consider the demands of a more positive policy towards, for example, agricultural improvement, they were obliged to look at their own system of native administration. Economic development and social improvement policies had implications for the system of government even before any obvious advances in the standard of living were noted. It was difficult to neglect considerations of constitutional change when contemplating social policy.

It is not surprising that these forms of embarrassment led some members of the Colonial Office to shy away from a more interventionist role in a manner which required changes in organisation at the centre. Some of the most telling evidence of the way in which the Colonial Office was thinking comes from the internal departmental arguments about organisation. The dispute about the methods of social development in the colonies had a direct effect on the conceptions entertained by Colonial Office staff about their own position. Some of them, such as the Permanent Under-Secretary, Sir Cosmo Parkinson, and the head of the Africa Division, Sir Arthur Dawe, were extremely cautious in taking any steps which might endanger the principles they cherished of their central activity as policy advice to the Secretary of State on the use of his powers of advice and approval. Dawe spoke of the Colonial Office as a central secretariat; he resisted any departure from the principle of holding together the generalisation and representation functions of the Secretary of State in a set of divisions organised by geography rather than by policy. He regarded the executive authority enjoyed by the new subject departments as a mistaken extension of central functions. The more conservative members of the Office hesitated to place

27

themselves in the position of having to generalise in policy matters across a number of colonies. They emphasised that the Colonial Office's principal *raison d'être* was to maintain standards of administration.

But this rather purist approach to the Secretary of State's functions sat rather uncomfortably with the realities of international politics. Whatever could be agreed in the abstract on social policy and central responsibilities had to be set against the constant temptation to think of the Empire only in terms of the interests of the United Kingdom. The anxiety about social development in the colonies was but one aspect of a wider concern for reducing economic and political instability. No British government could avoid looking at the Empire except in terms of the pattern of trade and the distribution of industrial capacity. Whatever their diagnosis of the depression, British industrialists in the early 1930s had been somewhat half-heartedly converted to a series of tariff reforms embodied in the imperial preference agreements signed at the Ottawa Conference, where the Federation of British Industries was represented; they had also been prepared to follow a 'selective development' policy within the Empire. But by the late 1930s they were so much more preoccupied with the consequences of competition from 'low cost' countries, particularly Japan, whose goods entered imperial markets in increasing numbers, that the British government was being pressed to consider ways of promoting agreements between all major individual powers, including Germany, whose products were then under attack, and to enter into cartels that would regulate trade. The Empire, in these conditions, was only important as a potential market, a site for low cost industrial capacity, or a source of supply.

Similarly, no British government in the 1930s could ignore the opportunity of treating Germany's claim to a restoration of colonial power status as a bargaining counter in negotiations for retaining peace in Europe. It began to seem that involvement in Europe was necessary in order to protect the Empire. By 1935, when the Dominions' Prime Ministers came to the King's Silver Jubilee, Foreign Office officials were contemplating posing some of the questions which might enable Britain to find arguments for conceding colonies to Germany. Even if there were grave political objections to the transfer of British territory to Germany, it was not practicable to refuse to discuss it. When Neville Chamberlain became Prime Minister in May 1937 he placed the colonial questions high

28

on the agenda of Anglo-German discussions. In January 1938 he put forward a plan for detente with Germany to the Foreign Policy Committee of the Cabinet; he wanted to see a redistribution of colonial territories in Central Africa by which Germany might be satisfied, but only if the German government would make a tangible concession in Europe.[3] The Empire had come to symbolise British weakness as well as British strength. The Dominions could not be relied upon by Britain to enter a European war, and the requirements of imperial defence ran counter to what were widely regarded as 'continental entanglements'. The policy of appeasement was prompted by a desire to reduce the number of potential enemies, and it took a long time to convice the defence planners of the need to prepare for a continental war. Both ministers and officials by 1938 were obsessed with the prospect of a Europe dominated by Hitler's aggressive policy, but not until March 1939 did they take the crucial decisions to switch resources.

In these conditions the Colonial Office began to formulate what it called 'a forward policy' for social improvement and to reverse its own approach to the formulas which it had developed in the late 1920s for making the centre into what Leopold Amery called a 'general staff'. Labour unrest in the West Indies and complaints from Governors about the debilitating effects of declining trade led the Office to reconsider how it might proceed, and Malcolm MacDonald's appointment as Secretary of State in May 1938 provided a strong ministerial backing to the whole exercise of examining the idea of colonial development in the light of events since the Ottawa Conference and Hitler's accession to power.[4] In 1938 civil servants at the centre looked back over the previous five years with a strong sense of the contrast between what Amery had intended and what events had produced. The centre had somehow to compensate the colonial peoples for an unanticipated failure in the process of wealth creation, as it was then understood, to supply the kind of social structure and development of technical skills which they all wanted to see. The essence of the Office's reappraisal of its own procedures and policy was exploring the link between economic depression and political instability.

It was characteristic of metropolitan thinking to stress the value of social welfare. In spite of its daily dealings with overseas territories, the Colonial Office was still strongly influenced by the arguments used in Britain for improving British social services. The difference between official thinking at the centre of the Empire in the late 1920s and in the late 1930s was a direct product of appreciating the social and political consequences of depression. Hitler's rise to power and the stance of Germany in Europe could quite easily be explained within the same set of theories as the strikes of colonial workers against a falling standard of living. In the 1920s colonial development policy had been discussed largely in terms of metropolitan economic difficulties — Britain's own social problems; in the 1930s it was presented in terms which recognised the worldwide effects of instability in manufacture, trade, and marketing. Unemployment and low wages were to be seen throughout the Empire. The Colonial Office felt that the strikes in the West Indies presented a timely warning of what might happen elsewhere. There were already signs of unrest in West Africa and among government workers in East Africa. It seemed important to take advantage of what could be regarded as a 'temporary lull' before social unrest provoked greater violence.

The documents circulating in the Colonial Office at the time included Lord Hailey's *African Survey,* which had received official support, and the report on nutrition in the colonies which was also the product of sponsored research. The Colonial Office was in the metropolitan fashion of using social survey techniques which had been widely applied to identify British social service needs. The *African Survey,* published in 1938, was undertaken by Lord Hailey after his retirement as Governor of the United Provinces in India.[5] He set out in 1935 to tour Africa by car with the aid of a scientist and a colonial service officer, and with support from a committee under Lord Lothian and a grant from the Carnegie Corporation. A Colonial Office Principal prepared the material for publication when Hailey fell ill. The survey summarised what needed to be done in many fields, and its main recommendations were incorporated into a series of subject files in the Office for circulation to heads of department. The Nutrition Survey was prompted by the publicity in 1935 of a League of Nations health organisation report.[6] The Secretary of State in 1936 asked all colonies to send in information about human nutrition, and the replies were examined by a special subcommittee of the Economic Advisory Council of Cabinet. That committee reported in July 1939.

The centre's conception of what it might do in the late 1930s was to develop a form of intellectual investment in organisation and communication. The Colonial Office wanted to see sound advice placed in the right hands among administrators in the field at the right time. Social improvement would be achieved as much by a better understanding of social services as by any deliberate promotion of industrial development. Capitalism could not be left to proceed without the moderating restraints of an administration equipped with a knowledge of social welfare. It was at the same time important to acknowledge the value of propaganda: all officers serving in the Empire should have a common sense of the commitment to welfare. The centre wanted to see a change in the psychological climate of imperial administration.

It would be wrong to suggest that all the officials at the centre shared the same views about an investment in social welfare. But it does seem evident that they all thought it right to switch the emphasis of the Colonial Office machinery towards a 'forward policy' by finding ways of subsidising local territorial efforts from central sources. The relative autonomy of the geographical department within the Office to handle generalising and representative functions was modified by the likelihood of a greater orientation towards subject specialisation. Officials had already accepted the practice of creating a subject department which, like each geographical department, enjoyed the Secretary of State's delegated authority. The first step had been taken in 1930 when the new Personnel Division was constituted to implement projected reforms in the Colonial Service. The Economic Division was created in 1934 largely to meet the demands laid upon the Office by the tariff agreements established at Ottawa in 1932.[7] The crucial point was reached in the departmental discussions of the late 1930s when a proposal was made to create a separate section of the Office which could administer a new policy of colonial development and another to bring together technical advisers on social welfare. The idea of a Social Services Department was first mooted in the spring of 1938 at a meeting on labour questions.[8]

Office reorganisation

The reorganisation of the Office in fact moved ahead of the preparation of legislation. A new Social Services Department began work in March 1939, to be a source of advice and guidance. Clauson, its first Assistant Secretary, who had also started off the economic department, was promoted an Assistant Under-Secretary in October. These arrangements symbolised the Office's reappraisal of its situation. It entered the war with an administrative centre for the social services without any special provision for economic planning. It was agreed that the most appropriate mechanism at the centre for subsidising colonies which needed metropolitan help was the well-tried formula of an advisory committee administering grants from a general fund. Nobody anticipated that the new subject departments would grow very rapidly, but there were difficulties in acquiring accommodation. When a lease was secured on a house in Queen Anne's Gate in August 1939, it was decided to try a system of 'horizontal' grouping which put together in this building the subject departments for Economics and Social Services with the Secretary of State's advisers, instead of the previous 'vertical' arrangement which had confined the advisers to sharing Richmond Terrace with part of the Personnel Department.[9] The Queen Anne's Gate grouping, which embodied the 'welfare' commitment, was moved en bloc to Park Street, Mayfair, in 1941.

The major public evidence of change lay in legislation. The Colonial Development and Welfare Bill of 1940 was prepared as a deliberate remodelling of the Colonial Development Act of 1929. When the Bill had had its second reading in the House of Commons just before the fall of France, it was the culmination of the Office's reappraisal of its functions. The contrast between the major provisions of the two Acts was regarded as an eloquent testimony to the increased importance of central functions.

The 1929 Act had embodied the reforms of Amery's tenure as Secretary of State. It was not until 1930 that Amery's intention of creating a new ministry to handle Dominion affairs was fully implemented. A division of responsibility between the Colonial Office and the new Dominions Office (which had been the Dominions department of the Colonial Office) was made in 1925, and a separate Permanent Under-Secretary for the Dominions appointed in 1926. Amery and Passfield, his successor, had each jointly held the two ministerial posts of Secretary of State for the Colonies and Secretary of State for Dominion Affairs, and Passfield only surrendered the latter in June 1930 in order to accommodate J. H. Thomas, then in some disgrace after being the minister who dealt with unemployment problems. Even then, until 1947 the two Offices continued to share the same building and to enjoy a common

32

establishment of staff which was technically interchangeable between the two.

The importance of a formal separation for colonial affairs was that the Colonial Office could henceforward specialise in the peculiar problems of trusteeship over the dependent Empire. Amery's account of his stewardship in defining what this meant was presented to the House of Commons in 1928 as a report of the achievements of four years in office which had marked the first major shifts in the character of departmental thinking.[10]

The political context of the specialisation in trusteeship was the changing role of arguments about imperial development in the domestic debate on the British economy. Milner and Amery as Secretaries of State had each tried to push for a more constructive and positive policy of government support for economic enterprise in the Empire. Both had been broadly sympathetic with the case for a system of imperial preference and with the arguments for using public funds to promote trade between the constituent members of the Empire. But they met with considerable resistance from those officials who feared any programme of imperial development which would foster British trade at the expense of colonial interests, or which would saddle colonial governments with debts they could not service.[11] In discharging their representative functions, the Colonial Office had always tended to shy away from moves which ran the risk of placing colonial budgets under direct Treasury control from Britain by the system of grants-in-aid. They thought aid should only be given to secure the self-sufficiency of colonial authorities. But the economic depression of the 1920s encouraged a climate of opinion favourable to the use of imperial government grants in the colonies, if they could be construed as instruments to reduce unemployment in Britain.

The Colonial Development Act of 1929, although passed by a Labour government, was conceived by Amery in November 1928. The publication of the report of the Commission on East African Closer Union helped to convince the Treasury that a new source of finance was required. The Act set up a fund into which Parliament voted sums up to an annual maximum of one million pounds, and from which grants or loans were made to colonial governments on the recommendations of a specially constituted Colonial Development Advisory Committee. That committee tended to adhere very strictly to the view that all applications from the colonies should be considered primarily in terms of the expenditure which they involved on the United Kingdom itself.[12]

Amery also secured a full consideration of the appropriate machinery for administering the Empire by appointing two special committees of outsiders: one in 1927-28 to examine the general organisation of the Colonial Office, under the chairmanship of its own Permanent Under-Secretary, Sir Samuel Wilson, whom he had brought to London from being Governor of Jamaica[13]; and another in 1929-30 to examine the reform of the colonial service, under the chairmanship of Sir Warren Fisher, the head of the home civil service.[14] The alternatives these two bodies explored and the recommendations they made provided the major basis for reconsidering central-local relationships before the war. There were no further official enquiries of this kind until 1941 on the Colonial Service[15] and 1948 on the Office.[16]

The Organisation Committee had been preceded by an internal enquiry, and the Secretary of State had taken decisions while its deliberations were in progress. He was particularly concerned with the definition of policy areas in which special advisers were required, the subject of the committee's first report. It considered the appointment of appropriate experts in the fields of tropical agriculture, veterinary science, finance, and railway development. Approaches were made to suitable candidates in agriculture and finance in June 1927 and the first appointments made in 1928. The second report, which dealt with administrative control over the colonies, recommended the setting up of a special sub-committee for further consideration of the work of the General Division. A third report dealt with the interchange of staff between the Colonial Office and the colonies. This and the further recommendation that a Personnel Department should be created from the General Division linked up with the work of the other committee.

The Colonial Services Committee supplied an official response to professional bodies in the United Kingdom which were interested in the design of proper career systems for expatriates in the service of colonial governments, and to those who were concerned to place the system of recruitment for service with the Empire on a regular footing. The ideas which the committee examined were part of the follow-up to the Lovat Committee on the agricultural services after the 1927 conference,[17] and a demonstration of concern about the position of the Appointments Department under Sir Ralph Furse. The solution proposed was to create schemes for the 'unification' of different branches of the civil services in the colonies by designating certain posts in each territorial administration to be filled by people from a defined cadre, and to tie the recruitment methods used in the United Kingdom more closely to those of the home civil service. The essence of 'unification' was that any officer who was offered membership of the service in his own technical field had the right to be considered for promotion to another scheduled post in any colony if a suitable vacancy occurred.

The most important elements in the Organisation Committee's reports to go forward for implementation were the appointment of permanent subject advisers to the Secretary of State and the establishment of subject departments which specialised in a functional area of responsibilities rather than a group of geographical territories. The General Division of the Office had hitherto held all the non-geographical subjects together. Although some advocated a more thoroughgoing reform of the Office by making divisions on functional lines, there seemed to be no serious alternative to dividing the work into geographical and subject headings, with subject advisers in residence who might occasionally make links between the two.

The appointment of permanent advisory staff received priority, partly because their presence could make an effective link between the specialist departments in colonial governments and professional bodies in the United Kingdom, which were often represented on the advisory committees which the Colonial Office encouraged. The best candidates as advisers were those who had both sufficient experience to command the respect of those still working in the field and adequate skills to handle the postures adopted by members of advisory committees at home. By 1938 Advisers on development subjects had been appointed in medicine, agriculture, and labour, as well as in the traditional field of law; and just before the outbreak of war consideration was given to the appointment of part-time Advisers in forestry, veterinary science, and public works or engineering, but not then pursued.[18] In July 1939 it was agreed that the joint secretaries of the Advisory Committee on Education should be replaced by an Adviser and an Assistant Adviser in Education.[19] The Advisory Committee on Education and the Medical Advisory Committee were joined in 1937 by a Committee on Penal Administration to make up the principal advisory committees in the social services field, with the special advisory committee on the administration of the 1929 Act.

The only subject department with which the colonies themselves had regular contact before the outbreak of war was the Personnel Division. This could not carry out its remit without extensive surveys of the establishment in each colonial government, because it was charged with the task of developing an appropriate system for managing the Secretary of State's responsibility with regard to the Colonial Service. As the process of 'unification' proceeded, the Colonial Service Department developed methods for recording and collating confidential reports on serving officers, as well as drawing up regulations for pensions and other conditions of service. Just as the Appointments Department handled individual applications for recruitment, the Colonial Service Department dealt with many day-to-day queries about individual officers whose personal files were in its charge.

Personnel work in the colonies was deliberately linked with a consideration of the organisation at the centre by associating the Assistant Under-Secretary in charge of Colonial Service recruitment and promotion with responsibility for internal office procedure as the departmental establishments officer. The Personnel Division, by encompassing both central and local interests, was the natural forum for assessing further proposals for change, and the Departmental Whitley Council was occasionally asked to look at organisational questions. As the reforms instituted by Amery began to bite, the Office started to acquire fresh accoutrements of expertise. In June 1935 the establishments officer issued the first edition of a code of office procedure which was designed to provide a work of reference on established practice; a sequel which was intended to cover subject departments and personnel was never completed.[20] In July 1935 the bulletin, which until 1932 had provided a guide to the joint establishment of the Colonial Office and the Dominions Office, was revived for use in the former alone, and from 1937 onwards a regular broadsheet on the distribution of work was printed.[21] Some Office committees under the guidance of the Personnel Division examined current problems, such as the survey of routine work in 1937 or office machinery in 1939.

This Division in the Department which linked the colonial and home civil services kept open a suggestion which both the Wilson and Warren Fisher Committees had rejected — that the Colonial Office should be staffed by Colonial Service personnel, and not exclusively by the home civil service — an arrangement which Wilson personally supported. Amery himself, interested in such a 'fusion', wanted the officials of the Colonial and Dominions Offices to be liable for periods of service overseas. But instead of pressing for fusion, which would have insulated the special nature of central-local relationships within its own professional cadre, both committees recommended the encouragement of a series of exchanges of staff between the centre and the localities. In 1935 a scheme was established to regularise the attachment of Colonial Service officers for two-year periods of secondment in London.[22] These men, who were known as 'beachcombers', were given their own senior representative in September 1937 when it was decided to bring in a Governor to serve as Assistant Under-Secretary.[23] The continued association of the colonial and home civil services was symbolised in the Appointments Board which was established in 1930 to regularise the patronage system which the Secretary of State had retained in his private office. This Board, which sanctioned all the appointments to the newly unified branches of the Colonial Service, was a device to use the reputation of the Civil Service Commissioners in Britain in order to diminish the accusation of patronage.

The staffing of the Colonial Office from the home civil service made the centre of the imperial administrative system vulnerable to domestic changes in at least two major respects. In the first place, promotion in London was subject to the vagaries of the United Kingdom labour market for civil service manpower. With the suspension of examinations for entry into the administrative class after the First World War, the Office by the late 1930s was largely in the hands of the 'reconstruction' generation who had not entered by open competition. The Civil Service Commission tried to avoid adding to the promotion blockage which that generation constituted by limiting the entry of new Assistant Principals (about two or three a year) after the examinations were restarted in 1925. By 1940 there were only eight administrative officers under thirty, and a real shortage of trained junior staff.[24] Some members of the 'reconstruction group' (such as Gent, Jeffries, and Lloyd) held important posts throughout the war.

In the second place, the grading of posts in London was subject to home civil service conventions, and the character of administrative supervision over the Empire had to follow recognised categories of Whitehall organisation. The Treasury kept the Colonial Office in step. Apart from the Appointments Department, which continued to use ex-military personnel in the job of assessing suitable recruits, all the other sections of the Office were easily divided into those which employed administrative officers on policy questions and those 'common services' which were almost exclusively clerical officer tasks, such as copying, registering files, or opening and sending despatches. In Whitehall parlance, the Office was organised without the middle-rank executive grade,[25] because its daily work was not considered to contain appropriate tasks for that rank. It depended for the greater part of its routine on senior clerical officers — staff officers — who remained in the clerical grade and had no opportunity of moving into the top executive pay scales. The only possible class-to-class promotion was to leap-frog directly into the administrative grade from the clerical. Any major modification in the tasks performed in the Office raised questions of grading and comparability.

The content of work at the centre was always an expression of the changing character of central-local relationships. Greater devolution of power to the colonies and a larger commitment to research and development meant that the centre had to equip itself with staff which could perform new specialities. The Colonial Office's concentration on the development aspects of trusteeship was a major reorientation of its style and type of work. Between the wars the application of a development policy had brought together at the centre three basic elements of organisation which had acquired little experience of working together — the geographical departments, the subject departments, and the advisers.

Commitment to a 'forward policy'

The preparations for the 1940 Act involved a deliberate reconsideration of these three elements in the light of contemporary assessments of the need for social welfare in the colonies. There were two sets of parallel enquiries, authorised by Malcolm MacDonald in 1938 but, because of the war, not reported in public. The first was an Office committee appointed in June 1938 to consider the workings of the colonial development fund established under the 1929 Act.[26] It constituted the Office's own response to social unrest in the West Indies, and was originally asked to consider how far the fund could be used for social services, particularly the improvement of education. The second was the appointment of the Royal Commission on the

West Indies under the chairmanship of Lord Moyne, which became the principal public commitment of the government to a reconsideration of both policy and administration.[27] In January 1940, largely because Chamberlain was concerned about the effects of the Royal Commission's views on American opinion, the War Cabinet decided to delay the publication of its report for the duration of hostilities.[28]

The most obvious connection between the two enquiries was the fact that any request for further expansion in the size and purposes of the fund would be influenced by the findings of an enquiry into an area where there had been considerable social unrest. The diagnosis of West Indian problems introduced a permanent bias into the consideration of colonial policy as a whole. Britain's standing as a colonial power in the West Indies was under the scrutiny of the United States, which took a close interest in what was happening in its off-shore islands where the colonial territories of other major powers were also situated. Worried about the inadequacy of its defence system, it began a series of secret negotiations in June 1939 about the lease of possible bases for American forces on West Indian islands. The Royal Commission, which had the privilege of using Lord Moyne's private yacht in order to overcome the difficulties of travel between the islands,[29] considered the setting up of a separate West Indian development fund to aid the British territories, but the Colonial Office preferred to examine the idea of a general fund on the lines of that already in existence under the 1929 Act, from which the West Indies could also benefit.

The distinctions made in these parallel enquiries involved a thorough appraisal of the system of central-local relationships, as it had evolved during the 1930s. Although there was a strong sense of building upon past achievements, the discussions also revealed the need for realism about the degree of management that could be effected from the centre. If there was to be any greater emphasis on social improvement in the colonies, the interdependence of the Colonial Office and colonial governments had to be reexamined. The majority of distinctions then made were concerned with the productivity of capital, and the fundamental anxiety which an examination of the West Indies had encouraged was the state of indebtedness which the weaker colonial governments could not avoid. The enquiries took place against the background of stagnation in world trade and a decline in commodity prices, although there was some hope that those commodities for which international agreements had been signed (such as tin, copper, rubber, sugar, and tea) would keep their value. The parallel enquiries called for a survey of the sources of income enjoyed by territorial governments, because any suggestion that social betterment should be pursued required some examination of the recurrent costs of social services in each budget. Nigeria, for example, the largest colony in Africa, was also the African territory with the largest budgetary deficit, partly because there had been serious falls in commodity prices for vegetable oils and oil seeds. The Governor, Sir Bernard Bourdillon, thought that the Colonial Office should lay down a more clear-cut policy on social development which would enable metropolitan subsidies to be granted for the health and education services.[30]

The Colonial Office was interested not only in seeing whether recurrent as well as capital costs could be met from United Kingdom sources, but also in drawing a sharp line between productive and non-productive purposes. It seemed possible to view the whole Empire as an aggregation of territories which could be arranged in a hierarchy according to their basic productivity. The Financial Adviser in 1938 suggested a three-fold classification which separated those territories such as Somaliland, which would never pay their way in the foreseeable future, from the richer colonies such as the Gold Coast, where only capital grants would be needed, leaving a large in-between 'border line' of those which would occasionally need support in the recurrent costs of maintaining services.[31] When the budgets of the colonial Empire for 1938 were analysed in aggregate, it was discovered that 25 per cent of local revenue was spent on administration, 25 per cent on social services and 20 per cent on economic development.[32]

Part of the Colonial Office's interest in the principles of the colonial development fund lay in its desire to find an alternative to grants-in-aid, which always entailed United Kingdom Treasury control over colonial governments. The Treasury was unlikely to consent to the abolition of the system of grants-in-aid, and the Colonial Office had primarily to find a means of persuading that department to consider methods of extending the scope of the purposes to which the fund could be applied. The enquiry into conditions in the West Indies sharpened the search and gave point to the argument for increased resources.

In designing more appropriate administrative machinery the Colonial Office clung to a model which had been popular in the 1920s — the fund voted by Parliament to be disbursed on the advice of a specially constituted committee. All the discussions on extending the purposes of the existing fund centred on the best means of administering it through a strengthened committee with a full-time chairman and a secretary.[33] When a proposal for a separate research fund was also entertained, it was formulated in terms of establishing a separate committee to judge the merits of research applications. In so far as there might be any formal planning for the allocation of such resources as Parliament made available, it would take place not at the centre but in the territorial government where some changes in the organisation of the Secretariat were contemplated.

The new Social Services Department in 1939 took charge of the discussions on draft legislation to improve colonial development and welfare. It was to constitute a source of advice on the social services which officers in the field could approach for guidance. It undertook to process applications for grants from the fund, and it began to consider what type of metropolitan expertise should be developed in order to help colonies find the most appropriate staff for health and welfare services.

There was no talk at this stage of appointing a full-time Adviser to the Secretary of State in either social services or economic development. Sir John Campbell remained Economic and Financial Adviser from 1930 until his retirement in 1942. Lord Hailey had already established himself as a major adviser on research questions, and he regularised his position when the Secretary of State decided to employ him as a consultant on native administration in Africa. After a number of interviews Hailey was commissioned in October 1939 to make a tour of Africa in order to write a report on native administration. The secret political purpose of his visit was to advise on the future of African unofficial representation in legislative councils. It was agreed by the Treasury that he should be paid as a senior adviser at the rate of £2,000 a year, and this was confirmed in May 1941 after his return from the Congo in March.[34] Hailey enjoyed the rather unusual status of a resident adviser on general trusteeship questions, and became chairman of the Research Committee when it was established in 1942. The proposal to appoint a full-time chairman of the colonial development advisory committee was never used as a way of introducing a figure of comparable standing into the deliberations of the Office. Although Lord Moyne, the Chairman of the Royal Commission on the West Indies, was approached to see whether he would consider acting as chairman of the committee which administered the fund, he declined when he became a junior minister in the coalition in May 1940 and it was decided that the committee should be established in 1941 only on an official basis under the chairmanship of a former Parliamentary Under-Secretary, Lord Dufferin and Ava.[35]

The Treasury was of course fearful that any new arrangements might replace Treasury control by advisory committee control. It could not easily abandon the suspicion that any provision which allowed colonial governments to meet their recurrent cost from United Kingdom sources would open up a number of limitless commitments and encourage a degree of reckless expenditure at the local level which was also non-productive. The aim of social betterment policy seemed a dangerous one to follow if it ran the risk of adding the burden of a continuous subsidy to poorer colonies. The Treasury even questioned whether a fund was necessary, and preferred to talk in terms of economic growth from private investment rather than the promotion of social welfare. After a number of rather difficult inter-departmental meetings, the Treasury made a gentleman's agreement with the Colonial Office that, if a fund was established during the war, half of it would be used to meet recurrent costs under the old conventions of grants-in-aid. The Secretary of State was fully aware that the size of the fund, which the problems of the West Indies alone would have increased in peace time, had to remain at the relatively modest sum of up to £5 million a year for ten years, with separate provision for research of £500,000 a year.[36]

While the main danger of subsidising recurrent costs in colonial budgets lay in supporting an unproductive social service bureaucracy, the debate on development could not leave out of account the future shape of the Colonial Service. Perhaps more than any other factor, the findings of the Royal Commission on the West Indies exposed the weaknesses of the schemes for the unification of technical branches. The governments of the West Indies were among the constitutionally more advanced which had given an increased measure of responsibility to unofficial members; the finance committees of their legislative councils had considerable influence over questions of establishments, remuneration, and conditions of service. The principles of unification had been applied throughout the Empire except in the West Indies, where, as was noted in May 1938, 'local legislatures have desired nothing better than to stew in their juice'.[37] Colonial governments which worked on the assumption that posts should normally be filled by locally recruited staff could easily refuse conditions of appointment which enabled the Secretary of State to send in senior officials from outside. The personnel of the Colonial Office was well aware of the trap into which a territory might fall if it secured higher constitutional status without a comparable change of attitude among leading members of the local community to economic and social development. Sir Ralph Furse, who was responsible for expatriate recruitment, used to ask how the poorer colonies could be given the services of first class men.[38] An interest in the relationship between local productivity and social improvement implied a certain degree of outside interference.

. While the Bill was in a preliminary draft form, Lord Hailey's suggestion, made originally in his *African Survey,* that special provision was required to finance research was incorporated into the Office discussions in May 1939. At a special meeting in July a proposal made in the context of the Royal Commission's investigations that a regional commissioner should be appointed to advise West Indian governments and coordinate their development plans was put by the Labour Adviser who had been in office for only a year. Labour questions had been uppermost in the discussions which preceded the appointment of the Royal Commission, and the General Secretary of the Trades Union Congress was appointed to be a member. It was not surprising that trade unionists pressed the Colonial Office to incorporate a condition into the machinery for administering the fund which would require colonial governments to establish proper labour departments. The Comptroller's office in the West Indies, when it was set up in Barbados in 1940, had a distinct bias towards labour and social service questions.[39]

The publicity which the West Indian inquiry attracted and the parliamentary interest which the colonial problem in international affairs aroused persuaded officials that they should design a colonial development bill with appropriate machinery to attract support from public opinion at home for the investment it entailed. In May 1939 the Secretary of State agreed to official suggestions that a Public Relations Department should be established inside the Office. No action could be taken before the outbreak of war, and the names considered for appointment between January and April

1940 were for a number of different reasons not pursued. Sabine, the 'beachcomber' who had been given the job of designing a scheme of work in this field, was therefore made the first acting Public Relations Officer in July.[40] The proposal to reestablish a strong advisory committee to administer the fund was also interpreted as an opportunity to gain support at home for a more progressive policy, and it even led to a revival of the idea that a special Colonial Assembly should be set up to represent the views of the Empire and educate British public opinion about its problems. The Secretary of State and his officials took seriously the suggestion that MPs might be appointed to the advisory committee and that the House of Commons should consider setting up its own committee on colonial affairs. The subject was discussed at a special dinner for the Parliamentary Under-Secretary and a number of senior officials in November 1938.[41]

The keynote of the new colonial development policy was that each side in the central-local relationship should be made more aware of the other's problems. This was stressed by the Secretary of State in his annual report to Parliament in May 1939,[42] which suggested that trust based on cooperation would have to replace the tradition of trusting the man on the spot. The message was repeated with some differences of emphasis in the White Paper of February 1940 which explained the new Bill and proposed the greater regularisation of contact between governments in terms of better coordination.[43] The implication of both these pronouncements was that a new idiom of administration was required.

The assumption of officials working at the centre when war was declared reflected a degree of uncertainty about how this cooperation was to be sustained. The White Paper at the time disguised some of the doubts and hesitations which would have found expression if the war had not intervened. In the first place, there was a strong feeling that the deployment of expatriate staff would be most openly discouraged by the representatives of local opinion where the required expertise was most needed in setting up social services. It was going to be difficult to reconcile the training of local staff for senior posts on European salaries and the raising of taxes from local sources. In the second place, there seemed to be a danger that metropolitan sources of revenue would be called upon to subsidise services in precisely those colonies where the local elite was the most resistant to change. The abandonment of the traditional doctrine that each colony should live off its own resources drew attention to the crucial importance of local social structures. However much the new policy required the centre to generalise across the Empire, civil servants still had to particularise in terms of whom the improved social services might benefit.

The presentation of the final announcement in February 1940 was delayed by differences between the Office and the Treasury over the forms of words to be used. The Office wanted its proposed legislation to secure the maximum political effect in the period of the phoney war; the Treasury wanted to emphasise that the Act would encourage economic development and provide financial returns on investment — a view which the Office thought smacked of exploitation. At one stage in the inter-departmental discussions the Treasury even wanted to jettison the term 'welfare', which the Office deemed essential. At the beginning of January Sir Horace Wilson, on behalf of the Treasury, complained that the draft statement was not far short of saying that 'the only thing to do is to put the Colonies on the dole from henceforth and forever'.[44] Ten days later the Secretary of State protested 'if we are not now going to do something fairly good for the Colonial Empire, and something which helps them to get proper social services, we shall deserve to lose the Colonies and it will only be a matter of time before we get what we deserve.'[45] The final text of the White Paper represented a compromise. The Treasury accepted the term 'welfare', and in return the Office agreed to drop the idea of a fund.

The White Paper managed to lay emphasis on the social costs of uncontrolled private capitalist activity without using any theoretical vocabulary, because it committed the British government to subsidising the recurrent costs of social services 'over a substantial period of years'. As an introduction to the Act, the White Paper showed how far thinking at the centre had been concentrated on what were seen to be the crucial factors in the localities — 'an improvement of the Government machinery and a reinforcement of the personnel of the development services . . . '. The vision of progress embodied in these discussions was founded upon expanding technical staff in the field, partly because only adequate research on the ground and appropriate social surveys would yield the necessary data on which to base agricultural or industrial improvement schemes, and partly because only properly trained officers would be able to build up the level of social services required. The Colonial Office stance in 1940 was that, while the 1929 Act had been directed towards material development, the new Act would give expression to the notion of 'welfare'.

THE TASKS OF WAR

2

THE ORGANISATION AT WAR

THE purpose of this chapter is to provide a broad picture of the way in which the tasks of war affected the Colonial Office's structure, procedures, and relationships, and of the resources available — human and non-human — for coping with the challenge. Some of the aspects discussed will be given fuller treatment in subsequent chapters, where the major functions are isolated and considered in detail. The first section sketches the pressures on the Office as a result of the large-scale developments of the war; the second looks at the organisation's expansion and the changing distribution of its responsibilities; and the third considers the leadership available during the war as a whole. There are clearly problems in fashioning a neat account of what wartime administration entailed, and it is hard to do justice to the multi-faceted, simultaneous, often chaotic character of the process itself. Some general sketch of the Office's experience of war does, however, have to be attempted in order to provide the organisational background necessary for a proper understanding of its policy deliberations.

The scope of the challenge

The Office accommodated itself to wartime administration in a manner which could not have been anticipated at the time of the major dislocations of 1940. The passage of the Colonial Development and Welfare Act took place largely during the period of the 'phoney war' and before the brunt of the enemy attack was felt. The Bill received its second reading in the Commons on the day that Churchill went to Paris just before the Allied armies began their retreat to Dunkirk. The fall of France and the closing of the Mediterranean to shipping after Italy's entry into the war brought a sharp shock to the administrative system of the colonial Empire at the beginning of June, and Somaliland was, in August, the first British colony to fall into enemy hands.

Although the immediate hardships had an important influence on the conduct of day-to-day business, the Office's work during 1940-43 developed characteristics which were largely determined by the changing methods of Allied strategy. In the first place, the arrangements made for the economic blockade of Europe were also applied to the colonies of the European powers, and as Hitler's armies advanced and colonies were separated from their metropolitan governments the British authorities had to decide how to handle the consequent disruptions of trade. The fall of France brought the additional burden of dealing with the French colonies, which were divided between those supporting the Vichy regime and those joining the Free French. An extremely active participant in the Whitehall Committee on French Resistance, the Colonial Office was obliged in December 1940 to set up its own French Relations Department.[1] This dealt with all the questions that arose as the Free French tried to persuade others to come over and join them. It also dealt with the Belgian authorities in the Congo, and with the Dutch authorities whose Empire was also in difficulties. The first year of war thrust the Colonial Office directly into handling the problem of colonialism at an international level.

In the second place, the United States, although initially not a belligerent, made its presence continually felt in the organisation of the war effort.There had been secret talks between the British and the Americans on security questions in the Caribbean even before war was declared; and in the summer of 1940 the negotiations for American bases in the British West Indies were opened. The Colonial Office became a fairly reluctant participant in what became known as the 'bases agreement', by which a number of reconditioned American destroyers were made available to Britain in exchange for the lease of Caribbean bases to the United States. It was also worried by rumours about possible territorial concessions to the United States in the Caribbean.[2] The supply of materials to Britain from America at the same time became subject to another 'lease' principle in the famous Lend-Lease arrangements by which American material was provided for use against the Axis.

The evolution of the Alliance after Hitler's invasion of Russia in June 1941 and the Japanese attack on Pearl Harbor in December left its mark on Colonial Office activity. The entry of the Americans into the war inaugurated the system of combined planning and subjected British war aims to the close scrutiny of an ally which was determined to avoid any appearance of fighting to preserve the British Empire. The loss of the Far East to the Japanese by

February 1942 also drew attention to the productive as well as the strategic potential of colonial possessions and led the Allies to reconsider their priorities. For the next nine or ten months Africa was not only the main theatre of war against Germany and Italy but also the area most likely to supply the raw materials which had hitherto been secured from the Far East. The American commitment to an Anglo-American landing in North Africa, which was agreed in July and executed in November 1942, reduced the likelihood of an invasion of Western Europe in 1943 and delayed an onslaught on the Japanese-occupied colonies in the Far East. The basic decisions of strategy and logistics influenced the shape and direction of administrative effort in the Empire.

The immediate casualties of the change of fortune in the summer of 1940 were the administrative routines themselves. The Legal Adviser in 1939 had already been given permission to restrict his scrutiny of colonial legislation in order to relieve pressure of work;[3] and the Personnel Department in 1940 abandoned its procedures for securing regular confidential reports on serving colonial officers.[4] The geographical departments had to proceed without the full panoply of legal advice, and the promotions committee which considered suitable candidates for senior colonial service posts had to meet without detailed dossiers on suitable individuals. The Office set up a small committee under Sir Alan Burns to investigate possible methods for reducing the volume of correspondence between London and the territorial governments.[5] By the end of 1940 the Colonial Service Department was regarded as so much reduced in status and activity that its Assistant Secretary was transferred to handle the new Department on French Relations. With the mobilisation of manpower for the armed forces the Appointments Department, with its head absent for long periods on sick leave, could hardly fill its vacancies or the Personnel Department consider the finer points of career development.

Another major casualty was the printed report — victim of the economy campaign to conserve the supply of paper. Colonies and their principal administrative officers in technical departments such as medicine or agriculture were discouraged from issuing annual reports. The Secretary of State's annual statement to Parliament for the Supply debate, reinstated by Ormsby-Gore in May 1938 and MacDonald in May 1939, was not submitted to the printer in June 1940.[6] Even the *Colonial Office List* itself, the standard reference

51

work for public use and guide to both the centre and the periphery in the administrative system, was not published between 1941 and 1946.

The burden of additional work fell largely on the defence section of the General Division with the military liaison staff and on the Economic Division which was responsible for handling the colonial consequences of the economic blockade of Europe. The measures which had been taken in 1938 to prepare for the defence of British colonies against an Italian invasion had in fact been relaxed in November 1939, and they were not reactivated until May 1940.[7] The Secretary of State had some difficulty in getting the service departments to keep him informed about the many facets of military planning which impinged on the Empire. He was not consulted about the appointments of regional commanders — the GOC East Africa and the C-in-C Far East — and his military liaison staff did not secure the right to make daily visits to the War Room of the Chiefs of Staff until November 1940.[8] The Economic Division in handling supply needs and imposing financial regulations on the colonies became closely associated with the Ministries of Food, Shipping, and Supply, particularly when it took the special action required to support those colonial economies which were heavily dependent on the sale of a single cash crop. The economic blockade played a part in persuading the French administration in Equatorial Africa to come over to the cause of the Free French. The initial impact of hostilities on the colonial administrative system was felt in the disruption of relationships between the European powers, whose metropolitan territory was in German hands, and their colonies, with all the implications which it carried for the threat of armed invasion; and also in the dislocation of the marketing of colonial products which had normally been sold in Europe.

On a narrower technical level the war brought the administrative burdens of security procedures and convoy arrangements to control the transmission of messages and the movement of people and goods. These included familiarity with the details of censorship over personal mail, news, and photographs, as well as with the methods of issuing identity papers and booking passages by ship or aeroplane. All the extra work fell on the General Division or on one of the common service departments. As if in acknowledgement of this extension of labour, when the King visited the Office on 1 October 1940 he inspected the very active code and cypher section.[9] A shortened form of air mail letter using telegraphic language (called 'savingram'), following the model of the Foreign Office, was introduced in November 1939 and 'special care' procedures for secret files in January 1940. The Office reviewed its security procedures at a special meeting on 24 May.[10]

The Office building itself became embattled. Preparations for evacuation in case of invasion played havoc with the storage and circulation of files. The staff were grouped for civil defence, Home Guard, and fire-watching duties, and an increasing proportion were asked or preferred to sleep on the premises. By December 1940 the numbers sleeping each night had reached about a hundred. The normal Whitley Council machinery for meetings between staff and management was wound up and replaced in September 1940 by a Staff Welfare Committee which handled all the problems of living conditions for the duration of the war.[11]

But the shock of handling great increases in the volume of work with a shifting body of staff immediately called into question the most fundamental feature in any office organisation, its established routine for the registration of papers. The Colonial Office had since the early 1930s maintained a system by which the papers on each subject were kept together under a recognised code number drawn from those allocated to that section of the organisation which seemed to have the greatest claim. Fresh files were opened each year but the same number retained. The General Division had argued even in 1935 that it would have preferred the introduction of a 'unit system' on the lines used by the Foreign Office which allocated a code number for each major document and its attachments, because that would have facilitated the discovery of papers dealing with subjects that cut across the formal allocation of office duties. The Establishments Officer in March 1940 suggested the introduction of a new system but had no success.[12] The more complicated a subject became, the more need there was for multiple copies which could be filed under different headings.

The main criticism rested on the argument that the supporting staff of registry clerks and other clerical officers would be more effectively deployed if they were not isolated in common service units but grouped around the administrative officers in each geographical or subject department. Those who had been temporarily seconded to other Whitehall departments and had seen other methods of work sometimes returned and expressed their dissatisfaction with a system which encouraged unnecessary conflict between different sections. A few confessed that they had frequently dispensed with the services of a registry or the despatch section in order to gain the benefits of speed and accuracy. In July 1940 a Principal in the Economic Division, J. B. Williams, criticised the centralised structure which channelled all its work through a single despatch section from a number of copying departments and registries. Caine, his Assistant Secretary, in submitting his criticisms for a wider discussion, secured a meeting of heads of divisions on 11 October to see how delays could be avoided.[13] The weight of opinion among the heads of geographical departments was against any change in practice; they were unwilling to recognise that the bias of the system towards a geographical treatment of any subject imposed an awkward handicap on those parts of the Office which bore the initial brunt of war-time arrangements.

In the massive increase in the volume of letters and telegrams exchanged between the Colonial Office and the colonies, there seemed to be a noticeable reduction in the kind of intimate contacts required by each side to foster understanding. Between 1937 and 1944 the number of despatches and telegrams sent and received in a calendar year increased from about 7,600 each way to about 40,000.[14] But the bulk of these exchanges dealt with matters decided in other departments or by negotiations between the Allies. Defence regulations imposed upon both the Colonial Office and territorial governments a form of correspondence from which neither drew any opportunity to consider development questions; international discussions sometimes called for circular telegrams or requests for statistical returns. This kind of correspondence hardly encouraged proper consultation. Pressure of work produced the paradox that constant exchanges inhibited the traditional forms of intimacy.

In addition, many colonies for the first time experienced the presence of representatives from departments of the British government other than the Colonial Office; they were often expected to create their own liaison arrangements if Whitehall did not send out its own officials. Those departments most interested in establishing colonial bases were the Ministries of Food, Supply, and War Transport. The armed services departments and the security services were also eager to take advantage of the strategic position which some colonies enjoyed if there were plans to control communications or launch an offensive. Intelligence officers wanted to be close to the French colonies which remained loyal to Vichy; the Ministry of Information also took an interest in all possibilities for extending the role of propaganda. The most momentous 'invasion' of the colonies by the apparatus of the British government consisted of the resident ministers which the Cabinet from time to time established in the Far East, the Middle East, West Africa, and North Africa. The Resident Minister in the Gold Coast in 1942 gave the West African colonies their first taste of a form of governor-general's department.[15]

The representatives of foreign governments or governments in exile also had to be accommodated on colonial soil if they were considered able to provide a smoother liaison between the different branches of the Allied machine. The Free French won the opportunity to send their own staff officers to colonies such as Nigeria which were close to their bases of support. American personnel were also sometimes posted to colonies even before the United States had entered the war. Arrangements made with the Americans in 1941 to ferry the aircraft required in the Middle East through West Africa brought the employees of Pan-American Airways, the principal contractors, to settle in that area.[16]

In spite of the great increase in metropolitan activity to promote better publicity and public relations on behalf of the Colonial Empire, the number of occasions when the Colonial Office could take the colonies into its confidence was not noticeably increased. Indeed, the multiplicity of negotiations between the Allies in the organisation of the war effort or in planning for a post-war settlement was a handicap to routine discussion between London and the colonies. The changes of mood and direction in wartime discussion could be so rapid and fundamental that any communication with the colonies might be not only quickly overtaken by events but also dangerously misleading. The Colonial Office hesitated to involve colonial governments in matters which it barely understood and on which it had scant information.

Even on questions which were more strictly confined to colonial policy, the status of information divulged to the colonies might be in dispute. Reports from advisory committees or speeches reported in the British press were likely to be misinterpreted in the colonies if they implied a degree of policy commitment. A recommendation might easily be given the appearance of a decision. If the Colonial

Office was obliged to take seriously the propaganda implications of its pronouncements and to consider their effects on public opinion abroad, particularly in the United States, it always ran the risk of being taken up by colonial governments on specific points which were not covered by a general statement.

It was ironic that the value of the colonies to the wartime alliance and the virtue of development policy for the colonies themselves had to be proclaimed without any stronger statistical analysis than a number of rough estimates. Another casualty of the 1940 crisis was the 1941 Census of the Empire. When officials decided on 24 May 1940 to abandon the arrangements they had made, thereby following the British government's own proposal to dispense with a decennial survey, they realised that they had foregone the opportunity to make some assessment of the progress made during the 1930s.[17] The results of the 1931 Census in the Empire were not particularly reliable in accuracy and uniformity, but they provided some kind of base-line in policy discussions. In 1939 the Permanent Under-Secretary doubted whether the Office could make use of a professional statistician.[18] The first attempts at an all-Empire survey were not begun until 1944 when Dr R.R. Kuczynski started work on a demographic survey to aid reconstruction planning; the first statistician joined the Economic Division in 1944 and tried experiments with economic surveys in the spring of 1945.[19]

Although the wartime system of economic controls brought the Colonial Office into closer contact with other departments in Whitehall and their counterparts in the combined planning agencies, there was often a considerable difficulty in getting colonial interests represented in the proper forum of debate. The major departments of state were not always ready to recognise that the Colonial Office had a standing obligation to speak on behalf of the colonies. The Secretary of State's 'dual role' — HMG in the colonies and the colonies in HMG — was not fully appreciated outside the Office and was particularly vulnerable to being slighted in the bustle of wartime activity.

The major policy areas in which the Colonial Office engaged with other departments were those associated with supply and production and to a lesser extent with questions of manpower for the armed forces. Before war was declared its officials sat regularly on six of the CID standing committees, and one of these — the Overseas Defence Committee — was normally chaired by its

Permanent Under-Secretary.[20] When war broke out it was represented on the food policy committees of Cabinet at both ministerial and official levels, and on the economic warfare committee at the official level. The only standing committees which continued normally to be chaired by its representatives were those handling imperial communications and overseas mails. The Treasury and Cabinet Office surveys of inter-departmental committees below Cabinet level undertaken in 1941 and 1942-43 suggest that the Office was largely linked with the economic departments (Treasury, Board of Trade, Ministry of Economic Warfare, and Ministry of Shipping and Transport), and the services departments, especially the War Office.[21]

There was one other major area which involved the Colonial Office in significant inter-departmental contact, and that was foreign policy, in which the Foreign Office naturally took the lead. The Deputy Under-Secretary of the Colonial Office was normally chairman of the Middle East Official Committee; the appropriate Assistant Under-Secretary played a major part in committee deliberations on the Far East when the return of British authority to Japanese-occupied colonies was being planned. The only major Cabinet committee of ministers which the Colonial Office could regard as its own creation was the Africa Committee, set up in 1942 to monitor the work of the Resident Minister in West Africa. This was the only significant Cabinet committee chaired by the Secretary of State.[22]

Paradoxically for a much smaller department, the Dominions Office was much more strongly represented in inter-departmental discussions.[23] The self-governing Dominions could make their voices heard in international debate, and the major British departments of state usually derived value from associating the Dominions Office in their discussions. In such fields as civil aviation or commercial agreements, the Colonial Office usually had to take the initiative and insist on being brought into consultation.

All these features of the conduct of business in wartime were a reminder of the fact that the innovations of the war machine were likely to influence the methods used in approaching post-war problems. It was particularly difficult to assess the consequences of technological invention, although all the advances made in weapon design and electronic detection equipment were likely to revolutionise security problems and patterns of communication in the Empire. By 1941 it seemed clear that the parochialism of the colonies would be much more easily broken down as the possibilities for extending travel by air became apparent.[24] The British feared that the Americans would take unfair advantage of the footholds they had gained in the imperial system in order to promote private commercial gain. An Anglo-American agreement on aircraft manufacture gave the Americans responsibility for the manufacture of larger aircraft which could easily be converted for civil aviation purposes. Even if an all-Empire route round the world had been established, only the American aircraft construction industry would have been in a position immediately after the war to provide the machines to fly it.[25] Pan-American and Trans-World Airlines gained a great deal of knowledge about imperial air space from the experience of operating ferry routes for military aircraft. In telecommunications the Americans had insisted as soon as they entered the war on opening up a large number of direct circuits between themselves and different parts of the Empire. The pre-war monopoly of Cable & Wireless was badly dented. The loss of the Far East in 1942 put 18,000 miles of cable out of action, and forced communication with Australasia to follow lines through either Canada and the Pacific or West Africa and Cape Town.[26]

As the theatre of war switched from Africa to Italy in the spring of 1943, the advances made in communication by air were immediately felt in the number of applications for travel made by officials both at the centre and in the colonies who wished to exchange views on the priorities for post-war planning. Governors wished to return home for leave and consultation with the Colonial Office; the advisers of the Secretary of State planned tours of inspection to report on territorial government activity. Advisory committees also considered which of their interests would benefit by a little foreign travel.

The contrasts between the London and territorial ends of the central-local axis provided in 1943-44 the principal evidence for contemporaries of the effects of the war effort on methods of operation. In the autumn of 1943 the British war economy was at full stretch; the mother country after four years of war had reached the maximum point in the mobilisation of its resources.

Territorial governments had also experienced administrative changes which were broadly comparable to those in Britain. Supply departments were created, customs departments expanded, food controllers appointed, and legislation introduced to institute rationing, control stocks, and set prices. But these controls did not lead to many basic changes in the organisation of territorial government, partly because a great number of the instruments whose development the mother country had encouraged, such as supply councils and marketing boards, were deliberately designed to deal with business at a regional level; and partly because the design of territorial government was closely bound up with notions of political advancement. The central government in many territories where the Chief Secretary continued to concentrate authority in his own hands had little opportunity to develop the range of subject specialisation which the war imposed on the Colonial Office itself. Sir Philip Mitchell's experiments in administrative reform were exceptional. As chief civil affairs officer on General Wavell's staff in the Middle East, he had devised a form of decentralised secretariat organisation which encouraged a subject specialisation among his staff. He believed that the basis of Cabinet government could only be reached in colonial territories if their secretariats were abolished and the business of government divided as far as possible among members of the Executive Council.[27] After experimenting in military administration, he was able to implement his ideas in Fiji in 1943 and in Kenya in 1945. Similarly, Sir Bernard Bourdillon in Nigeria had requested the appointment of a commission to examine his secretariat because he wanted to see what he called 'the Indian system' of Cabinet secretariat introduced into colonial affairs.[28] Part of the reluctance on the part of Colonial Service officers to consider improvements in the organisation of colonial government was the skeleton nature of their establishments in expatriate postings. The officers in the field rarely enjoyed the stimulus of new work and expanding career opportunities, and they certainly bore the brunt of local discontent about the imposition of controls.

Staffing and the expansion of the 'subject' side

The weight of the administrative burden brought by the outbreak of war fell initially on those parts of the organisation which were not strictly in the main stream of colonial policy formulation. The Defence and General Division, as its name implied, handled the collection of miscellaneous obligations that were not easily divided on a geographical basis. Even the Economic Division at the outbreak of war was not the major focus for the discussion of development.

The emphasis in policy considerations was as much on research and welfare as on economic growth. The Division's initial *raison d'être* was the imperial preference system, and its extension to include the development of international commodity agreements. As the war progressed major decisions on strategy and logistics altered the balance of advantages inside the Office towards a much greater subject orientation. The following chapters provide a detailed account of these administrative changes in the context of the events in which they took place. Subject departments were created by continuing the process of 'hiving off' sections from the General Division, and making provision for greater specialisation in the Economic Division.

The principal Colonial Office expansion of staff took place during the year which followed American entry into the war. The loss of the Far East to Japan gave such increased importance to the position and products of the African colonies that the volume of central department work increased at a rapid rate. During 1942 the centre of activity in the Allied supply system switched from London to Washington, but the vast increase in its volume and complexity required an expansion of staff at the London end. The whole-time non-industrial Civil Service which bore the main burden of wartime operations was expanded until it reached its peak of 686,000 in the spring of 1943.

The difficulties brought on by the increase of work at the centre were compounded by the withdrawal of experienced staff for service in the armed forces or elsewhere. In 1940 eight Assistant Principals were already serving in the forces, five Principals were on loan to other departments, and two Assistant Secretaries and the third Legal Adviser had been sent to the Ministry of Supply.[29] Unlike those home departments which were obliged to recruit large numbers of temporary officers directly from civilian occupations, the Colonial Office had the advantage of being able to call upon members of the Colonial Service. Some on leave in England were hurriedly summoned to the Office by telephone, and several recruited in this manner came to occupy key positions. Sabine became Public Relations Officer; Sabben-Clare went as representative to Washington; Benson was transferred to the Cabinet Office and then returned to work on post-war planning; and Thornley, who succeeded to the post of Principal Private Secretary in September 1941 when Eastwood was knocked down by a tram, stayed in that post for the remainder of the war.

Even retired Governors were recruited to perform duties for which an administrative officer could not be spared. Those Governors who fell into enemy hands were detained for the duration of the war, but those who escaped were employed. Sir Vincent Glenday, the Governor of Somaliland at the time of the Italian invasion in 1940, was not allowed to return on its recapture in 1941 because the War Office insisted on a military administration, and he remained a temporary Principal in the Eastern Department. Lord Hailey commissioned a few retired officers to prepare memoranda on post-war problems. The custom of taking 'beachcombers' had acquired the additional virtue of supplying for temporary employment a pool of manpower which could be relied upon to be familiar with colonial affairs.[30]

The permanent staff secured additional authority to improve the despatch of business. A ruling of 1925 that minutes written by those below the rank of Assistant Under-Secretary had to be signed and not just initialled was waived. Assistant Secretaries could now initial on all occasions, while lesser officials could do so in those instances where they wrote 'at once' on a paper — that is, where they could authorise immediate action.[31]

Any established officer in the department considered capable of handling the increased volume of work was given promotion, or at least placed in a position where promotion was deserved, even if the Treasury declined to approve it. In September 1942 the Establishment Officer recorded: 'we have reached rock bottom in the matter of the promotion of clerical officers to replace the Higher Clerical Officers being used....'[32] When the Permanent Under-Secretary visited the Treasury in December 1942 to discuss his staffing problems he felt that he was in a strong position to recommend major changes.[33] Sheer pressure of work had compelled an increase in the number of staff dealing with defence and economic matters, even if some savings in manpower had been effected in the personnel and geographical departments. The report submitted to the Cabinet committee on manpower showed that since the outbreak of war there had been 293 additions to the General and Economic Divisions and to the advisory staff, while the Appointments Department had lost 25 and the geographical departments 14 staff.[34] The total figures available for the number of staff in post show that the increase in staff during the first ten months of 1942 was roughly equivalent to that for the thirty previous months and the thirty following months.

NUMBER OF STAFF IN POST

	Administrative Executive and Clerical	Support Staff	Total
1938	255	185	440
April 1939	297	174	471
January 1942	367	249	616
October 1942	442	323	765
August 1945	480*	357*	837
1948	634	650*	1,284*

*estimated numbers

There was no equivalent increase in the size of the Dominions Office. Although the latter was closely involved in the discussions which took place between departments on post-war questions, it had no supervisory duties and no development policy to pursue. The size of its staff remained between 120 and 160 throughout the war.[35] By contrast, the Colonial Office was four times this size in 1944 and five times in 1947.

The Permanent Under-Secretary of the Colonial Office secured Treasury approval for a major reconstruction which came into force in March 1943 with the creation of two new posts of Assistant Under-Secretary, bringing the total at that level to seven. There was no further addition of this kind in the history of the Office except the creation of a eighth post in February 1948.[36] The two new posts in 1943 provided an Assistant Under-Secretary to supervise the General Division in association with Social Services, Public Relations, and the West Indies; and another to supervise the Economic Division which consisted of two Assistant Secretary departments and the Financial Adviser. Clauson, the Assistant Under-Secretary who had hitherto supervised the economic work, was released in order to specialise in long-term economic questions. This regularised a *de facto* situation which had been working since the economic staff had moved in September 1942 to separate accommodation in Dover House, near Horse Guards Parade and close to Downing Street; the heads of the Production and Supplies Departments had begun their respective duties while they were still Principals. The Treasury had been reluctant to grant full Assistant Secretary status to some of the new specialisations breaking away from the General Division. Sabine, the first Public Relations Officer, and Colonel Cole who took charge of the Prisoners of War Department — both of whom began in the General Division — and Keith who separated welfare work from social services, were all on an intermediate salary between Principal and Assistant Secretary.[37]

The structure of the Office in the spring of 1943 therefore reflected the alteration in the balance between subject and geographical work which had been brought about by wartime administrative developments. The proportion of administrative staff arranged on the two sides can be seen by comparing the figures for April 1939 with those of December 1942 after the main expansion. Between these two dates the number of administrative officers on the geographical side had been reduced from 73 to 53 and in personnel from 83 to 53, while those in the subject departments had increased from 66 to 170.[38] The steady increase in the volume of subject work after 1942 can also be measured by the number of files registered on each side of the Office. That number can be estimated from the register sheets filled out each time a new file was created. (See diagram.[39]) This major change can be illustrated in the difference between the structure of the Office in 1938 and in 1948. The number of geographical departments had increased during that decade from seven to nine, but the subject side had expanded from the General Division and three Departments to the General Department and eighteen additional ones. Of these new Departments, ten were created during the war.

The growth of subject specialisations in the Colonial Office had been encouraged by the distribution of governmental functions at home. The majority of official committees at Cabinet level which the Office was invited to join called for Assistant Secretaries from within the Defence, General, or Economic sections. Those responsible for defence questions extended their former CID roles to cover such subjects as censorship and allied forces manpower; the Economic Division was brought in to the commercial and commodity discussions. A Principal from the Economic Division, H. T. Bourdillon, who became the expert on relations with the Free French and economic aid to the French colonies, was moved to the Foreign Office and then to the Cabinet Office to take charge of the African Economic Affairs Secretariat, which acted as part of the machinery set up with the combined planning boards to deal with questions of supply for the whole of the former French Empire, whether

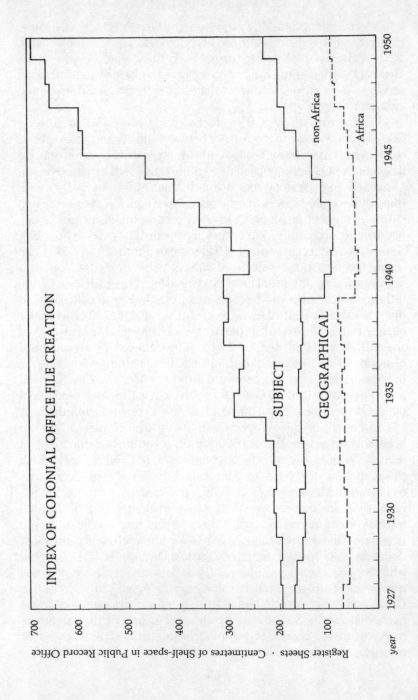

INDEX OF COLONIAL OFFICE FILE CREATION

SUBJECT

GEOGRAPHICAL

non-Africa

Africa

Register Sheets · Centimetres of Shelf-space in Public Record Office

year

or not it was in Africa, as well as the Belgian Congo and Liberia.[40]

But the changing character of administration was effecting something more than a shift away from geographical specialisation at the centre; it was also gradually undermining traditional distinctions of grade and rank. The tasks performed during the war did not fit neatly into the division of labour between administrative officers and supporting staff. A striking feature of the 1942 expansion was the proportionately high rate of increase in clerical officers, typists, and messengers. Many of the new routines did not call for administrative personnel, although such a grade was often employed on work 'below' its expected skills whenever there was a shortage of experienced juniors. Assistant Secretaries occasionally complained that they were obliged to undertake 'Assistant Principal chores'. War regulations required the handling of large numbers of sub-files on individual territories or specific commodities, and a great deal of time was consumed in the initiation of surveys, checking figures, and writing brief summaries of regular returns.

The promotion of clerical officers to fill key posts in the organisation raised the question whether the new control procedures called for staff in the middle rank which corresponded more closely to the executive grade found in other Whitehall departments. Those who left the Colonial Office on secondment to ministries where executive officers were in regular use returned with ideas to deploy the available manpower in a different manner. As soon as the departmental Whitley Council was reconvened at the end of the war, the issue of introducing executive posts into the department was raised by the staff side, who wished to participate in general discussions about the future shape of the home civil service organised by the National Whitley Council.

The subject was also allied to the future of the Colonial Service-Colonial Office relationship.[41] Some continued to argue for the 'fusion' of the two, ending the recruitment of staff for the Colonial Office through the mechanisms of the home civil service and staffing the department entirely from those who had served in the field. Even those who rejected 'fusion' were concerned to regularise the employment of Colonial Service 'beachcombers'. The Permanent Under-Secretary told the Treasury in May 1944 that a decision had not yet been reached on the issue, but that the 'peculiar problems' of the department 'should hardly affect the measures deemed to be desirable for the service as a whole . . . '.[42]

Wartime leadership

The 'peculiar problems' referred to by the Permanent Under-Secretary were not derived from any drastic changes in the composition of the senior personnel during the war: the majority of Governors remained in post at least until 1943, and the same group of senior officials managed the Colonial Office throughout the period 1939-45. Nothing can be ascribed to a 'new generation' thrown up by the battle — at least not in the top echelon. There was, in fact, only one retirement at the senior level during the war: Sir John Shuckburgh in March 1942, the 'senior' and therefore 'Deputy' Under-Secretary, who was replaced by Sir William Battershill, a 'beachcomber' and already Assistant Under-Secretary, leaving a vacancy to which Sir Gerard Gent was promoted. Dawe, Clauson, and Jeffries all held Assistant Under-Secretary posts for the whole period of the war, to be joined by Lloyd and Creasy with the new posts created in March 1943, and by Caine in April 1944 when Jeffries embarked on an African tour.[43]

The only serious attempt to create a 'new generation' of leadership at the official level took place before the war, as part of the policy discussions on colonial development. The Secretary of State for Dominion Affairs, Malcolm MacDonald, accepted appointment for the second time as Secretary of State for the Colonies in May 1938 on the resignation of his predecessor, Ormsby-Gore, after the Cabinet had rejected a plan for the partition of Palestine which had strong departmental backing. MacDonald combined the two ministerial posts — Colonies and Dominions — for a few months during the Munich crisis and its aftermath (October 1938-January 1939) and only gave up the Dominions Office to accommodate Sir Thomas Inskip when the latter was removed from the post of Minister for the Coordination of Defence. MacDonald was anxious to get rid of both his Permanent Under-Secretary, Sir Cosmo Parkinson, who was an internal promotion made by his predecessor in July 1937, and his Deputy Under-Secretary, Sir John Shuckburgh, who had been in charge of the Office's management of the Palestine Mandate since 1921. He secured the transfer of Parkinson to the Dominions Office, whose Permanent Under-Secretary had been selected as the next High Commissioner in South Africa, and designated Shuckburgh to be the next Governor of Nigeria in succession to Sir Bernard Bourdillon who had been nominated Governor-General of the Sudan. Perhaps afraid of a 'leak', he shocked the administrative staff of the Colonial Office by not giving them confidential notice of the name of Parkinson's successor, which they read in their newspapers with considerable surprise in July 1939. The Clerk of London County Council, Sir George Gater, a man only two years younger than Parkinson, was appointed to take charge.[44] Although totally unfamiliar with colonial affairs, he had a reputation for efficiency and drive, and had been closely associated with the LCC Labour Party group's policy programme under Herbert Morrison as leader, which some argued would stand him in good stead now that the Colonial Office had decided to extend social services in the Empire.

But the outbreak of war prevented this dramatic change from taking place. Bourdillon had to stay in Nigeria, and therefore Shuckburgh remained in London. Gater did not take up his appointment on 7 November as arranged, because he was called to be a second Permanent Secretary in support of Sir John Anderson at the new Ministry of Home Security. Parkinson, instead of spending the anticipated two months to achieve the transfer to his new post, found that he had to spend six months working with the Minister who had secured his removal and almost three years in the rather humiliating position of a *locum tenens* for Gater. Parkinson went to the Dominions Office in January 1940, and Gater took up his new appointment on 1 February, but on 25 May was again removed to the Ministry of Supply to assist the new Minister, his old chief, Herbert Morrison, with whom he returned to Home Security in October. Parkinson was therefore called back to the Colonial Office to take charge until such time as Gater could be released.

When Gater finally returned to resume his duties in April 1942 the new Secretary of State who had just been moved from the Dominions Office, Lord Cranborne, refused to prevail upon his successor there, Attlee, to take Parkinson back,[45] and the latter was therefore appointed as the Secretary of State's personal representative who was required to make systematic tours of the Empire and to report on the circumstances he found. Parkinson undertook four such journeys before his retirement: the West Indies in 1942-43, Africa in 1943, the Mediterranean in 1944, and the South Pacific in 1945.[46] His memoirs, *The Colonial Office from Within,* show a remarkable restraint. Cranborne, who had the opportunity of nominating Shuckburgh's successor as Deputy Under-Secretary, chose Battershill.

Gater joined the Office just as it was beginning to expand to meet the major pressures arising from the changing fortunes of war, and until his retirement in January 1947 he enjoyed almost five years of office which witnessed all the important changes of structure. Although he had at least one short sick leave (December 1943-January 1944) because of trouble in the sight of one eye, he presided over all the major post-war planning meetings. His appointment was unpopular with many junior officials in the Office who sympathised with Parkinson, and he never seems to have gained their complete loyalty. With an outstanding record in the First World War and promotion to brigadier at the age of 29, he used to say that he had always 'run his own show' since the age of 35; he organised the Office in a very centralising manner, which some thought deprived the administrative staff of their traditional freedom to handle problems which interested them. Gater liked to sit with the Secretary of State and face his fellow officials across the table. He prided himself on his sensitivity to parliamentary opinion, just as a good council clerk listens to town hall gossip.[47]

But the Coalition Government had no systematic policy on colonial affairs for Parliament to consider. Sometimes parliamentary debates raised the status of a colonial issue to Cabinet level debate — such as the question of compulsory labour[48] in East Africa in September-November 1943 — but this happened rarely. While the Secretary of State was drawn from the House of Lords (May 1940-November 1942) debates in that House, where some expertise on colonial affairs was displayed by peers who had served in the Empire, were occasionally able to mobilise the government. Lord Halifax's combination of the posts of Foreign Secretary and Leader of the House of Lords, which ceased with his departure to be Ambassador in the United States in January 1941, was replaced by a similar conjunction of Leader of the House and Secretary of State for the Colonies, when Lloyd, Moyne, and Cranborne in succession held both posts. The majority of parliamentary information came, however, through questions raised in the Commons by the Fabian MPs and their associates. The major colonial items submitted to the War Cabinet were concerned with either constitutional advance in individual territories which required formal approval, or 'high policy' questions which were usually prompted by American pressure and Dominions' interests. The major collective discussions at Cabinet level on the colonies centred on American proposals for a joint declaration, Palestine, and post-war organisation, subjects not initiated in the Colonial Office. The main occasion when the latter insisted that Cabinet approval should be secured, although the Treasury did not think it necessary, was in submitting the scheme for Colonial Service reform in June 1942. The Colonial Office argued that it could not open negotiations with colonial governments on this question without the authority which only War Cabinet approval would confer.[49] The principal initiatives taken to submit important questions to Cabinet were confined to the proposed constitution for Malaya and the renewal of the Colonial Development and Welfare Act in 1945.

With the possible exception of Cranborne, who held the office for a short period during 1942 between the Cabinet reshuffle which brought in Cripps in February and that which left him out in November, no Secretary of State carried weight inside the coalition. Cranborne's pre-war association with Churchill and Eden usually meant that he could secure a War Cabinet hearing for any matter which he pressed on its attention. He knew a great deal about colonial affairs through his tenure of the parallel office of Secretary of State for Dominion Affairs from October 1940 until he entered the Colonial Office, and again from September 1943 until the 1945 general election. Indeed, his brief stay as Secretary of State and his subsequent posting as Lord Privy Seal were part of the balancing of forces which the Prime Minister had to perform in order to maintain the coalition in being. Even after the reshuffle in November 1942 Cranborne continued to speak on behalf of the Colonial Office in the Lords, and was detailed to look after its interests while the Secretary of State was away on tour in 1943. The Labour Party leader, Attlee, occupied the Dominions Office post in Cranborne's absence. Cranborne had the courage to protest very forcefully in November 1941 when he thought the Prime Minister was failing to keep him informed and thereby making impossible 'the only part of the work of the Dominions Secretary which is of the first importance'[50] — discretion to keep the High Commissioners of the empire in London properly briefed.

The initial impact of the war fell on the Colonial Office when it was under ministers who, like Cranborne, were short-lived in their management of its affairs. When the coalition was formed in May 1940 MacDonald was offered the Ministry of Health, and was succeeded at the Colonial Office by Lord Lloyd, a former Governor of Bombay and High Commissioner in Egypt, who flew to France in an unsuccessful attempt to persuade the French government to keep fighting.[51] Lloyd, as Chairman of the British Council, had been critical of the Colonial Office, and MacDonald ordered certain files to be destroyed when he learnt who his successor was to be. Although he had been an MP, he had never before held ministerial office, and, according to Sir Alan Burns, 'effected a startling change',[52] shocking Parkinson by insisting on discussing telegrams before they had been handled in the Office and summoning junior officers to his presence without telling their superiors. A strongly entrenched Anglo-Catholic and an indefatigable worker, he died at his post from a disease of the blood on 5 February 1941, after less than nine months in office. He kept a bed in the basement of the Downing Street building during the blitz, and only left his post for literally his final hours in hospital.[53]

Lord Moyne, who succeeded him, had been Parliamentary Secretary at the Ministry of Agriculture and Fisheries since the coalition was formed. As the former chairman of the Royal Commission on the West Indies, he was already familiar with colonial policy and administration. Parkinson wrote later that none of the Secretaries of State whom he remembered had 'inspired greater respect and won such affection. Wisdom he had, and kindliness, and humanity; and none could have had a higher sense of public duty. He was keenly interested and happy in his work at the Colonial Office . . .'.[54] Moyne, however, refused to have a scrambler telephone installed in his country home, and was therefore out of touch when officials required a quick decision at the weekend, such as giving permission for the surrender of Hong Kong which was requested on a Sunday.[55] It was suggested that he had only accepted office to help the Prime Minister with whom he had been associated as a Conservative MP and junior minister in the 1920s. Whatever the reason, he remained in the Colonial Office for only a year, and in the reshuffle of February 1942 agreed to go as deputy Minister of State to Cairo where he was later assassinated by Jewish terrorists.

The office of Secretary of State during the critical period of planning post-war reconstruction was held by a single occupant, Oliver Stanley, who had then not held office since the downfall of Chamberlain. He was brought into the coalition in November 1942 to replace Cranborne at the Colonial Office and he remained there until Labour won the general election in 1945. He was the first Secretary of State to spend more than two years in the Office since L.S. Amery's tenure during the Baldwin administration of 1924-29. Stanley's name has been regularly associated with all the important declarations of policy made during the second half of the war, but his personal influence is hard to assess. He left no private papers; he rarely wrote minutes on the official files, and, when he did, was normally terse. His private secretary hesitated to substitute his own interpretation of the minister's wishes and compromised by pinning on the files his own notes, most of which have not been preserved.[56]

There is likewise little evidence of initiative taken by the Parliamentary Under-Secretary, except for the short period in 1942 when the post was occupied by Harold Macmillan. The latter, who subsequently described his entering the Colonial Office from the Ministry of Supply as 'leaving a madhouse in order to enter a mausoleum',[57] made a powerful combination with Cranborne as Secretary of State during the period of Office expansion. Each was a meticulous worker, and a writer of clear and succinct minutes. Eastwood told Burns in August 1942 that Cranborne's presence suited the Office admirably, and Macmillan was responsible for making a major speach in the House of Commons which directed attention to the notion of 'partnership'.[58] While the Secretary of State was in the House of Lords, the Parliamentary Under-Secretary enjoyed a degree of importance in the House of Commons. The only Labour minister in the wartime Colonial Office was George Hall, a mine-workers' MP from South Wales, who was Parliamentary Under-Secretary from May 1940 until he was transferred to the Admiralty and replaced by Macmillan in February 1942. He became the first Labour Secretary of State in the Attlee administration. As soon as a Secretary of State was appointed from the Commons and Macmillan sent to be Minister of State in North Africa, the new Parliamentary Under-Secretary came from the Lords — the Duke of Devonshire, who, like Ormsby-Gore, was Cranborne's brother-in-law. Devonshire, like Stanley, remained in office for the duration of the war.

Stanley and Devonshire did not constitute a very powerful combi-nation of minsters. Stanley suffered from an incipient cancer of the throat, wrongly diagnosed as mumps, for which he had a long sick leave (January-March 1944) and he had a private office reputation for being 'moody'. He had a sharp mind and was a fast reader but many thought he was too prone to reflect the views of the last person to whom he had spoken.[59] Devonshire's contribution is hard to assess.

Apart from taking a number of routine chairmanships, he seems to have made little comment on the progress of departmental work.

There was no strong direction of the Office's policy from the ministerial level, largely because its original distinctive specialisation — the trusteeship of dependent territories — could hardly be a subject for regular collective consideration at Cabinet level in that form, while all the interests of the coalition were centred upon the international order which might emerge from the peace settlement. The Secretaries of State who had given such a firm leadership between the wars were working within the idiom of imperial preference *versus* free trade — an issue which had considerable force in domestic politics — or in terms of the effect of colonial possessions on the balance of power, because they had been able to relate the management of the Colonial Empire to a set of domestic issues. While wartime necessity relegated responsibility for the colonial peoples to the speculative area of post-war planning, their successors could not provide the same positive drive for which political support would be forthcoming. If Cranborne was the sharpest wartime Secretary of State in perceiving what should be done and giving precise instructions for its execution, his skill was not so much in developing the distinctive characteristics of the Secretary of State's formal authority but rather in handling the high policy questions from outside which impinged on his department's work. The war took the colonies 'out of politics' in the sense that trusteeship did not seem to have a place in future party differences on affairs at home.

As there was no ministerial drive or collective Cabinet interest in colonial development, and as the senior personnel had not been drastically changed, the war machine made itself felt in the Office through a series of experiences for the permanent staff who were familiar with the formal aspects of the Secretary of State's authority. The following chapters spell this out in detail. The officials responsible for the Office sense of continuity and commitment to CDW came to appreciate what their administrative system might do as a result of performing tasks which sometimes did not seem closely related to its interests, and what its limitations might be when the assistance of defence regulations and the pressure of wartime emergency was removed.

3

THE MOBILISATION OF RESOURCES

THE experience of participating in the war effort tested the Colonial Office's capacity to apply standards of bureaucratic efficiency to an empire defined for these purposes as part of a wider, integrated system of resources and demands requiring generalised instruments of control. The impact on the organisation was far-reaching, affecting alike its shape, routines, and size. New skills came to be valued and new patterns of consultation employed. The need to enter the mainstream of Whitehall activity produced a significant shift of emphasis in the 'dual role', towards the representation of metropolitan interests or more precisely towards a metropolitan interpretation of common interests. With the effective prosecution of Allied strategy accepted as a value in its own right, the department became acutely sensitive to criticism made inside Whitehall or beyond that the colonies were failing to make their maximum contribution to the war effort. Existing obligations were subjected to close scrutiny whenever they appeared as obstacles to this goal, a process which gave rise to internal friction on more than one occasion.

Although supervision of defensive or military functions occupied its fair share of the Office's attention, this was in no way comparable in its organisational ramifications to the task of administering economic mobilisation.[1] Measures of central or centrally-inspired control came to embrace almost every aspect of the colonies' economic life. After the outbreak of war previously prepared schemes for the maintenance of the blockade and the preservation of resources and supplies were communicated to the colonies in a steady stream of circular telegrams. Territorial administrations were 'invited' to enact the necessary measures for conserving gold and foreign currency reserves, reducing the import of inessentials, and ensuring that vital commodities did not find their way into the enemy's war machine. The chief administrative tools used to achieve these ends were those of exchange control and of import and export licensing; they were for the most part implemented by invoking the special powers available under Defence (Finance) Regulations. The Colonial Office soon found itself snowed under with the work of advising

73

colonies about the particular applications of these policies, while at the same time struggling to keep abreast of the demands and requirements of the other Whitehall departments involved, particularly the Ministries of Food, Supply, and Shipping.

It was impressed upon the Governors that the needs of the Empire as a whole took precedence over those of any individual unit. The working of controls served to restrict a trade already severely disrupted by the closing of European markets, and wartime conditions also gave rise to a burst of activity at the centre to safeguard the supply of essential goods, especially food, and to protect the position of colonial producers and traders. Purchasing arrangements were made for all or part of a crop at guaranteed prices, beginning with sugar (most of which came from the West Indies) and West African cocoa and vegetable oils, and in due course covering such leading products as West Indian bananas, Palestinian citrus fruit, Ceylonese tea, and East African cotton and sisal. By the end of the war nearly all major exports had become the subject of bulk purchasing schemes by agencies operating on behalf of the British government.[2]

In some cases, most notably that of bananas, United Kingdom purchase was undertaken primarily as a relief measure to prevent social and economic hardship. What could not be sold or stored was frequently destroyed. More commonly, however, such schemes were designed to meet central as well as local needs by their incorporation into the British government's supply machinery, although, even in such cases, shortage of shipping space occasionally meant that commodities so purchased were never exported from the colonies. This was the case with a large proportion of West African cocoa during the war years. Arrangements for marketing produce were as complicated as they were time-consuming, calling for a great deal of coordinated activity between government departments. It was not always easy for the Colonial Office to make its voice heard. In March 1940, for example, it complained bitterly about not being properly consulted before a decision was taken to extend United Kingdom import control to all foodstuffs, with the result that the Ministry of Food agreed to prior consultation before taking any action in future which would limit imports from colonial sources.[3]

The necessity for a large measure of inter-departmental contact was equally a feature of the Office's responsibility for seeing that adequate provision was made to meet colonial supply needs, especially in food. Besides calculating colonies' shipping requirements, alternative sources of supply had to be identified and tapped. As United Kingdom resources became increasingly scarce, greater reliance was placed on the productive output of the United States through the provisions of Lend-Lease and the Allied supply machinery in Washington. Local production for import replacement was encouraged and rationing schemes were introduced wherever possible to take some of the pressure off metropolitan authorities. Even so, the pace of work in London was never less than furious: a test check over the period 24 May to 21 June 1943 revealed that the Supplies Department had to deal with no less than 34 per cent of all telegrams passing through the Office.[4]

Territorial governments, under the close prompting and supervision of the Colonial Office, embarked upon economic management with a wide range of interventionist instruments for the control of prices and wages, the direction of manpower, and the storage, movement, and distribution of goods. Supply departments were created and food controllers appointed. Taxation of incomes was greatly extended and, more importantly, used for the first time specifically as a fiscal device to help deal with the inflation arising from a combination of military expenditure and excessive demand. The most contentious aspect of intervention was undoubtedly the conscription of labour, which, though confined to Tanganyika, Northern Rhodesia, and Kenya, produced much adverse comment in Britain and prompted the Cabinet in 1943 to request that Stanley should determine whether effective safeguards existed against the exploitation of the system for private profit in the application of compulsory labour for war production in East Africa.[5]

In so far as they were both firmly locked into a common framework of wartime categories and priorities, the Colonial Office and the colonies became more strongly bound together. Never before had a periphery been expected to keep in such close step with metropolitan decrees. The colonial system became more regularised and colonial societies more regulated. Yet in a paradoxical way wartime centralisation had the effect of introducing a greater degree of remoteness into relationships between London and 'the man on the spot'. The sheer volume of communications may have increased, but the content was largely procedural. Regular correspondence with Governors was cut back sharply and Colonial Regulations were modified to allow them greater personal initiative without reference back to London.[6] Both the Office and the local administrations were, for the most part, functioning as agents for policies decided elsewhere. They did so with the full consciousness that a tightening of central control with a minimum of consultation was necessary and right in the special circumstances of war.

Certain parallels clearly existed between the central administration of wartime controls and the new initiative for a centrally inspired development policy. Given the competition for resources and the need to adapt to changes in Allied strategy, however, it is hardly surprising that officials were much more aware of the way their existing priorities and objectives were frustrated by the war effort than of the implications it contained for future applications of their forward policy. Because war diverted more conspicuously than it reinforced, the process of organisational learning occurred incidentally rather than consciously. It was really only after 1942 that the task of making conscious connections between the experience of current war work and long range planning had to be tackled. The head of the Supplies Department observed in June 1943 that there was a great deal to be learnt if only someone were appointed in his department 'with the necessary qualities and time to spare for dealing with those problems which affect both the present and the future'.[7]

Central management

By the summer of 1940 the system of economic controls was virtually complete.[8] But it was only afterwards, and especially during the following year, that the Colonial Office was forced to come to terms with changes in the pattern of its responsibilities which arose from the working of this system. The 'blitzkrieg telegram' of June 1940 called for a general direction of all effort towards the survival of the colonial empire in conditions of total war. Colonies were asked to reduce their demand on resources to a minimum by restricting non-essential imports, particularly those using iron and steel. They were also encouraged to produce raw materials for the war effort and foodstuffs for their own consumption. The need for curtailment of social services was recognised, and the recently unveiled policy of Colonial Development and Welfare was for the time being placed in cold storage.[9] As early as 1939 cocoa and sisal had become serious marketing problems because of the loss of the large German market in those commodities.[10] As the availability of shipping deteriorated and materials became more scarce in the latter part of the year and into 1941, the United Kingdom authorities adopted an increasingly selective approach to trade with the colonies. The reduction in United Kingdom imports placed a number of colonial producers in a very difficult position, which had to be met by guaranteed purchasing arrangements, such as that instituted in late 1940 when the Treasury agreed to buy the greater part of the West Indian banana and citrus crops, in the full knowledge that they would probably never be shipped.

The problem of export surpluses was by this time beginning to receive serious attention. An interdepartmental meeting had been held at the request of the Colonial Office in June to consider the disposal of primary products in excess supply; and in July another meeting, this time held at the Ministry of Economic Warfare with Leith Ross in the chair, decided in favour of a ministerial committee to examine the problem of surpluses. Colonial Office concerns became tied to general Whitehall activity directed towards closer Anglo-American economic cooperation. An official committee on export surpluses was established in January 1941 under Leith Ross, and in due course memoranda were submitted by the Colonial Office representatives covering a wide range of commodities, including bananas, citrus, sugar, and cotton. At the same time a new body inside the Office known as the Scientific Committee for examining Alternative Uses of Colonial Raw Materials (SCAUCRM), staffed by officials, scientists, and a few businessmen, was brought into operation at Lord Lloyd's direction.[11]

The Colonial Office did its utmost to maintain the United Kingdom import quota of colonial products at as high a level as possible. This was primarily a matter of conducting negotiations with the Ministry of Food. To improve the methods of communication Melville was sent to this department in July 1940 to serve as the Office's liaison officer there. In order to make forceful pleas in London for the protection of colonial interests, it was clearly essential that the colonies should be seen to be playing their full part in the war effort. This was the new face of the traditional Colonial Office problem concerning its 'dual role'. The key factor was the effectiveness of colonial regulation, given even greater importance after November 1940 when metropolitan controls on United Kingdom food exports were replaced by colonial controls on food imports.

By the beginning of the following year the Office was under considerable pressure to impress the need for stringency upon territorial administrations. They were told that the level of food supplies might have to be reduced still further, and were asked to submit estimates of the extent to which existing import licences could be reduced.[12] Those on the economic side of the Office were becoming convinced that something more was required to bring home to those who had not suffered the privations and dangers of life in Britain the seriousness of the economic situation. It was difficult to know what standards were appropriate in judging the colonial contribution. The Economic Department formed a view that the colonies should go much further in tightening their belts but failed to reach any firm ruling whether these territories were to be governed by conditions similar to those prevailing in the United Kingdom, or whether they should all be allowed to maintain their pre-war standard of life. Shortages being experienced at the centre, especially in iron and steel semi-finished goods, were becoming acute. The burgeoning of the Lend-Lease scheme made it doubly important to insist on restrictions in colonial consumption, as it would be courting widespread criticism to give the benefit of American aid to areas where the enjoyment of luxuries appeared little diminished. Nor was it simply a question of the economic benefit to be gained from savings in shipping, foreign exchange, and resources. As powerful as all economic arguments was the 'moral' one favouring an equality of sacrifice. This created considerable resonance among senior Colonial Office officials who, concerned about the way certain expatriates in the colonies continued to live with all the pre-war comforts, added their voices to the demand for a tightening of controls.[13]

By the end of February 1941 the time was obviously ripe for 'a great drive' to compel the dependencies to improve their 'deplorably lax' implementation of import licensing. The Treasury was told that big changes were in the wind.[14] At Parkinson's suggestion, the Economic Department prepared a draft telegram underlining the hardship being experienced in Britain, and calling for greater equality of sacrifice. The means to ensure this were spelled out as stricter import licensing, income tax closer to British levels, and a purchase tax on non-essentials. Caine, as head of the Economic Department and chief architect of the policy, had by this time established a substantial reputation as an economist within the Office and in the wider reaches of Whitehall: copies of the draft were sent to Keynes at the Treasury and the economic section of the War Cabinet secretariat.[15]

The Colonial Office, like any complex organisation, could contain more than one ordering of its obligations at any one time. A tension between positions which had not formerly been appreciated might surface only when each side had made a substantial commitment of time, energy, and principle. Thus, when the Economic Department's initiative began to encounter serious difficulties in the spring of 1941, it was the result not of external pressures, but of an unresolved incompatibility between the Office's efforts to make progress with its forward policy and its administration of economic controls.[16] The 'blitzkrieg telegram' had, as already noted, given war measures absolute priority over social and economic development. As the threat of imminent invasion started to fade after the summer of 1940, however, Lord Lloyd began to grow restive about the generally negative tone of the directives which had been sent out to the Governors, particularly a circular telegram of 10 September in which it was stated that as Secretary of State he would not feel 'justified' in asking the Treasury for money unless the scheme in question was of exceptional urgency and importance. This condition, he declared, 'delivers me bound hand and foot to the tender mercies of the Treasury in respect of almost any scheme that I may desire to push forward'.

Lloyd did his best to rally the support of his officials by appealing to their sense of organisational and constitutional propriety. He was, however, at something of a disadvantage in having had too short a tenure of office to acquire a feel for interdepartmental relationships. As his Permanent Under-Secretary pointed out, tactfully but firmly, relations with the Treasury were very good at the moment. The circular, like everything else relating to the Colonial Development and Welfare Act, reflected a series of private understandings with the Treasury that had informed regular discussions taking place for the past year.[17] There was little likelihood of Treasury opposition so long as the Office had a reasonable case.

Parkinson thought it best to wait for a specific case to arise, but Lloyd preferred to see development policy shaped by central initiative, rather than being allowed to emerge a bit at a time from the periphery. The Secretary of State accepted the impossibility of cutting out the Treasury altogether (since Treasury approval was written into the Act) but remained determined that something should be said to the Governors to encourage them to put forward schemes of the desired kind. A draft to this effect was prepared in the Social Services

Department, though with the caveat that such schemes must not interfere with the war effort.

The Treasury's reception of the proposed circular was cool. It seemed too much like telling the Governors not to bother with the restrictions they were being urged to make. The issue appeared capable, as Parkinson obviously feared, of producing some friction between the two departments. For example, the Treasury's pointed reminder that it was spending large sums of money to subsidise colonies and purchase surplus raw materials drew forth the observation in the Colonial Office that the Treasury had been only too willing to accept over £15 million from the colonies in the form of voluntary contributions.[18] The Permanent Under-Secretary, well aware by now of the strength of Lloyd's feelings on the matter, remained hopeful that some compromise would be achieved: it was 'all a question of presentation and degree'.

Lloyd's sudden death in February 1941 threw the future of the proposed circular once more into doubt. The campaign had been a highly personal one. Indeed it was made clear to his successor, Lord Moyne, in an unusually candid account of the background to the issue, that Parkinson did not altogether share Lloyd's views, even given the fact that the circular of 10 September, like the 'blitzkrieg telegram', was 'a very negative document'.[19] What emerged strongly from this incident was that the Office recognised the need to preserve Treasury goodwill in dealing with the urgent difficulties which arose directly out of the war. Moyne, however, had his own reasons for taking up where Lloyd left off. He told his officials in March that he had been asked by Churchill to become Secretary of State, to meet the new situation created by the grant of military bases to the United States in the West Indies. The Prime Minister, worried by the prospect of comparisons being drawn between the leased areas and those under British administration, was keen to see that the welfare proposals of the West Indies Royal Commission, over which Moyne had presided, were implemented without delay, and what was granted here would hardly be withheld elsewhere in the colonial empire.

Moyne's position was stronger than that of Lloyd, for he was able to argue for increased development activity in terms not simply of high principle or obligation, but of the war effort itself. Those at the Treasury, according to the new Secretary of State, would quite simply have to reexamine their 'sense of proportion in this matter'. When the Social Services Department submitted the required draft of a circular despatch, it did so in the confident belief that Moyne had something larger in view than the proposal drawn up for Lloyd. The only obstacle appeared to be the 'gentleman's agreement' with the Treasury of the previous year, of which the colonial governments had not been informed.[20] But even here estimates made it appear unnecessary to impose any formal limitation on expenditure.

It was precisely at this time (March 1941) that the Social Services draft came face to face with the 'drive' of the Economic Department for a reduction in colonial consumption. It was recognised that the two documents in question would have to be 'harmonised'. In contrast with the pre-war pattern, when the dividing line in deliberations usually lay between geographical departments or on the subject-geographical border, this dispute was firmly fixed within the confines of the rapidly-growing subject side. The proprietary interest taken by the Social Services Department in the rapid implementation of the Colonial Development and Welfare Act stemmed directly from the responsibility it had been given for the work of drafting, consultation, and negotiation which preceded the successful appearance of the measure. There was some irony in the fact that the Economic Department was generally seen to be just as closely associated with the progress of this policy: MacDonald had told Creech Jones that he would have enlarged the Economic Department even if there had been no war.[21] But there was a war, and its effect had been to differentiate the purposes of each department. They had come to operate in contrasting organisational worlds, even though, to the outsider, the dramatic expansion of the economic side was understood both as a function of the war effort and at the same time as a symbol of the Colonial Office's continuing commitment to a development policy.[22] Changes in the shape of an organisation could obscure the nature of its internal difficulties.

Caine made no effort to conceal his objections to the Social Services' draft. It was time that people in the colonies, 'like people in this country, learned that it is not money, but real things that matter in this emergency'. If the colonies needed taxation measures as 'a lesson in elementary economics', he was no less willing to deliver such lessons to those around him:

The general improvement of standards of living is dependent on either economic development or doles from this country, open or concealed; and frankly I think we are going to have a hard enough task to maintain standards in face of the stark difficulties of the present circumstances.

This view continued to attract considerable support among senior officials, a number of whom had identified an inconsistency between the two drafts. No one was more anxious about this than Parkinson, who was anyway worried about generating expectations which could not be satisfied. The only way out, he told Moyne, appeared to lie in placing the decision 'solidly on a political basis' and treating the West Indies as a separate case.[23]

The Secretary of State's task of adjudication was not made any easier by his known commitment to one side of the argument. But he did not see why there should be concern about inconsistency, since each of the two circulars was aimed at a different section of the colonial population. The important thing was to make sure that those who enjoyed an English standard of living limited their consumption, while help would be forthcoming for those services, particularly health and education, designed to improve living standards of the 'native communities'. The Permanent Under-Secretary had one more card to play in his effort to maintain the appearance of consistency in his department's policy output. Making shrewd use of his authority to determine procedure, he asked Caine to amalgamate the two circulars into a single draft, removing any suggestion that views on the two subjects had been prepared without sufficient collaboration. The new draft reached Moyne eleven days after its original submission, and it would seem that only then did he learn that what had been two documents was now one. In keeping with the tone of its reception among his officials, however, Moyne's reaction to the draft was favourable.

If the Treasury offered no further resistance, it was largely because the Economic Department of the Colonial Office had already done the bulk of work in expressing its views. The despatch, sent to nearly all colonies on 5 June 1941 as Circular (2), was to be widely accepted as one of the Office's leading wartime statements of policy.[24] The origin of its drafting was evident in its design and content: the section setting out the case for reducing inessential personal consumption was given pride of place and occupied nearly two-thirds of the total space. One strand running through the entire despatch was the attempt to persuade colonial administrations to look at their territories in broad resource terms and to educate themselves in the essentials of resource management. The chief problem was 'how to regulate the use of those resources' in the interests both of the war effort and of social and economic development. The former set of interests was described in detail, with reference made to the disappointment felt over the rather lax administration of import controls. Nor was the note of moral exhortation about the need for a 'common sacrifice' absent. The appearance of colonial endeavour was as important in its own way as the substance.

When the circular turned its attention to the raising of living standards for those existing below a reasonable minimum, it reflected Moyne's attitude towards Office doubts by stating confidently that this was 'in no way inconsistent with the present necessity for restricting consumption by the better off'. It was no longer appropriate to adhere strictly to the rigid view of the previous September: some progress in wartime was possible, and it was desirable that plans be submitted for central vetting. The common emphasis on resource management, implicit in the approach to development planning, had clearly acquired a more powerful bite and meaning in the context of the war effort. Although there was an institutional tension between these two aspects of metropolitan initiative, it was none the less true that the two sides shared many of the same assumptions and categories.[25] The circular argued for 'schemes of economic development which, while improving the long-term economic position, are also expected to produce commodities or materials of special wartime value, including the development of local production of goods to replace imports'. While the majority of those reading the circular would have recognised it as an attempt to accommodate the claims of two separate policy areas, they would not have been able to know that in its organisational dimension it served as a monument to a series of deliberations inside the Office which illustrated how responsibility for the war effort had impinged on existing roles and values.

It was one thing to press for the partial implementation of forward policy in wartime, but quite another to seek an extension of that policy itself. The suggestion of such a change came from a subcommittee of the Advisory Committee on Education in the Colonies which, after considering a despatch from Stockdale setting forth building and teacher-training programmes, expressed the view that it was a waste of time considering such proposals without some assurance of metropolitan financing beyond the official CDW terminal date of 1951. The Social Services Department, eager to follow this up, tried to convince the Treasury and the Office generally that some informal arrangements could exist between the two departments whereby plans could be made for a longer period than ten years in the firm expectation that extending legislation would be passed in due course.[26]

There was as little enthusiasm within the Office as in the Treasury for such a cutting of constitutional corners. Although the Social Services Department had counted on Moyne's continued backing after the issuing of Circular (2), it had failed to grasp his view of the balance of political advantage. He was quite happy to agree with his Permanent Under-Secretary that in this case the matter should go no further. The extension of the Act beyond 1951 was not so vital to its success as a policy to make a battle with the Treasury worthwhile.

The stricter application of import controls, which was necessary to reduce imports and save shipping, also had a bearing on the growing problem of colonial inflation. The need for central guidance here was crucial, since local attempts at a solution, made without benefit of the latest advances in the practice of economic management, could fail to avert and might even increase the associated hazard of labour unrest. Circular (2), in advocating taxation as a means of soaking up purchasing power rather than of raising revenue, represented one of the first, rather tentative, steps taken in London to meet increases in the cost of living. During the following month a memorandum on price stabilisation by the economic section of the War Cabinet secretariat was circulated to colonial administrations.[27]

By November 1941 it was becoming accepted within the Office that more effective means were required without delay to deal with the *effects* of inflation.[28] A number of officials agreed with Orde Browne, the Labour adviser, who on the basis of his recent tour advocated a system of wage bonuses linked to rises in the cost of living, like the one operating in Malaya. It had the appeal of appearing the response best calculated to prevent labour unrest. To Caine, however, this was unrealistic and inadequate. No increase in money wages could do anything about the underlying problem of a shortage of goods, though it could well serve to increase the rate of inflation still further. The best hope lay in subsidising prices. Caine's objection was sufficient to counter-balance the arguments of a number of senior colleagues. The temporary stalemate was broken early in 1942, with the result that a circular despatch was sent to the colonies on 9 February. Although the document mentioned the possibility of granting bonuses to lower-paid workers where necessary, it was

Caine's policy of price subsidisation and control that formed its central core.

The responsibility for giving guidance to the colonies was greatly complicated by the sheer difficulty of getting adequate information about what was happening on the ground. Even by the summer of 1942 it was hard to know what effect the circular despatch of 9 February had had. Nor was it any easier to substantiate the Office's general impression that the terms of trade had turned against the colonies. Though requests were made for quarterly returns of changes in the cost of living and for the information needed to devise an index of trade, these moves were taken against a background which induced the Office to refrain from adding to the burdens of already overworked colonial officials.[29] There was little inclination on the part of those bound up with the day-to-day job of administering controls to use their capacity for giving guidance for purposes not directly related to furthering the war effort. Clauson, with his eye fixed firmly on post-war reconstruction, circulated a long memorandum in March 1942 on 'The Problem of Raising the Standard of Living in the Colonies'. He was well aware of the way in which war had given a new relevance to the longstanding aim of articulating a common economic doctrine for the Empire.[30] But those around him did not share his feeling that the time was ripe for using the powerful network of central-local communication for the dissemination of general principles. Nor was there much interest in opening a discussion on this question inside the Office itself.[31]

Colonial Office officials, especially those in the Economic Department (or Division, as it became in 1942), were quite simply too busy to shift their attention from the short-range for very long. A great many economic files, thick with communications and memoranda, contained only the most perfunctory comments on the minute pages. Keeping in touch with the rest of Whitehall was essential, and if rows with other departments occurred the Colonial Office did not always assume the part of the injured party. Not long after the colonies had been asked to tighten their import controls in June 1941, for example, the Board of Trade issued a strong complaint that it had not been properly consulted over a matter which was bound to have a serious effect on the United Kingdom export policy. Though it received a full apology from the Office, the Board of Trade went on to insist that some working compromise must be found between considerations of wartime necessity and those of post-war trade. Such an approach was highly unpalatable to the Economic Department; in the words of one official, 'in deciding these matters we should be governed only by wartime considerations'. In the end H. D. Henderson was called in to settle the dispute. A change in the import licensing arrangements was agreed which left the Office with little cause for complaint.[32]

The work of assuring essential supplies for the colonies, which merited the creation of its own subject department by 1943, had always to take into account the impact which its work might have on British export interests. Indeed, the United Kingdom system of export controls 'had been built up on the basis that trade should continue to flow, as far as possible, through normal trade channels, and adherence to those channels was thought to be more likely to maintain a proper flow of normal supplies'.[33] For this reason colonial bulk purchase was never greatly encouraged or used, and even in the summmer of 1942, when the Colonial Office was having to produce programmes of all foreseeable calls on American production for the next two years, the Board of Trade made clear its continued reluctance to see wholesale bulk ordering by colonial governments.[34]

When it came to the question of colonial food requirements it was as important to look at the possibilities of extending and diversifying local production as it was to consider the problem from the supply angle. A nutrition research survey had been attempted, based on replies to despatches issued in 1940, with an additional expert in Mrs Culwick employed in 1941 to help in the work of what in due course became referred to as a 'Scientific Food Policy'.[35] Also in 1941 colonial governments were requested to make regular returns of their monthly minimum requirements of food which would have to be met from external sources. These returns (known as the 'Perio' series) were examined carefully by the Office in consultation with other departments: in January 1942 an informal office committee with representatives from the War Office and the Ministry of War Transport began to hold monthly meetings. It was expanded in July to meet the growing difficulties in the supply situation, and it was not until almost exactly a year later that matters had improved sufficiently to prompt a suggestion from the Permanent Under-Secretary that the 'Perio' returns continue in a simplified form and that the committee be allowed to run down gradually.[36]

There is little doubt that the area of greatest innovation concerned the use and marketing of colonial commodities. The early interest in dealing with export surpluses led to the establishment of the Leith Ross official committee and the Office committee to examine the alternative uses of raw materials (SCAUCRM).[37] In 1941 the latter's deliberations produced the proposal for a semi-independent institute to give full-time consideration to research into colonial products. As a result the Colonial Products Research Council was established early the following year under the chairmanship of Lord Hankey.[38] During 1942 the question of surpluses became linked increasingly with the creation of an Anglo-American scheme for post-war rehabilitation and relief. By August the Leith Ross Committee had adopted the new title Post-War Commodity and Relief and the Colonial Office's contribution to its proceedings had fallen off significantly. Near the end of 1942 Leith Ross was informed that cocoa was now the only genuine colonial surplus; and, with the obvious exception of the Far East, the Office's function by this time was chiefly one of keeping in touch with the activity of determining Allied relief needs, and considering where and how such needs were related to its current commodity policy.[39]

As the work of dealing with surpluses declined with the growing success of Allied fortunes, that of handling marketing arrangements continued to enjoy a position of some importance in the Office's ordering of priorities. The applications of wartime experience and machinery to the strengthening of colonial economies were clear, particularly since the wartime mood of international cooperation seemed likely to lead to the creation of an economic order characterised by commodity agreements much more extensive in scope than the rather limited pre-war schemes. But, even during the emergency of war, political considerations were capable of preventing too radical a change. At the same time as he was leading the Economic Department's drive against excessive colonial consumption in the spring of 1941, Caine proposed a rationalisation of existing West African commodity control schemes to allow the entry of new firms and the introduction of greater flexibility into the quotas. The system appeared less than fully efficient since a fixed share of purchases had been allotted to particular firms and individuals in trade before the war, with cost cutting discouraged by the fact that the margin needed to cover marketing costs was the margin of the least efficient firm.

Although the schemes left something to be desired from the economic point of view, they had the great virtue of having proved politically workable; and Caine's willingness to risk European hostility by admitting more African or Syrian shippers was unpalatable to those around him.[40] The cause of wartime efficiency was difficult to maintain when it could be shown that serious local division might occur as a result. Nor was there much liking for the idea of using the new commodity arrangements as a means of fostering social reform. The attempt by Creech Jones, assisted by Arthur Greenwood, to obtain Office backing for the notion of having social welfare provisions written into commodity control agreements came to nothing.[41]

The Office could ignore such outside pressure, but it could hardly fail to become closely involved with interdepartmental discussions which were taking place about Britain's future trading policy. Colonial Office representatives sat on the official committee established in the summer of 1941 on Post-War External Problems and Anglo-American Co-operation. As the committee's proceedings continued into the following year, the organisation was compelled to clarify its thinking about present and future policy: a Colonial Office memorandum was submitted in August 1942, for example, on the need for a 'Permanent Economic Rescue Service', based on the British emergency relief schemes, which would be part of an international post-war machinery on commodity marketing.[42]

This was the arena which really mattered when it came to representing the colonies and colonial policy at the metropolitan end. The work was exhausting and sometimes frustrating, but also stimulating. Personal letters flowed back and forth between senior officials on the Office's Economic side and such men as Keynes, Henderson, Harrod, and Robbins about the future shape of external monetary and economic policy. The war had given the Office a role to play which altered its frame of reference as much as its daily routines.

Machinery for coordination

The organisation of the war effort was accompanied from the outset by a general recognition of the need to improve the machinery for inter-territorial coordination. The Secretary of State told his officials in 1939 that he was anxious to see all possible arrangements made during the war for the closer grouping or association of colonies.[43] In many cases the individual colony was poorly suited as a unit to meet the economic and strategic demands of total war. Where a number of territories occupied a distinctive geographical region, sharing similar needs and resources, it appeared only common sense to provide machinery whereby the import quotas or production plans of any single unit were related to those of all the others. Far from being adverse to such collaboration, the colonial governments, faced with a mass of highly complex operations, led the way in pressing for special regional authorities in which all the available information could be pooled, collated, and studied by those with the most expert knowledge to devise uniform programmes. Such authorities could be no less useful in dealing with other Whitehall departments which on the whole preferred to negotiate with one agency representing a coherent territorial grouping.

With the possibility of enemy attack remaining very real in some colonies until 1943, a significant number, especially in Africa, found it necessary to sustain British or American military forces stationed within their borders. Whether it concerned supplies, civil defence, intelligence gathering, or matters of strategy, the contact between civil and military authorities in the colonies was of necessity frequent and close. As a result an incompatibility was identified between a highly centralised military command structure on the one hand, and a civil arm composed of a collection of separate units on the other. It provided another powerful argument in favour of more effective regional machinery, especially in view of the fact that in an emergency it would be imperative for the military commander-in-chief to work in close conjunction with a single civilian counterpart for the area in question.

The early years of the war saw a remarkable growth in the creation and strengthening of regional bodies. Resident ministers were appointed for the Far and Middle East and for West Africa. In East Africa the Governors' Conference machinery was greatly expanded, while more effective inter-territorial links were established for the colonies of Central Africa. A regional organisation for the purposes of Anglo-American cooperation was constructed in the West Indies. In Ceylon an admiral was appointed Commander-in-Chief and given supreme powers of direction over all civil and military authorities in the area. Colonies, or groups of colonies, became closely involved with the special wartime activities of the Middle East Supply Centre and the Eastern Group Supply Council.[44] In the United Kingdom the West African Cocoa Control Board (and later the West African

Produce Control Board), containing metropolitan and colonial representatives, acted as a central marketing agency for the leading products of this region.

These developments became intertwined with the web of existing commitments in a way which tended to pull the Office with varying degrees of force in different directions at the same time. The virtues of coordination were associated not simply with wartime efficiency, but also with the new central policy of social and economic development. The 1940 White Paper on Colonial Development and Welfare proclaimed that 'the need for co-ordination is clear'.[45] The creation of the Stockdale organisation in the West Indies underlined the importance attached to the idea of having bodies working on a regional basis. But the improvement of coordinating machinery could hardly avoid giving a new meaning to the whole debate about closer union which had been such a prominent feature of the inter-war years. Here the other facet of representation contained within the 'dual role' made the Colonial Office cautious about supporting change in circumstances where local privileged minorities might latch on to wartime necessity as a disguise for achieving their own political ends. In practice, it proved far from easy to separate local pressure for more effective coordination into political or non-political categories. If it was difficult to resist altogether arguments based on principles of rationalisation, it was no less important to preserve the stability of existing relations in and with the colonies.

The areas of greatest sensitivity were East and Central Africa.[46] The continuing debate about closer union in the late 1920s and the 1930s derived its force from the growing trend towards inter-territorial consultation, the outstanding example of which was the administration of common services in East Africa. So impressed was the Hilton Young Commission of 1928 with the benefits accruing from the coordination of policy, that it recommended the appointment of a Governor-General for East Africa with full executive powers. Sir Hilton Young himself was in favour of an amalgamation of the Rhodesias, though his fellow members thought this too radical a step. But if there was a good deal of support in Britain for the idea of closer technical cooperation, the bulk of informed opinion shared the caution about political union expressed by the Joint Select Committee of Parliament of 1931 when it reported that the realities of race, historical development, territorial pride, and tribal composition rendered proposals for formal union in East Africa impracticable.

There was no popular demand for and considerable local opposition to such a step. While the Bledisloe Commission Report of 1939 was more sympathetic to the concept of an amalgamation of the Central African colonies, it thought moves in this direction were fruitless as long as Southern Rhodesia's racial policies continued to be so markedly out of step with those of the colonies further north.

Economic cooperation was a different matter however. The Bledisloe Commission, keen to demonstrate its appreciation of the advantages to be enjoyed by larger units, called for the creation of an Inter-Territorial Council with two standing boards to coordinate government surveys and plan economic development. Some progress had already been made in this direction. Occasional conferences of Central African Governors had been held during and after 1935, as had conferences of technical officers on such matters as education and health. The obvious model was provided by the three East African colonies which during the 1930s had established a customs union and cooperative machinery for transport and postal services. By the outbreak of war the East African Governors' Conference had become well enough established to have a permanent headquarters and secretariat in Nairobi.

War was to accelerate the growth of regional coordinating machinery to a degree where it became increasingly difficult to keep the consideration of economic and political cooperation in separate compartments. The creation of an East Africa Command, covering the whole of East and Central Africa, gave rise to demands for the establishment of a single civil headquarters to facilitate communications. Furthermore, the problems of supply, distribution, and war production added their own pressures for centralisation. By the time of Italy's entry into the war in June 1940 the Governors of Kenya and Uganda, Moore and Mitchell respectively, were pressing hard for improvements in the collaborative machinery for East Africa. The demand for a 'central authority' produced considerable uneasiness in the Colonial Office, particularly since it found Mitchell's 'centrifugal tendencies' politically suspect in the light of his excessive enthusiasm for establishing good relations with the Union of South Africa.[47]

The plan which eventually met with the Office's approval and was adopted later that summer saw a restructuring of the East African Governors' Conference with the Governor of Kenya appointed as permanent Chairman and Mitchell vacating the governorship of

Uganda to become permanent Deputy Chairman with special responsibilities for maintaining contact with military authorities in the area, and for planning and coordinating the East African war effort. Parkinson told the Secretary of State that neither he nor his officials were enamoured of the scheme, but that in the face of the unanimous backing given to it by all the Governors there was little option but to agree.[48] The way was now open to develop the Governors' Conference as the focal point for coordinating wartime activity, and during the next two years in particular a rapid expansion of its administrative machinery took place.

In August 1940 an Economic Council was established to secure common action between the three East African territories and to speak with a common voice on their behalf to other authorities and organisations. Northern Rhodesia and Nyasaland, both formally members of the East African Governors' Conference, were invited to join the Council but declined. In due course War and Civil Supplies Boards, composed mainly of representatives of the Governors of Kenya, Uganda and Tanganyika, were brought into being; the former was also staffed by military members, the latter by commercial advisers. The office of Deputy Chairman came to an end in January 1941 when Mitchell left to become Chief Political Officer with the Middle East Command. But this took nothing away from the growing authority of the regional machinery. The secretariat of the Governors' Conference had assumed a new importance as the channel of communication through which messages were passed between the Colonial Office, the Conference itself, individual colonial governments, and the East African Command. Later in 1941 the War and Civil Supplies Boards were absorbed by the secretariat as its economic section.

After the fall of the Far East the pace of events on the ground quickened still further. Once again demands for a more powerful form of centralisation were greeted with some alarm in London. General Platt, as Commander-in-Chief for East Africa, wasted no time in pointing to the dangerous military implications of the new situation, and suggested to the Secretary of State the appointment of a military overlord who, with the assistance of a civil adviser, would assume full powers in case of an emergency. At the same time Moore, always sympathetic to closer union, weighed in with the proposal for a civil High Commissioner. He based his call on economic as well as military considerations: questions of production and supply, bulk purchasing, and transportation in Kenya, Uganda, and Tanganyika were, he claimed, 'proving increasingly unmanageable in the absence of an over-riding civil inter-territorial authority'.

The Colonial Office was greatly relieved when the Governors' Conference eventually agreed to settle for a scheme, similar to the one just implemented in West Africa, granting emergency powers to the Chairman. Nevertheless, the Office still thought it vital to ensure that the public announcement neither gave the impression of imminent attack nor — and here it followed the advice of the Governor of Tanganyika — suggested that they were 'moving rapidly towards Closer Union under the guise of war necessity'. There were already signs of local discontent. The operations of the East African Civil Defence and Supply Council, formed over the preceding months to meet the new economic pressures, had aroused some inter-territorial tensions by dint of its poorly defined constitutional position and its method of dealing directly with the colonial departments concerned.[49]

The danger of the British government being faced with an East African Dominion as a *fait accompli* at the end of the war was emphasised at a special Colonial Office meeting presided over by the Secretary of State in June 1942.[50] Closer union was alive once more as a topic of office deliberations, one which might well merit the attention of the War Cabinet. In August Moore arrived in London for a series of discussions on short- and long-range questions. Since the Governor of Kenya remained as firmly attached as ever to closer union, Dawe, the Office's senior official with African responsibilities, put forward the suggestion that war might in fact be the best time to introduce constitutional change, before the white settlers of Kenya had a chance to consolidate their power any further. It was a conscious attempt to break the existing pattern in which local forces had possessed the initiative, and to exploit the trend towards larger units for the political as well as the economic purposes of the centre. Such a gamble appeared altogether too risky to Dawe's colleagues, who replied with the argument that war was the wrong time for constitutional change precisely because the cooperation of the settlers was essential for maximising the productive capacity of East Africa. In the end Moore was sent back with instructions to sound out local opinion about the possibility of appointing a High Commissioner, and to report back to the Secretary of State about the feasibility of introducing such an office in the near future.[51]

But something more tangible had been achieved at the same time. Having been told of the Secretary of State's desire to see the Civil Defence and Supply Council reorganised on a more uniform basis under the Governors' Conference, Moore also returned to East Africa with a set of proposals which led in due course to the replacement of the Council by a new body entitled the East African Production and Supply Council in January 1943. It derived its authority from the Governors' Conference, and, although it was capable of taking decisions effective throughout East Africa, these could be questioned by individual governments and referred to the Conference Chairman. Armed with an Executive Board and seven directors, each responsible for different functional aspects of the regional economy, the Production and Supply Council was a sophisticated and powerful centralising instrument.[52] While the question of East African closer union remained in limbo, the experience of cooperation and of administrative innovation ensured its place on the agenda of post-war reconstruction.

The same pressures which lay behind the strengthening of regional coordinating machinery in East Africa had a similar effect upon the colonies to the south, only this time with even more marked political complications. The situation was administratively awkward to begin with, since Southern Rhodesia, unlike Nyasaland and Northern Rhodesia, was a self-governing colony falling within the purview of the Dominions Office. Discussions about the possibility of amalgamation in the light of the Bledisloe Report were held in London during the summer of 1939 between the Prime Minister of Southern Rhodesia, Sir Godfrey Huggins, and United Kingdom representatives but they were cut short by the outbreak of war. No official reply could be accorded by the British government to the Bledisloe Commission's proposals, though it was agreed between the two sides in the latter part of the year that Lord Hailey should visit Southern Rhodesia during his 1940 tour of African colonies to assess the degree to which that colony's native policies represented a stumbling block to closer political union.[53]

The Colonial Office was keenly aware of the explosive potential of this issue among the colonial lobby in Britain. On 14 March 1940 MacDonald, Eden, and their officials received a deputation from the Anti-Slavery and Aborigines Protection Society which was firmly opposed to amalgamation in Central Africa and clearly fearful that the government's lack of comment on Bledisloe might reflect a willingness to take steps in this direction during the war.

Assurances were given that no decision had yet been reached; indeed Huggins was to say more than once that he had a gentleman's agreement with the Dominions Office not to raise the amalgamation issue during the war.[54]

But developments on the ground made it difficult to still such fears. The decision by the Governors of Northern Rhodesia and Nyasaland not to join the Economic Council of the East African Governors' Conference reflected their natural tendency by this time to look to the south and not to be drawn into the orbit of East African economic activity. In October 1940 a meeting of the three Central African Governors held in Salisbury to discuss the coordination of the war effort decided in favour of an enlarged Governors' Conference on a permanent footing and with a proper secretariat. The Colonial Office found this step far more ambitious than the simple machinery for economic cooperation it had anticipated: 'we shall have to be careful about this' commented one official, appreciating the difficulty of dismantling institutions established during the war. It was particularly irritating that the initiative for enlarging the Central African Governors' Conference came from their own 'man on the spot' in the person of MacKenzie Kennedy, the Governor of Nyasaland, whose motives were cast into doubt still further when it was noticed that his covering despatch had very little to say at all about the 'war aspect'.[55]

As well as internal political difficulties, there was always the question of South African aspirations further north to be borne in mind. 'We must have amalgamation or be absorbed by the Union', Huggins told Lord Lloyd in January 1941.[56] It was the fear of isolating Southern Rhodesia that accounted for the Dominions Office's desire to see approval given to the Salisbury proposals. The hope persisted in London during the first few weeks of 1941 that a successful outcome in the North African campaign might remove altogether the need for creating more elaborate machinery in Central Africa.[57] But by the end of March a decision could be delayed no longer, and Moyne gave his approval to the creation of a secretariat as a war measure.

Given the emphasis on administrative efficiency during wartime, the trend of the previous decade towards greater coordination, the pervasive example of East Africa, the backing of both governors in question, the need to placate Southern Rhodesia, and pressure from the Dominions Office, the Colonial Office could hardly have declined to give its blessing to some form of regional authority for Central Africa. The fear now existed that, in Dawe's words, 'once this Secretariat gets going it will flourish like a green bay tree'.[58] The Office's public declarations on the subject were qualified at every turn by references to the machinery's temporary character and limited scope. Privately, however, Moyne accepted Cranborne's prediction that it would probably prove impossible to jettison. Following the formal establishment of the secretariat at Salisbury in July 1941, urgent consideration began to be given to the implications for amalgamation. While Dawe visited Salisbury to test opinion on the spot, Moyne, Cranborne, and Hailey conferred together in London. In the report he had prepared on his findings of 1940, Hailey was forced to the conclusion that there was a very deep divergence of policy between Southern Rhodesia and its Central African neighbours.[59] The two Secretaries of State succeeded by October in persuading the Prime Minister that the problem was urgent enough to invite Huggins to London once more with a view to persuading him to modify his government's position.

While preparations for a new round of discussions were being made at the centre, the changing pattern of the war produced significant repercussions on the ground. In Central as in East Africa the fall of the Far East provided colonial governments with a fresh opportunity for seizing the initiative in a way which threatened to upset the existing political *status quo*. The root of the problem was that although Northern Rhodesia and Nyasaland lay within General Platt's East Africa Command, Southern Rhodesia did not. The emergency powers conferred in 1942 on the Chairman of the East African Governor's Conference immediately raised the question of what would happen in Central Africa in the event of a similar emergency. Did the establishment of the secretariat at Salisbury make it advisable that such powers be given to the government of Southern Rhodesia? Such a suggestion was made, albeit tentatively, by Waddington, the Governor of Northern Rhodesia, in April 1942. He and MacKenzie Kennedy favoured the convening of the Central African Governors' Conference to reconsider the whole position: 'we are concerned that our security may be jeopardized by the lack of co-ordination between Southern Rhodesia and East Africa in military command.'

The Colonial Office's reaction was predictably wary. Accepting the arrangement suggested by Waddington, the Secretary of State was warned, could mean entering 'the deep waters of the amalgamation controversy' as there would be many who would argue 'that under the guise of wartime necessity you were taking a step towards amalgamation.' Although not encouraged to do so by the Colonial Office, the War Office, or Platt, the Governors of Northern Rhodesia and Nyasaland then attempted to see if Southern Rhodesia could be persuaded to place itself under the East Africa command. Although Platt favoured this in the event of hostilities, he expressed himself quite happy with things as they were at the moment. London officials agreed that the Governors' initiative was unnecessary and possibly dangerous. In the end the question was resolved at the Pretoria Conference of June 1942, where it was agreed that Southern Rhodesia would come under the jurisdiction of the South African Command in the event of an emergency. Cranborne refused to allow Waddington to cancel a previously planned tour of the Copperbelt, where there had been strikes in 1940, in order to attend the conference. The Secretary of State clearly had no wish to involve the Central African colonies so overtly in the affairs of the southern part of the continent. Though resigned to accept it, neither he nor his officials had much liking for the Pretoria decision. It heightened fears that, with Southern Rhodesians naturally inclined to look towards the south, amalgamation with Northern Rhodesia and Nyasaland could result in all three being pulled firmly into the Southern African orbit.[60]

The possibility of closer union for the West African colonies had been considered but never taken very seriously before the war. Efforts by the Secretary of State in 1936 to promote the adoption of a governors' conference system produced nothing tangible until 1939, when a meeting of the four governors concerned (Nigeria, Gold Coast, Sierra Leone, and Gambia) appointed the Governor of Nigeria as permanent chairman of a conference to meet once every two years. A Colonial Office committee of the same year looking into the prospects of West African closer union favoured greater use of the governors' conference machinery with the addition of a permanent secretariat. Both committee and Governors agreed, however, that a federation or Governor-General was out of the question for reasons of geographical separation, differences in size and populations, and longstanding territorial jealousies.[61]

Such considerations lost a good deal of their weight in the

economic and military circumstances created by the fall of France, the closing of the Mediterranean, and the imposition of economic controls. The establishment of a command in West Africa in 1940 produced demands for a single channel of communication with the military authorities. In June Sir John Dill, newly appointed as CIGS, used the difficulties being experienced by the military commander in West Africa (General Giffard) in communicating with four separate Governors, as an argument for the appointment of a Governor-General. Lloyd rejected this proposal out of hand.[62] What was done was to enact the recommendation for giving the West African Governors' Conference its own secretariat at Lagos headed by a permanent Deputy Chairman. As was the case in East and Central Africa, the Colonial Office took some pains to issue the reassurance that no commitment had been made about the acceptability of such measures outside the context of the wartime emergency. A new telegraphic code, WAGON, was added to the rapidly growing list as the outward sign of another change in the traditional pattern of communications.

The terms of reference of the secretariat had been very broadly defined, and in 1941 it was able to create an organ known as the West African Supply Centre with some executive powers to meet the pressing demands for a central body to coordinate the region's import and production policies. In the same year the West African Cocoa Control Board, chaired by the Parliamentary Under-Secretary and composed of representatives of the Colonial Office, the West African governments, and the cocoa trade, was established in Britain to manage the purchase and disposal of the cocoa crop. Later, as the West African Produce Control Board, it assumed responsibility for a much wider range of commodities, particularly ground-nuts and palm kernels and oil.

Yet for all these changes, the civil and military leaders in West Africa continued to believe that something more drastic was required. Sir Bernard Bourdillon, as Governor of Nigeria and Chairman of the West African Governors' Conference, adopted a stand not unlike that of his counterpart Moore in East Africa in calling for the appointment of a Governor-General. The proposal was considered by the Office at various times throughout 1941 against the background of a possible invasion following an Allied collapse in the North African theatre. Dawe discussed the idea with the Governors' Conference during his visit to the region.[63] A more acceptable alternative to the idea of a

Governor-General, from the Colonial Office point of view, was for some extension to be made to the existing powers of the Conference's Chairman. A scheme embodying this alternative was devised in London in November 1941, and refined in subsequent consultations with Bourdillon.

The new provisions, brought into operation in March 1942, conferred special wartime powers on the Chairman of the West African Governors' Conference which permitted him to act on behalf of, give directions to, and where necessary overrule, individual Governors in matters relating to supply, transfer of foodstuffs between colonies, food reserves, civil/military requisitioning, manpower requirements, propaganda in occupied enemy territory, or anything else deemed relevant to the needs of an extreme emergency.[64] The irony was that, by the time this scheme was finally unveiled, the situation on the ground had altered so drastically as to throw its sufficiency into doubt. America's entry into the war, the collapse in the Far East, and growing British misfortune in North Africa had combined to endow West Africa with a new strategic importance. Not only did it appear much more vulnerable to attack but, considering its key position in the Allied supply chain and its productive potential in replacing the tin, rubber, and oil seeds formerly obtained from the Far East, it became much more important to protect. A special meeting on the maintenance of West African production had been held in the Colonial Office even while the Japanese were advancing towards Singapore.[65]

The Chiefs of Staff Committee in London became increasingly agitated about the lack of unified control in West Africa, and in April proposed the appointment of a military Governor-General with powers similar to those held by Admiral Layton in Ceylon. The plan had been put to them by General Giffard, who was critical of the Governors' reluctance to surrender their authority to him over key areas. The Colonial Office reaction was that such a revolutionary change could hardly be contemplated without more evidence that the present system was working badly. Since the Chiefs of Staff Committee could not be persuaded to modify its scheme, however, the whole question dropped into the lap of the War Cabinet, which settled eventually on the solution of creating the post of Resident Minister, on the lines of the one in the Middle East. In the directive sent to the Governors on 8 June 1942 it was stated that the step was necessary to 'ensure the effective co-operation, in the prosecution of war, of all services, Civil and Military, in West Africa': once again the Colonial Office was determined to underline the fact that there was no long-range political significance in the establishment of a wartime regional body.[66]

A special War Council was to be formed under the Resident Minister, although on the civil side he would work through the Governors and the Governors' Conference, over which he would preside. The list of his duties bore eloquent witness to the range and complexity of the problems by now associated with West Africa. They included dealing with the rapidly expanding American activity, overseeing policy on the needs and resources of the region as a whole, and exercising general control over propaganda, intelligence, security, and economic warfare. Although officially serving under the War Cabinet — from which he was to receive a weekly letter — the Resident Minister's channel of communication would be through the Secretary of State for the Colonies.

Lord Swinton's arrival in Achimota as Resident Minister early in July 1942 marked the beginning of a transformation in the style and structure of British administration in West Africa. He set out at once to rally spirits and boost morale, declaring in his broadcast to the people of the area: 'What is this cause for which we fight? It is the cause of freedom.'[67] But the Colonial Office, among others, did not find the adjustment altogether easy. By September its representative on Swinton's staff was reporting that the allocation of subjects between the Governors' Conference and the Resident Minister had become one of their 'major headaches'.[68] Since the Governors' Conference was supposed to deal only with non-war matters, and since nearly everything had some relevance to the war effort, it found itself with less and less to do. In December it faded away altogether, to be replaced by a Civil Members' Committee of the West African War Council consisting of the four Governors under the chairmanship of the Resident Minister. This gave the central coordinating machinery the structural balance it had hitherto lacked, for the new committee formed a natural counter-weight to the Service Members' Committee, which acted as a kind of miniature chiefs of staff organisation under Swinton.

The immediate problem for the Colonial Office in conducting its relations with the Resident Minister was concerned with the amount of information it could afford to give him, without running the risk of prompting him to take initiatives which could prove difficult to check. Complaints arose in late 1942 that the Office representative in Achimota was not sufficiently well-informed to be able to defend his department against adverse criticism encountered in his day-to-day functions. From the viewpoint of those in London, however, this official owed his loyalty to the Resident Minister rather than to the Secretary of State: 'In that sense', it was observed, 'he is not a true "representative" of the S of S and we cannot really differentiate between sending information to him and to the Minister.'[69]

Yet, as things turned out, Swinton experienced little difficulty in applying himself after 1942 to broad questions of economic and development policy.[70] In May 1943 he created a third committee of the War Council — the Supply and Production Committee — to assume supervision of planning and action in these areas. In West, as in East and Central, Africa, efforts to improve the machinery for inter-territorial coordination had led to administrative innovation which had a relevance extending beyond the immediate context of the war effort. New routines became ingrained, and old assumptions about the value of larger units were given substance. The growth of regionalism within the colonial empire suited central purposes in smoothing the path for a policy of coordinated development, but at the same time it placed the Office in the uncomfortable position of trying to see that local interests were prevented from gaining the political advantage which might be found in the administrative initiative they were authorised to assume in wartime conditions.

Allied cooperation

Participation in total war brought with it more than the necessity for making changes in the machinery of the Colonial Office and the dependent Empire. It was no less important at certain times to cooperate in arrangements with other Allied powers or representatives which were designed to assist the common cause. The most striking and most important instances of this occurred in the Western hemisphere, in the associated settings of American strategic interest in the West Indies and Anglo-American supply machinery in Washington. There were other examples. Cooperation with the United States began well before Pearl Harbor. Along with the leasing of bases in the West Indies and the establishment of the Colonial Supply Liaison in Washington, arrangements were made whereby the Americans assumed much of the responsibility for the ferrying of aircraft across the Atlantic to West Africa, as well as for air transport on the trans-Africa route. By the end of 1941 American companies were operating no fewer than five services weekly between Takoradi or Accra and Khartoum.[71] The Americans' entry into the war acted as a powerful spur to their growing involvement in the life and work of various British colonies. Their military presence in West Africa was powerfully increased, while the creation of the Anglo-American Caribbean Commission was symbolic of the role they had chosen to play in the economic and social development of the West Indies. The United States also came to wield full authority in all matters relating to defence and military strategy in the Western Pacific, an area which contained a large scattering of British island colonies.

Anglo-French colonial cooperation was more complicated. MacDonald's visit to Paris in March 1940 was part of a series of discussions between the two governments which accepted the need for close collaboration on both sides, especially in the area of joint economic planning. After the fall of France machinery was created in London to keep the British Government in close touch with the Free French and Belgians.[72] Relations between colonies themselves were inhibited by the insistence of the Belgian government in exile and the Free French National Committee that all questions of policy should be dealt with in London.[73] Yet for all this there was a steady if limited strengthening of ties. After French Equatorial Africa had declared for de Gaulle in 1940 it became incorporated into the general framework of the British West African supply effort. A Free French Liaison officer was appointed to British military headquarters in the Gold Coast, and a mission (the 'Fighting French') set up in Accra.

Neither the overtures for collaboration nor the Free French propaganda, directed successively from British colonies towards French West Africa, had any more success than de Gaulle's attempted seizure of Dakar in overcoming the loyalty of this region to the Vichy regime. Only after the Allied invasion of North Africa in November 1942 had the situation improved sufficiently for the United States and Britain to send an economic mission to Dakar, which Pedler headed as Chief British Economic Representative, with the purpose of mobilising the resources of French West Africa. But even here Swinton's attempt to achieve a thoroughgoing coordination of supply and production for French, Belgian, and British territory in West

Africa was frustrated by the Americans' desire to make this area economically 'subordinate' to French North Africa.[74] Syria and Lebanon, partly because of their close economic ties with Palestine, proved a good deal more compliant as Vichy colonies than those of West Africa. The change of control in 1941, following their seizure by the Allies which brought these two territories under the direct administration of the Free French, opened the way for their much closer economic integration with Palestine and Trans Jordan.[75]

The cumulative effect on the Colonial Office of all these developments further stretched its already strained manpower resources. Much of this effort was taken up with meeting the growing demands for office representation on interdepartmental bodies, such as the Committee on Allied African Economic Affairs whose task was to monitor Anglo-American economic cooperation in North and West Africa after late 1942.[76] Against this background of heightened activity at the centre, messages were received about particular difficulties of Allied cooperation being experienced at the periphery. The influx of American personnel into the West Indies and West Africa — by the middle of 1943 there were roughly 8,000 in the latter region, the equivalent of the entire pre-war European population[77] — had troublesome social and economic repercussions. Wherever there was friction with the local population, officials on the spot often found it difficult to define with precision their scope of authority in the event of a dispute, and the sudden increase in demand taxed the resources of colonial administrations, adding to the existing burden of economies experiencing severe dislocation and rapid price inflation.

Beyond these immediate worries was the nagging fear about Britain's ability to maintain her former position in these colonies after the war. The outstanding example again was the West Indies, although even in West Africa the impression of American dominance was sufficient to give rise to rumours about the likelihood of an American takeover after the war. In both areas the degree of penetration by the United States into the sphere of communications and transport, particularly civil aviation, held ominous commercial implications for the British in the post-war period. Roosevelt's son, James, while visiting the Middle East in June 1941 had proposed the establishment of an American air base at Bathurst in the Gambia.[78] The Western Pacific was not immune from these concerns, since it seemed likely that the military balance there could give the United

States the extra leverage necessary to make good its claims to a number of islands. Anxiety about Britain's future sovereignty in colonial areas did not accompany contact with the Free French — indeed the latter suspected the British of designs on their territory — but the political necessity of accommodating the Free French in the Middle East certainly added a further complication to the already daunting task of settling Arab-Jewish differences over Palestine.

Only in the case of the West Indies, however, did the necessity for Allied cooperation produce any notable tension within the Colonial Office itself. It revealed another aspect of the running debate within the organisation between those committed to serving the war effort and those whose principal sense of obligation was to maintain good relations with, and social and political order in, the West Indian colonies. In time, as experience of dealing with the Americans first-hand modified earlier fears about their intentions, the example of a wider 'regionalism' in the West Indies came to provide a useful model for the Colonial Office in defining the form of international colonial cooperation it would be prepared to accept in the post-war world.

The establishment of the development and welfare organisation under Stockdale in 1940 was evidence of Britain's inclination to see the West Indies as the testbed for the new development initiative. In contrast to the African experience, West Indian regionalism only became associated with war purposes gradually and in a limited way. The prevailing metropolitan fears were concerned with sovereignty rather than closer union. In spite of its being singled out in the Moyne Commission recommendations as 'the end to which policy should be directed', West Indian Federation remained largely dormant as an issue during the war.[79] The West Indies was not adjacent to a theatre of war and did not possess the pervasive centralising example of a military command against which the multiplicity of civil authorities might be compared and found wanting. From the beginning it was the United States which gave first priority to the strategic requirements of the region; and military activity, largely external from the British point of view, was always more likely to pose a threat than to set a standard.

The negotiations which resulted in the preliminary agreement of September 1940 granting the United States the right to lease naval and air bases in return for fifty destroyers were conducted between the British and American governments at the highest level. The

Colonial Office was little more than a spectator. Although Churchill gave assurances about the preservation of British sovereignty, his declaration that from now on 'the British Empire and the United States will have to be somewhat mixed up together in some of their affairs for mutual and general advantage' made plain his determination to see new forms of cooperation take root.[80] The Colonial Office did not have an easy time during the London discussions which settled the exact terms of the Bases Agreement. Faced with expressions of local disgruntlement — mostly forcibly from the Governor of Trinidad — on the one hand, and remarks like the one of Colonel Knox, a member of Roosevelt's cabinet, that the British West Indies would some day 'be ours . . . . by willing consent' on the other, the Office sought to have a further, authoritative assurance issued about American intentions. After overcoming the Foreign Office's initial opposition to such a move, it saw its parliamentary question prepared for the purpose vetoed at the last minute by the Prime Minister.[81]

In the early part of April 1941, only a few days after the formal signing of the Bases Agreement, an initiative for an entirely new kind of venture came from the American government in a memorandum for Churchill's immediate consideration. After expressing fulsome praise for the Moyne Commission recommendations, the paper referred to the probable creation of an advisory committee for the American Caribbean territories of Puerto Rico and the Virgin Islands, and proposed that this body and the Stockdale organisation work in close harmony, specifically by forming a joint committee. Although a certain trepidation was expressed in the Colonial Office about this being 'the beginning of internationalisation of colonies [sic]', Moyne, already aware of Churchill's desire for progress on the development front in this region, saw no reason to be obstructive and informed the Prime Minister that he found the idea of a joint committee attractive. There was little to which the Office could object at this stage, especially after it was learned that Stockdale, having discussed the proposal with the United States Secretary of State, Welles, and others in Washington, favoured its acceptance. It was also known that Roosevelt took a special interest in Caribbean social and economic development in general and this initiative in particular. All the same, the Colonial Office was careful to make it clear that its agreement in principle, as well as that of the Governors, was dependent on the understanding that the new body was to be strictly advisory in character, composed only of officials and exclusively Anglo-American (although the Canadian government was consulted before the British reply was delivered). These terms were included in the draft joint communiqué sent to the American government in July.[82]

While the stage was being set for further negotiations, important developments of another type were taking place in Washington. In view of the growing importance of the United States as a source of supplies for the colonies, especially after the enactment of Lend Lease, it was decided to institute some form of direct Colonial Office representation within the rapidly expanding supply machinery being formed there by the British government. In July 1941 Melville was appointed head of the Washington-based Colonial Supply Liaison, a small section officially charged with advising and assisting the British Purchasing Commission. The Liaison was soon deluged with work whose main components were arranging bulk purchases, deciding on colonial priorities, and obtaining export licences.[83] The machinery seemed scarcely adequate for meeting such demands. Caine, who had been in Washington to assist at the birth of the new body, returned to London in the autumn determined to see improvements made.

Once back in the Colonial Office he began to argue for the appointment of a high-ranking, permanent Colonial Office representative in the American capital (Melville was a Principal) to deal with all questions about the colonial economy in which the Americans shared an interest. As a leading practitioner of the functional approach, Caine considered Anglo-American cooperation in the Western hemisphere as a single coherent enterprise. It appeared logical, in view of the amount of time already devoted by the Liaison to West Indian supply, to pull all the threads together in Washington in a way which allowed the Office to coordinate policy and conduct relations with some authority. Significantly enough, he had devoted much of his time in Washington to discussions with two key figures in American West Indian affairs: Rex Tugwell, the new Governor of Puerto Rico, and Charles Taussig, head of the American Molasses Company and chairman of an economic mission which had toured the West Indian islands the year before. Both were numbered among Roosevelt's 'brains-trusters', Taussig enjoying a position of trust and intimacy with the President on Caribbean policy second to none.[84]

The benefits of making such an appointment were less apparent to most officials than the risks and practical difficulties such a step would involve for their organisation. One of the very few to support the idea was the Principal who had special responsibilities for matters concerning the establishment of United States bases in the West Indies. Given the difficulties of trying to oversee policy and conduct relations under existing administrative conditions — only recently the Office had been in the uncomfortable position of having to face criticism of the West Indian Governors' attitude to the bases which emanated from the British Embassy in Washington — he favoured an initiative of this type as a means of strengthening the colonies' interests. The West Indies Department, on the other hand, led the way in opposing the appointment as a 'needless complication' which, in view of Stockdale's presence, would function as a 'mere fifth wheel'. Beneath the surface of the discussion lay a threat to this Department's role as the hub of metropolitan-local communications with the West Indies. Responsibility here meant preserving an established set of relationships through which it was possible to instil confidence that colonial interests and views were being properly represented at the centre.

Senior officials were equally diffident about establishing more powerful representation in Washington. As Moyne had told Halifax earlier, the establishment of bases had 'necessitated a very drastic re-orientation of the whole outlook of the people of the islands and their governors'. It was clearly felt in this case that cumbersome procedures were preferable to an administrative streamlining which could add to the impression that policy questions for the West Indies were being decided in Washington rather than London. Furthermore, the Cabinet favoured reducing the size of British missions in the United States, and far too few men of the right calibre were available to be spared for anything that was not of the greatest urgency.[85]

In November the American government ended its long silence over the British terms for an Anglo-American Caribbean Commission (as it was now termed) by submitting a revised version of the joint communiqué. Although most of it appeared acceptable enough, the inclusion of 'finance' among the Commission's terms of reference added to the suspicions of some officials about American motives. Once again the lead was taken by the West Indies Department, which by the beginning of December succeeded in gaining the approval of senior officials, most Governors, and Stockdale to its omission. Enough was now known about the business activities of Taussig, the American choice for the body's co-chairman, to lend credibility to the argument that behind the lofty sentiments about cooperation lay the ugly hand of commercial advantage. Indeed the inclusion of 'finance' could be explained by Taussig's well-known enthusiasm for a Caribbean customs union.

The Japanese attack on Pearl Harbor came in the midst of the Colonial Office's deliberations about the content of its formal reply to the American terms. Caine, already chosen as one of the three British representatives for the first meeting of the Commission, could scarcely conceal his impatience with the caution displayed by his colleagues. He was able to use his close knowledge of the West Indian economy to squash many of the fears regarding Taussig and a customs union as either misinformed or unjustified. He also seized the opportunity to enter a renewed plea for a high-powered representative in Washington, 'a matter not merely of West Indian interest'. 'If we really want collaboration with the United States', he declared, 'I think we must be prepared to discuss all manner of proposals, some of them completely impracticable, and must be prepared to do things very differently from those we have been accustomed to doing in the past.'

If those on the economic side of the Office were sensitive to the advantages of closer links with Britain's new ally in the West Indies, events in the Far East had the effect of making its hierarchy that much more reluctant to divert time and resources into what was anyway seen as a low priority venture. It was decided to retain the amendment excluding 'finance', although the wording was altered to remove the impression that the object was to keep the United States away from something that was not its concern. The Commission was still seen as essentially unrelated to the demands of the war effort, and, as such, an inadequate justification for making the complex arrangements to allow Caine to cross the Atlantic, especially since the Office could ill afford to do without his services in London for long.[86]

As it soon became abundantly plain, however, this was not just a matter of Colonial Office interest. The Foreign Office by now attached the very highest importance to avoiding any appearance of coolness when faced with American offers of collaboration. Nowhere was this more important than in the West Indies, on which Britain's record of colonial administration was particularly vulnerable to criticism. It was with some irritation, therefore, that the Foreign

Office was informed at the end of December of the Colonial Office amendments and its request that the United States postpone the first meeting of the Commission. The Colonial Office's stand was recognised as in part a reflection of traditional West Indian suspicion of the United States, but this hardly made it any easier to accept. This was not a time for central government organs to adopt positions representing local points of view. In consequence pressure was brought to bear on the Colonial Office to drop its insistence on the exclusion of 'finance'. On 2 January 1942 Parkinson admitted defeat, remarking to Moyne: 'I suppost we must give way, though I am uneasy about it'.[87]

The creation of the Anglo-American Caribbean Commission coincided almost exactly with the outbreak of enemy submarine warfare in the West Indies.[88] But since the nature of the connection between the two was not immediately appreciated in London, there was some disquiet in the Office during the preparatory period about the American urgings that the first meeting should take place as soon as possible. Their case was based on the deteriorating food situation in the Caribbean area, but, as the head of the West Indies Department denied the existence of such a problem, it was natural that more sinister ends should have been suspected. Only slowly did it begin to be recognised that the economic impact of American entry into the war and of the fall of British territory in the Far East upon the Colonial Supply Liaison merited some special attention. As a result Caine was given permission to combine his attendance at the first meeting of the Commission with a visit to Washington to gain a first-hand impression of the problems facing Melville.

The linking of these two spheres was hardly fortuitous, and marked the beginning of an increasingly powerful trend. The first meeting of the Commission, held at the end of March in Trinidad, was itself devoted mostly to the immediate shipping and supply problems of the wartime emergency. It recommended the setting up of a permanent secretariat in Washington and regional offices in the West Indies. Caine, writing from Washington on 21 April 1942, left the Office in no doubt that the Americans regarded the Commission as 'a bigger thing than we do'. They were more powerfully represented, and at times appeared to toy with the notion of investing the body with executive powers. If Britain were to prevent the Commission from withering away or becoming totally dominated by the United States, it had to respond to the challenge effectively. A more powerful reason now existed for appointing a person of 'high status', one who could also serve as a permanent member of the Commission.[89]

This time the suggestion was given an altogether more sympathetic hearing inside the Colonial Office. It was recognised that Melville and his staff, faced with an increasingly complex priorities system, the severe shortage of shipping, the technicalities of Lend Lease, and the marketing of colonial raw materials, were overworked and poorly equipped: Harold Macmillan stated that the Office was entitled to the level of representation enjoyed by other government departments.[90] While the Principal in the West Indies Department was among those who were leaning in favour of a high-status representative, his Assistant Secretary, Downie, remained as adamantly opposed as ever. Although by then he had recognised the seriousness of the food situation in the islands and accepted the case for a permanent secretariat of the Commission in Washington, Downie thought that anything more was incompatible with the constitutional position of the West Indian governments and the functions of Stockdale's organisation.

The Secretary of State and the Permanent Under-Secretary, both recent arrivals at the Colonial Office, were faced with a difficult decision for which there were few real departmental precedents. It was vital not to arouse colonial fears. Yet it was impossible not to have a certain overlapping of war effort cooperation centred in the West Indies. As Cranborne observed, to make a great display of preventing the Commission from doing what had to be done would have appeared 'an example of British officialdom at its worst, hobbled by red tape'.[91] It was a point given extra meaning by the chorus of American criticism of British colonial administration which by then was at its most strident.

While the Secretary of State agreed that the answer probably lay in appointing a high-powered representative to act on both the Commission and the Supply Liaison, no precise formula could be devised until Caine had returned in June 1942 from the second meeting of the Commission. The Foreign Office, which had kept in close touch with Colonial Office thinking throughout this period, was generally pleased by what it saw as a growing sense of realism.[92] But although the case for more powerful representation in Washington, as well as the style of the Commission's approach, may have been generally accepted in the Office, there was still substantial resistance to the notion of linking the two sets of activities. Caine was 'horrified' by the attitude displayed at a meeting he attended shortly after his arrival in London, where his arguments for making the new man a permanent member of the Commission failed to find much favour. Leading the opposition was the redoubtable Downie, who warned that this would merely 'serve to confirm the pernicious American conception of the Caribbean Commission as a body permanently active in Washington'. The issue was settled only after a powerful series of exchanges between these two officials, a struggle unusual for its lack of compromise and the total commitment of personal reputation displayed on both sides.[93]

Encouraged by what Cranborne had said earlier and knowing that both Halifax and Stockdale supported his position, Caine defended the American conception of the Commission as occupying an area of competence between the advisory and the executive. Traditional priorities and assumptions had to be adapted to allow the Office to perform the full range of functions for which the war had made it responsible. The experience of West Indian supply problems had demonstrated the advantages of joint operations, and it was 'political expediency' to preserve goodwill with the Americans on which the long-term prosperity of the region was so dependent. Policy had to be based on something more than the avoidance of risks:

The procedure for canalising everything through Sir F. Stockdale's office seems to be admirably suited for preventing American penetration into the administration of the British West Indies, but since I take it that our object is to achieve Anglo-American co-operation, even at the cost of some penetration, I cannot think that it is a procedure so well devised for that purpose.

Making the new Washington representative a member of the Commission could actually strengthen Stockdale's position by providing him with a direct channel of communication with American interests.

In the end it was this conception of an interlocking Washington-West Indies system of economic collaboration and support which carried the day. At a meeting called by the Permanent Under-Secretary on 16 June it was agreed that the balance of advantage lay in making the new senior appointee a permanent member of the Commission. To underline the finality and importance of the decision, it was recorded by Downie in a revised version of an earlier minute from which, presumably at Gater's request, his harsh words of

111

criticism for the proposal were expunged.[94] The possibility of giving the new representative ministerial status was considered but quickly abandoned in the face of Foreign Office objections.[95] In due course Sir John Huggins, the Colonial Secretary of Trinidad, already in line for a governorship, was selected and appointed as head of the upgraded and re-styled British Colonies Supply Mission.

From this time onwards the Economic and West Indian sections of the Colonial Office were able to perform their respective duties without coming into serious conflict with one another. The Supply Mission continued to expand steadily during the next year as controls were applied to more and more American products and the system of programme licensing was introduced. Although established as an extension of the Office, the Mission's work was largely analogous to that of the Crown Agents; and for this reason it was decided in the latter part of 1942 that the colonies should bear its cost through a percentage commission charged on all orders placed. By June 1943 the Mission's total staff, which had been 42 the previous year and 22 in December 1941, numbered 110. Its peak of about 150 was reached later the same year, after which its work began to taper off until its operations were wound up for good in July 1946.[96]

Concern about American interference in the West Indies continued to make itself felt during and after the summer of 1942. The combined effects of anti-British sentiments in the United States and volatile social and economic conditions in some West Indian islands (notably Jamaica) created by the cessation of work on American bases and supply difficulties, prompted the Colonial Office to send Parkinson on a special tour of the West Indies and Washington in 1942 to collect information and conduct discussions. At about the same time the rather high-handed action of the United States Department of War in whisking away suspected fifth columnists from British Honduras caused some annoyance in the office. Sir R. I. Campbell, the Foreign Office Minister in Washington, rubbed further salt into the wounds by calling for the improvement of conditions in the British West Indies. He also reported that some Americans were demanding the handing over of the whole Caribbean as payment for wartime assistance. A protracted and rather pointless exchange of letters between Foreign and Colonial Office ministers about colonial administration in the West Indies took place in late 1942, in which the latter department did its utmost to refute accusations made in the United States.[97]

In a sense this argument had more to do with the past than the present, for by this time the Office was beginning to find its feet in the new setting of regularised Anglo-American cooperation. In October 1942 Gater and Caine arrived in Washington for talks with high-ranking authorities, including Taussig and Roosevelt himself. Taussig returned the favour when he led an American delegation which came to London in December to conduct talks with the Colonial Office and Stockdale. The meetings succeeded in fostering much greater mutual understanding. No one reflected the change in attitude more strongly than Gater, who displayed a sympathy for the American position over the West Indies in explaining to his department the fear that unrest among the black population there could ignite similar unrest in the United States itself. He also wished officials to appreciate the legitimate strategic interest that country had in the British West Indies:

I think it is essential to the establishment of good relations between ourselves and the United States that we should realise the direct American interest in the Caribbean and in all that happens there. We may dislike it intensely, but, in the present circumstances, we cannot avoid it.[98]

When the American State Department issued a statement shortly after which appeared to carry the suggestion that the Caribbean Commission's functions were more than advisory, there was little enthusiasm in the Office for resuming the battle over this issue. It was well understood by now that 'the Americans do speak an entirely different language from us'; the whole thing was 'a storm in a teacup'.[99] The Commission had proved its worth, and would continue to do so, in establishing an organisation for bulk purchases of imported food, assisting local administrations by developing a system of inter-island distribution using small local schooners and steamers (the 'schooner pool'), and encouraging local production by guaranteed purchase schemes.[100] Suspicion of American intentions did not disappear, but where it surfaced during and after 1943 it tended to be focused on particular instances where post-war commercial interests were at stake, such as the exploitation of airfields constructed under the bases agreement for the advantage of American civil aviation.[101]

The experience of cooperating with the Americans in Washington and the West Indies had forced the Colonial Office to relate the hitherto separate concerns of Allied collaboration and regional development to each other. It provided a formulation of regionalism which was to prove valuable when seeking machinery appropriate to the requirements of Allied diplomacy. In coming to terms with this change, the Office had acquired a much more sophisticated view of the possibilities of working with other powers towards a common goal.

4

WAR AIMS AND PUBLIC
RELATIONS

IT was a common enough experience for British government departments to be tested to the limit of their physical capacities during
the war. Few, however, were tested as exhaustively as the Colonial
Office in their ability to frame and articulate their public purpose.
The application of general standards was required not simply for the
administration of wartime controls, but also for the enunciation of
policy in the singular conditions of a wartime alliance. Accountability became as crucial an issue for the Office as efficiency; and
bureaucratic innovation in devising administrative instruments was
accompanied by similar innovation in formulating doctrine. Indeed
there was never a hard and fast separation between the two areas.
War lessons could be put to the Office's service in redefining the
nature of metropolitan responsibility. The process established the
broad framework within which post-war planning could occur and
provided the foundation for a later approach to the United Nations.[1]

The fundamental difficulty for the Colonial Office lay in the need
to re-state objectives in a manner which reconciled the demands for
a more powerful, reforming central initiative with those for greater
local responsibility and participation. The adoption of CDW at the
beginning of the war had given the Office some appreciation of
this dilemma, but only during the war itself did it become necessary
to pull the two threads together into what appeared as a properly
integrated policy. With the proclamation of the Atlantic Charter
and subsequent calls for a Colonial Charter, the organisation could
scarcely avoid relating the hitherto uneven and unplanned pattern of
political change towards responsible government on the Dominions
model to the more recent central commitment on social and economic
improvement.

The Office's problems were compounded by the fact that it did
not control the agenda for discussions, and that it was necessary
to take account of the attitude of other Whitehall departments,
particularly the Foreign Office, and of the Dominion governments.

Nor was the 'audience' for colonial policy any longer as narrow or as familiar as had once been the case. Those in Parliament and among the British public who took an informed interest in colonial questions, no matter how critical their approach, were generally willing to agree with officials about the danger of a statement which ignored the essential diversity of the colonial Empire. The Americans were entirely different. They could not be understood within the framework of common assumptions. They displayed none of the British reluctance to generalise about political progress. If these critics tended to overstate their case, they were nevertheless successful in touching a nerve in British circles, both official and unofficial, that led to a call for something fresh, a bold statement to capture the imagination. The Foreign Office, keen to capitalise on the anti-isolationist mood in Washington in order to draw the United States into lasting defence arrangements, made it plain from the beginning that it would not take kindly to any obstruction by the Colonial Office in the course of Anglo-American negotiations. Thus while the Office was doing its best to enlighten opinion on the one hand, it was drawn into a series of discussions in which it represented colonial interests but from which all direct colonial participation was excluded.[2]

In circumstances such as these, public relations came to assume a defensive rather than an aggressive posture. The Colonial Office's desire to meet criticism, as it had previously sought to meet indifference, by more and better information, frequently appeared an inadequate recipe for successful propaganda to those in other departments, particularly the Foreign Office and the Ministry of Information, concerned with Britain's image as a colonial power at home and abroad. Yet differences of approach notwithstanding, the war gave a tremendous stimulus to the development of public relations inside the Colonial Office. By 1945 the Public Relations Officer headed a department of about a dozen officials, responsible for dealing with publicity in the United Kingdom, the Dominions, the United States, and other allied countries; for arranging photographic exhibitions and film showings; for collecting newspaper and magazine cuttings; and for coordinating policy with the Ministry of Information and the BBC. A full-time Press Officer was eventually appointed and given a small staff. In 1943 Elspeth Huxley was made BBC Liaison Officer.[3]

The really knotty question, for the Office's own Public Relations

Officer as for others in Whitehall, was how to discuss the improvement of Britain's image without dealing with the substance of colonial policy itself. As one official told Gladwyn Jebb at the Foreign Office in 1943, the Secretary of State for the Colonies was 'positively allergic to any arguments based on the desirability of placating American opinion'.[4] Yet ministers as well as senior officials at the Colonial Office came to recognise that a new kind of language was needed to demonstrate the relevance of their objectives to Allied war aims, colonial aspirations, and the emerging international order.

What the Office needed and, in the end, managed to do, was to alter its image without sensing that it was being made to conform to public relations criteria. This meant in practice that the organisation, while prepared to make changes, would only do so at a rate where what was expected of it could be reconciled with what it expected of itself. If public opinion had to be educated, so did the Colonial Office. Thus the new formulations which emerged during and after 1941 were not created according to a simple, recognisable pattern: rather, from the uneven process of interaction between the Office and its environment, ideas and messages were picked up, chewed over, made familiar, and in due course took shape as working hypotheses. By the middle of 1943 the worst was over: a feeling of equilibrium with the outside world was returning. For the preceding two years public relations and policy had been kept strictly apart in organisational terms. In reality, as will be seen, the two were closely bound up with one another.

Charters and declarations

From the outbreak of the war the Colonial Office had anticipated that peacemaking would entail unwelcome demands.[5] In fact, 'external' pressure began to be felt from a relatively early point, when the Prime Minister expressed a personal interest in seeing the welfare proposals of the West Indies Royal Commission enacted without delay. The catalyst was the agreement to create American military bases in the British West Indies.[6] In this instance, however, what the Office was being urged to do was in harmony with existing policy. With the Atlantic Charter, things began to change. Not only was the Office caught off guard; the demands became much more threatening.

There had been no prior consultation about the form of the British draft presented to the Americans on 10 August 1941, a paper which contained the essential features of what in due course was to appear as Article Three, with its promise to 'respect the right of all peoples to choose the form of government under which they live'.[7] The Office was confronted by a novel kind of difficulty. The Atlantic Charter opened up questions of colonial rights and constitutional progress which had lain largely dormant amid the wartime emergency. The Office was to be caught in the backwash of the lofty declarations thought necessary to woo American opinion closer to acceptance of an outright alliance. Even though it had acquired some knowledge of high policy, international relations, and American opinion through its administration of Palestine, this was not much use in the present situation. Palestine had been treated from the beginning by the Office as a special case, an unwelcome burden whose peculiar character made it an inappropriate responsibility for the Colonial Office. The success of German propaganda had induced Lord Lloyd in August 1940 to press for the implementation of the constitutional provisions of the controversial 1939 White Paper but this had at no point created reverberations in Cabinet or elsewhere about the political future of the dependent Empire generally.[8]

The worrying implications of Article Three were rapidly appreciated within the Colonial Office, particularly after Leo Amery at the India Office had begun to press for the submission of a joint memorandum to the War Cabinet on this very point.[9] Article Four, which had dealt with free access to trade and raw materials by all world powers, did not present the same threat, partly because its terms had been carefully limited by the British government to protect the Ottawa agreements and partly because it did not possess the same potential for arousing political discontent among interested parties in Britain and the colonies. Although it was known in the Office, as elsewhere in Whitehall, that Article Three was a reference first and foremost to the political reconstruction of Europe, there was every likelihood that it would be thought applicable to colonial conditions unless a qualifying statement were issued.

The Colonial Office had developed a rhetoric for dealing with the question of political progress in the colonies, but it was far removed from the stark phraseology of Article Three. References could be made to the ultimate goal of 'self government'; there was, however, no question of a uniform pattern, of timetables, of the timing being dependent wholly or even mostly on local choice. The goal would be achieved, rather, in the ripeness of time, as the last in a series of recognised stages. In Kenneth Robinson's words, 'If British policy was certainly not opposed in principle to any idea of eventual self-government it equally certainly did not during the inter-war years conceive it to be part of its duty "officiously to strive" to bring self-government into existence.'[10]

Statements of high purpose like Article Three might have been necessary to woo the Americans and underline a shared repugnance for totalitarianism but they opened a Pandora's box for Moyne and his officials. According to the development philosophy, greater central direction was necessary before the preconditions for colonial autonomy could be achieved. A preliminary memorandum drawn up for Moyne by the General Department as the basis for a submission to the War Cabinet, described the crucial passage in Article Three as 'frankly an unfortunate one from the Colonial point of view'.[11] The Office's reasoning was conditioned in part by the legacy which made generalisations about political development vague and limited: 'In the past, in so far as we have had any conscious constitutional policy for the Colonies, it has been based on the assumption that the aim must be the gradual development of local institutions leading up eventually to fully responsible self-government as separate units.' Yet such a tradition mattered less than the conviction that it was Article Three, and not British colonial policy, that was out of touch and backward-looking. The Office had learned well from the findings of the inter-war anthropologists and in particular from Lord Hailey, whose recently published Romanes Lectures were cited at the beginning of the memorandum.[12] Thus 'freedom' was not to be seen as synonymous with 'democracy', even though it was thought to be so, 'especially by our friends across the water'. The dangers of imposing western institutions and habits of mind on areas with radically different traditions were underlined, as were the virtues of variety and the need to break down 'the parochialism and narrow-mindedness that are often the worst bars to further advance'.

There were other reasons why the 'centripetal' tendency could appear more in tune with the times than the 'centrifugal'. Rapid advances in air communication would make the Empire a more manageable unit. Moreover, 'one of the morals of the present war is that the small unit can only survive by association with others.' Here was the germ of an argument which was to become an essential part of the Office's position in the period that followed. The war's lessons were in effect being used to qualify war aims. The ideology of the burgeoning Anglo-American alliance stressed self-determination; the practice stressed the value of large blocs and technical expertise. One way of responding to calls for greater control at the bottom was to emphasise the advantages of greater cooperation at the top.

The preliminary memorandum was for the most part a mind-clearing exercise and only the bare outline of it was incorporated into the final document presented to the War Cabinet.[13] The Colonial Office position was cautious indeed: not only must any suggestion that Article Three had colonial implications be removed, but also 'we should be careful not to commit ourselves to fully responsible government as the goal for the whole Colonial Empire'. The mere reference to 'self-government', which appeared in Leo Amery's parallel memorandum covering India and Burma, could be dangerous: 'It is not necessary to the argument and we should avoid any implication that the free choice of the peoples of the Empire would necessarily be for self-government.'

Perhaps the Colonial Office hoped to carry the day by touching Churchill's sensitive nerve on this question. But the Prime Minister and his Cabinet agreed with Amery. There was no disagreement anywhere, however, over the need to remove any impression that Article Three applied to the colonies.[14] In the statement he made to the House of Commons on 9 September 1941, Churchill said that this article had been framed with Europe in mind and referred to 'quite a separate problem from the progressive evolution of self-governing institutions in the regions and peoples which owe allegiance to the British crown'. In his efforts to shut one door, however, Churchill inadvertently opened another. On his own initiative, he went on to add the following gloss about the issue of colonial self-government:

We have made declarations on these matters which are complete in themselves, free from ambiguity and related to the conditions and circumstances of the territories and peoples affected; they will be found to be entirely in harmony with the high conception of freedom and justice which inspired the joint declaration.[15]

This assertion was to pass almost unnoticed until the following year. For the moment, the crisis appeared to be over. It had forced the Colonial Office to engage in some tentative self-examination, but nothing beyond this. The occasional complaints that were heard from the Left about the exclusion of the colonies from the terms of the Atlantic Charter gave the organisation little cause for concern over its public image.

Until the end of 1941, aside from the more limited questions of economic coordination in Washington and the establishment of an Anglo-American Caribbean Commission in the West Indies, there were no developments on the international scene capable of causing the Colonial Office much concern. It was a deceptive and short-lived calm before the violent storm which burst in 1942. The Japanese onslaught in the Far East, whose first effect was to turn the Americans overnight from friendly neutrals into firm allies, ended with a collapse of power in Malaya, Singapore, and Hong Kong of such proportions that it called into question the governing principles of British colonial administration. If this were a military failure, 'there would be little for us to say. But there is an uneasy suspicion in many minds that there is more to it than that.'[16] The apparent indifference of the indigenous populations and the incompetence of local officials in the Far East undermined faith in the quality of British colonial administration. This sense of disquiet in Britain was accompanied increasingly by a chorus of criticism from the United States. The fall of Singapore was the worst moment for the Colonial Office in the war,[17] and it found the pressure growing from this point on to produce the kind of declaration which would seize the imagination and inspire confidence about the future. In Britain a mixture of shock and embarrassment prompted Margery Perham and other members of the 'colonial lobby' to urge that the 'reforming spirit, to which Lord Hailey had done much to give substance' be reinforced by 'the new intolerance of official delay and privileged incompetence which the present crisis has aroused'.[18]

British critics may have railed against the apathy, even arrogance, of officials in the colonies and called for a Colonial Charter; but they did not reject the need for continued British rule (or 'responsibility' as they were more apt to call it). 'The future lines of colonial policy are being struck out now in the furnace of war', stated a *Times* leader written by Miss Perham: 'What has been destroyed cannot be rebuilt in its former shape.'[19] American critics tended to reject the idea of rebuilding the colonial empire in any shape. In May Vice-President Wallace made his famous reference to the 'century of the common man', and shortly afterwards, Sumner Welles, the Under-Secretary of State, told a Memorial Day crowd that 'the age of imperialism is dead. The right of people to their freedom must be recognized. . . . The principles of the Atlantic Charter must be guaranteed.'[20]

Language like this, of course, sent shivers down the spines of Colonial Office officials. The Office had always had its critics, of course. In the years before the war, however, such criticisms operated within a well-defined arena and seldom attracted widespread attention. Aside from the handful on the extreme left who would settle for nothing less than the total dismemberment of the Empire, most radical critics attacked specific policies which undermined or failed to serve the interests of colonial peoples. The Labour Party may have committed itself formally to the concept of international supervision but, for those within its ranks who followed developments in the dependent Empire, the bulk of the membership appeared all too content to accept orthodox imperialist views.[21] The discussion of colonial questions took place within a relatively small circle, largely drawn from the 'official classes'; critics and supporters were united in deploring the lack of concern with the colonies shown by Members of Parliament and society at large.[22]

When Malcolm MacDonald accepted his officials' recommendation in 1939 that a public relations department be established inside the Office, the object in view was an attack on public indifference. At this stage the relationship between public relations and policy seemed straightforward enough. The underlying assumption was that what ministers and officials had, in their wisdom, decided was right and necessary could gain the backing of the public so long as a sufficient amount of information was made available in an arresting way. Although Noel Sabine, a 'beachcomber' who had recently been seconded to the Office from Kenya, was appointed as acting Public Relations Officer in July 1940,[23] it was to be more than two years before he was given the rank of Assistant Secretary and a proper department of his own. His work during the early phase was devoted chiefly to maintaining high morale, and here he worked closely with the Ministry of Information to project a picture of the colonies and the mother country enthusiastically combining their forces in a great campaign to defeat the common enemy. All the available instruments of propaganda were employed: for example, a Colonial Film Unit, established under the aegis of the Ministry of Information, produced documentary-style films especially aimed at African audiences.[24]

The Colonial Office would have been pleased to concentrate its publicity efforts on encouraging local-metropolitan cooperation while it gradually educated public opinion about the purposes of its new development policy. The disasters of the winter of 1941-42 and the onset of the American alliance played havoc, however, with such a strategy. What the Office wanted to say and what the public wanted to hear were now likely to be at variance; indeed, the very fact that the public wanted to hear anything was unusual enough. As early as February 1942, while Singapore was teetering on the brink of disaster, representatives of the Office and the Ministry of Information met to consider means of educating American opinion about the colonial Empire.[25] If hostility was based on ignorance, then more information was clearly the answer. A series of articles written by authorities like Hailey, Sir Donald Cameron, and Sir William McLean was soon being planned and appeared in due course in the *Bulletins from Britain* produced by the British Library of Information in New York.[26] In May 1942 an Advisory Committee on Long Range Publicity was instituted in the Office.[27] Yet something was still lacking. It was all very well to talk about social and economic improvement, but the war had raised the question of what the improvement was for, where it was leading to. As *The Times* noted, it was necessary to reconcile 'a centralized economic policy' with the steady advance of self-government.[28]

This concern was felt in other Whitehall departments which took an active interest in the making and keeping of friends abroad. The Foreign Office and the Ministry of Information were especially anxious to make the Colonial Office realise that effective public relations was a two-way process: to influence an audience one had to take into consideration its wants and prejudices. Harold Butler, the newly-appointed minister in charge of the work of the British Information Services in the United States, added his voice to those which suggested that 'there was a real need for a new definition of Colonial policy or something like a Colonial Charter.'[29] Starting in the spring of 1942 the Colonial Office began to experience in earnest the tension created between its recognition that some public act of assurance was necessary and its determination not to dance to the tune of others. These contrary pulls were well expressed in two minutes written on the same day by the Assistant Under-Secretary given oversight both of Far Eastern planning and the Public Relations Department.[30] He agreed, on the one hand, that a policy declaration was required 'which will frankly face the political problem and will not take refuge in economic ideals of material betterment'. In the second minute, however, he deplored the 'defeatism' of the Foreign Office's Far Eastern Department in the face of 'uninformed' American criticism: 'They suffer from what to my mind is a quite fatal lack of belief and confidence themselves in our position in the Colonies...'.

What was particularly worrying was the Foreign Office's disposition to take at face value the criticism which ascribed military failure in the Far East to defects inherent in the colonial system itself.[31] While it was important to take into account serious American opinion, the Colonial Office felt certain that it 'should not necessarily allow our policy to be formulated for us by that opinion'. The key question revolved around the extent to which the pre-war *status quo* should be restored, especially in view of the American wish to accommodate Chinese interests as fully as possible in the eventual settlement.

On 30 June a meeting took place between the two departments which made explicit the fundamental difference of approach separating them. The Foreign Office declared that it would be necessary to give up 'non-essentials', a term which might be used in this context to describe Malaya and Hong Kong, to 'maintain the really important things'. The Colonial Office, however, took exception to a view which saw territories whose interests it felt bound to represent, treated as 'pieces in the game of international politics'. There was little to be gained at this time in simply appearing negative, and the note which the Office's Eastern Department prepared as a result of this meeting was careful to take account of Foreign Office sensibilities:[32] Thus although it was described as essential that full sovereignty be restored to Britain in Malaya, the possibility of restoring Hong Kong to the Chinese was not ruled out. The United Nations might be accommodated by the establishment of a multinational commission to control the port of Singapore, and being made party to the new treaties which would have to be negotiated with the Malay·Rulers.

The Permanent Under-Secretary and the Secretary of State both felt the note went altogether too far in its attempt to meet Foreign Office views. Gater's reservations were, by his own admission, reduced in force by his lack of knowledge of the Far Eastern colonies. It fell to Cranborne, therefore, in a remarkable minute of 14 July, to argue the case for abandoning the defensive. There had been no failure of colonial administration in the Far East, merely a failure of defence for which the United States bore no small part of the responsibility. To come forward now with unilaterial concessions would be tantamount to an admission of failure.·He went out of his way to remind his officials of Britain's achievements in her eastern colonies: 'We made of Malaya one of the richest and most vital producing areas of the world. We brought her peoples law and order, happiness and prosperity.' It is difficult to know how different the outcome might have been had the Secretary of State been a less assured and forceful personality. Certainly there can be little doubt that after the batterings it had received since the beginning of the year, augmented by reports that even official opinion in the United States was referring to the liquidation of all empires,[33] Office morale was sorely in need of the kind of boost Cranborne was equipped to provide. The impact of his intervention was evident in the final version of the Office note on Far Eastern policy sent to the Foreign Secretary in the middle of August.[34] For example, while the question of Hong Kong's sovereignty was not 'beyond the scope . . . of discussions', neither was it something which could be conceded simply for the asking. Gone too was the provision for direct United Nations participation in the settlement and internal administration of Malaya and Singapore and in its place, broached cautiously for the first time, was the possibility of some form of closer union. If the United Nations were to have unquestioned rights anywhere, it would be in assuring the defensive security of the whole area.

This was the approach which informed all the Office's subsequent labours in Far Eastern planning and in the framing of machinery for international cooperation. Later in the year an Office committee was formed to consider what lessons, 'from the point of view of colonial administration in war-time, can be drawn from the experience of Hong Kong and Malaya'. Its report (the 'Singapore Report') was a reflection of the organisation's recovery of nerve during the summer. Much of the criticism of the Malayan civil service was rejected as 'misguided', military weakness was identified as the chief factor contributing to Japanese success, and some interest was displayed in the idea of a regional authority to coordinate military and civil policy for the area. If there was an admission that those on the spot were not well prepared for the emergency of 1941-42, there was also a conviction that with improved contact between London and the officers in the field and more time devoted to forward planning, some 'clearer definition of policy' might emerge from the war.[35]

During this period of the war Colonial Office officials, their sense of security shaken and their sense of isolation heightened, looked to Cranborne as one of their two chief sources of strength. The other was Lord Hailey. His direct contribution to the Office was seen most obviously when he agreed to lead a Chatham House delegation to a conference sponsored by the American Institute of Pacific Relations in the autumn: it was hoped by the Foreign and the Colonial Offices that this would serve as a useful opportunity for correcting misconceptions and spiking criticism.[36] It was, however, Hailey's indirect contribution, as a phrase-maker, that mattered most during the first half of 1942. In an attempt to convey 'a new vision of the future', which might serve as the basis of a Colonial Charter, Hailey suggested that the time had come to replace the term 'trusteeship' with that of 'partnership'.[37]

'Partnership' had just the right kind of ring for the times. It reflected the wartime mood for a greater local participation in the affairs of the Empire, yet not in a way which questioned the order of priorities laid down by London. *The Times* saw the term as marking a 'new stage' in the history of the British Empire, though it added that 'a change of terminology is valuable only so far as it reflects a change of spirit'.[38] The Colonial Office wasted no time in incorporating Hailey's concept into its evolving vocabulary. During a Commons debate on 24 June, Harold Macmillan, the Parliamentary Under-Secretary, stated that it was his intention to develop the idea of 'partnership'. He linked it to the argument which stressed the future world importance of large units.[39]

Signs like this that the Colonial Office was sensitive to changing expectations only whetted the appetite of those who had been calling for a Colonial Charter. By the summer of 1942 it was 'no longer questioned that some such statement has become necessary'.[40] A major barrier lay in the way, however, and this was Churchill's statement of the previous September. It was only a matter of time before someone demanded to see just what the 'declarations' were which justified exclusion of the colonies from the terms of the Atlantic Charter: 'If they exist at all', commented *Empire* acidly, '[they] are buried in Blue Books and White Papers, perhaps a generation old.'[41] Finally, on 1 July, the leading voice of the Fabian Colonial Bureau in the Commons, Arthur Creech Jones, extracted from Macmillan a promise to consider the publication of 'a comprehensive set of declarations on this subject'.[42]

The framing of a Colonial Charter was a daunting prospect for the Office, and the hope clearly existed that it could be avoided by drawing on statements from the past. There had been no prior investigation, however, of what the record actually contained. The gamble proved a dismal failure.[43] As the Office's General Department began its search for broad statements on constitutional policy it was made aware of the fact that there had been 'no practice of keeping a register of declarations of policy either relating to the colonies generally, or to particular colonies'. A 'great weakness in the Office machinery' had been revealed. This only reflected the fact that before the war the topic of political progress had not been defined by the organisation as an independent area of policy with its own recognised niche, like social and economic development. The general statements that were assembled were in fact located in large part by Miss Eyre Crowe, an 'outsider' who had been brought in to deal with constitutional questions for the Hailey Committee on Post War Problems.[44]

By the last week of August the preliminary draft of a White Paper on 'Constitutional Policy' was circulated round the Office. It consisted of extracts from speeches made by various ministers since 1919 on topics ranging from closer union in East Africa and West Indian political federation, to broad statements of intent about the ultimate goal of self-government. This was supplemented by a list of references to the principal policy statements made over the same period concerning particular territories. Although most officials and advisers confined themselves to relatively minor criticisms, the members of the Africa Division had no reservation about launching a blistering attack on the whole enterprise. Such 'unctuous' and 'shop-soiled platitudes' would merely 'call attention in a formal and pretentious way to the barrenness of the ground'. Indeed critics' reaction to such a rag-bag was likely to be an insistence on something more substantial.

That the greatest resistance to the White Paper should have come from the Africa Division of the Office was hardly surprising, since its officials had not had to take account of external criticism in their day-to-day work to anything like the same degree as their colleagues responsible for the administration of the West Indies or the Middle and Far East. As Gladwyn Jebb, head of the Foreign Office's newly created Reconstruction Department, pointed out, the

Colonial Office thought of Africa as 'the one area in which at the end of the war we shall be physically able to protect our interests'.[45] It undoubtedly appeared supremely foolish, in the eyes of the Africa Division, to risk stirring up the kind of public discontent capable of undermining the political and social order which sustained these interests.

In the end, such arguments proved more telling than the view that the White Paper was the only way to meet Creech Jones' perfectly fair request. Macmillan accepted straight away that the document was untenable: 'The declarations are not complete in themselves, nor are they free from ambiguity. They are scrappy, obscure and jejune.' He was clearly irked at having replied to Creech Jones' question without then realising, as he now discovered by some detective work in the files, that Churchill's reference to the 'declarations' had been made without consultation with the Colonial Office. But this was not the main point. Officials had known all along that the Prime Minister had not based his words on Moyne's draft answer. The really significant revelation of the White Paper episode was the Office's inability to test the premise of Churchill's claim without conducting a search for the supporting evidence. 'We wrongly assumed', Gater told Cranborne a little mournfully, 'that the material at our disposal was much more valuable than it actually is.' Still new to Colonial Office procedures, he gave the assurance that steps were being taken to improve the Office's recording machinery with the aim of maintaining a complete list of all pledges and commitments on the constitutional front. It seems a reasonable assumption that Gater's experience of the confusion caused by a lack of centralising machinery contributed to his determination to institute a secretariat for post-war planning the following spring.[46]

The Secretary of State, while certain that a response of some kind was unavoidable, agreed that the White Paper was the least happy of solutions and hence would have to be scrapped. Whatever else it may have taught the Office, the work on this abortive document drove home certain fundamental lessons about its capacity for political generalisation. No amount of rummaging around in the past could produce a coherent policy if the circumstances in which previous statements had been made bore no relation to this kind of aim. The result simply served as a mirror in which the organisation could see reflected the essentially reactive, *ad hoc* character of its approach to constitutional change.

The alternatives facing the Colonial Office by September 1942 were limited not only by the failure of the White Paper. Developments during the summer had thrown into question the feasibility of making any kind of unilateral declaration. 'In the framing of future policy,' remarked *The Times*, 'a large place must be given to the closest co-operation with the United States', a sentiment of some relevance in the light of reports that Roosevelt was concerning himself with the question of international trusteeship after the war, particularly in the Far East.[47] During July the American Secretary of State, Cordell Hull, had given public support to the doctrine of 'liberty' as the entitlement of all peoples who were properly prepared; and shortly after, a special State Department committee on international organisation began to consider the question of trusteeship.[48] Hull was far from happy when he heard from Halifax that Cranborne was planning to make a statement on colonial policy, and responded by broaching the possibility of a joint Anglo-American declaration.[49]

Far from appreciating Halifax's premature disclosure, Cranborne regarded it as having robbed him of the option of overcoming the impasse created by the White Paper by resorting to some form of Colonial Charter. He had little real liking for the idea of a joint declaration, but his sense of political realism made him acutely aware of the fruitlessness of pursuing a strategy of simple resistance. Hull's proposal had already gained considerable support among Foreign Office officials, largely as a result of the favourable reports sent by the Parliamentary Under-Secretary, Richard Law, during his Washington visit. Since they were 'in an embarrassing situation anyway', Cranborne noted, no path the Office took was likely to be an easy one; and a joint declaration might well offer the best way out.[50]

The projection of policy

In this new phase of policy formulation, the broad objective of educating opinion was to be overshadowed by the narrower one of finding a negotiating position for diplomatic exchanges with the American government. The two areas of activity, while functionally separate, were closely linked to one another. The Office's Public Relations Department, created as such in November, continued to gather information and plan publicity campaigns, whereas the really creative work of formulating new definitions of purpose took place in the context of high-level ministerial deliberations concerning a joint declaration. The Secretary of State was always keenly aware of the propaganda value of what was done here, and those responsible for public relations shared this recognition. As a result, Sabine's position remained awkward, dependent as he was for much of his information and expertise on the Ministry of Information and its various offshoots, while conscious at the same time of his organisation's desire to defend its traditional policy-making authority against the intrusion of others in Whitehall.

At the 'high policy' level, interdepartmental deliberations got effectively under way in early September with a meeting, anticipated for some weeks, to consider the next stage in the planning of future policy for the Far East.[51] Attending were the four ministers most directly concerned: Cranborne, Eden, Amery, and Attlee, then Secretary of State for the Dominions. They had before them a Foreign Office memorandum which incorporated most of the Colonial Office's proposal for a Pacific Regional Council, conceived by Cranborne as forming the basis for mutual defence arrangements with the Americans. The model was clearly the Anglo-American Caribbean Commission, though it was hoped that the Council could serve as a means of making possible United Nations participation in the area.

The subject matter may have been familiar enough, but Hull's recent overture had given a new meaning to the discussions. It was no longer merely a question of providing guidance for the British delegation to the Institute of Pacific Relations conference or of making preparations to educate opinion in the United States and Britain. Nor could the main determination of policy be delegated any longer to permanent officials. The composition of the forum ensured that much of the discussion would be highly political in nature. Amery and Attlee stood at opposite poles over most of the issues involved, the former repeating his warnings about the dangers of going too far in appeasing foreign opinion, while the latter proclaimed that 'in the view of the Labour Party the British electorate would not be content to go on bearing the financial burden in respect of the Colonies for which the advantage mainly accrued to a capitalist group.' Attlee reflected a long tradition of Labour thinking in advocating a full system of international administration possessing sovereign authority. Eden and Cranborne occupied positions in the middle ground, stressing respectively the need to involve the Americans in collective defence arrangements and the establishment of a regional council as a way of allowing wider involvement without threatening internal British authority.

The prospects for agreement at this stage appeared remote. The meeting broke up without reaching a decision and without any plans for further discussions. For a short time the Foreign Office hoped it might succeed in gaining Colonial Office backing for a scheme which would bypass the wider questions of colonial policy and simply approach the American govenment with a proposal for two associated regional bodies in the Pacific area. But the Colonial Office, with the experience of the Anglo-American Caribbean Commission fresh in its memory, was uneasy about the implication of executive powers for these bodies, and rejected the idea of establishing contact with the Americans until there had been agreement inside the government about Britain's post-war policy for the colonies.[52]

As there was a common reluctance among the ministers to take the matter to Cabinet, the only worthwhile strategy for resolving the deadlock lay in the conduct of informal negotiations. Nearly the whole of October 1942 was taken up with impromptu meetings between all or some of the parties involved, punctuated by the steady exchange of notes between their private offices. There can be little doubt that the willingness of the ministers to work in this way and their ability to persist in face of substantial disagreements may be attributed in some part to the fact that all, with the exception of Attlee, had formed bonds of understanding through their common association with the views and position of the 'Eden group' in the late 1930s.[53] They could therefore act with a lack of bureaucratic constraint which for once gave them the edge in inter-departmental consultations over their civil servants. Besides Cranborne, Amery, and Eden, the participants included Law at the Foreign Office and Emrys Evans, Parliamentary Under-Secretary at the Dominions Office.

The Foreign Office at first thought that it might be possible to gain Attlee's support for the scheme rejected by the Colonial Office. But although Attlee certainly seemed much more pliant when approached by Eden and Law, he looked to Cranborne as the man best able to devise a solution. If agreement could be reached between the Foreign, Colonial, and Dominions Offices, there was not likely to be much difficulty in dealing with Amery. Cranborne, congratulating Emrys Evans and Law for having 'done wonders with the Dominions Secretary', wasted no time in coming forward with a proposal of his own. He argued for the creation of consultative committees in all the main colonial areas. This, he suggested, would meet Attlee's desire for some kind of world-wide arrangement without giving away anything essential. The committees, which would be purely advisory and unconnected with any outside body or the United Nations, would confirm the participation of the United States in areas where she was involved already, but would exclude her from Africa where she had no clear-cut interests. 'You may think all this is a great nonsense', Cranborne told Emrys Evans, 'but it seems to me to have in it the germ of something on which we could work, and it might well be acceptable to Attlee and the Left, for it has in it the element of internationalism.'[54]

The idea of transferring the regional committee concept from a Far Eastern to a worldwide context represented a crucial step in the formulation of an agreed and workable British position; and what evidence there is suggests strongly that its originator was the Secretary of State rather than his department. Cranborne was actually holidaying in Dorset when he learned of Attlee's interest in a compromise solution, and his reply was sent almost immediately, apparently without his consulting officials in London. It is also interesting to note that, if the ministerial discussions took place against the background of Hull's offer, the scheme for a worldwide system of regional bodies arose in the first place to meet the views of Attlee and the Labour Party.

At first Cranborne's Conservative colleagues were distinctly jittery about the tack he was taking. Eden, though all for taking the initiative to avoid being confronted suddenly by an American draft declaration, was nonetheless in favour of confining the discussion with Attlee to the Far East. Emrys Evans went further, questioning the need for 'elaborate schemes' at this stage, and reminding Cranborne that 'when the views of the Left are put forward so vigorously we must not forget our own Party whose attitude we are bound to represent.'[55] But such objections did not last long. By the latter part of October ministers were giving consideration to a draft Cabinet paper, prepared by Colonial Office officials under the watchful eye of Cranborne, which took the form of a telegram to Halifax based on the format used by the Foreign Office in setting out its earlier scheme for two Pacific regional councils. Amery had dropped out of the deliberations by now, and Gater's absence in Washington during this vital phase may also have been significant in the light of Jebb's observation that the Permanent Under-Secretary was 'not in favour of our joining in, far less suggesting, any declaration if we can possibly avoid it'.[56]

When friction did occur it did not involve Attlee at all, but centred on certain amendments Law made to the agreed version of the draft. Although Law had assured Eden that these merely 'fleshed out' the draft, Cranborne and his officials disagreed, as the Foreign Secretary learned in a sharply worded letter from the Colonial Office. By some rather injudicious wording the Law version had succeeded in stirring up all the old Colonial Office fears about regional bodies being given executive powers. No less objectionable was the phrase 'unable to bear the full burden of complete independence' used to describe the condition of colonial peoples. It drew from Cranborne a rebuke which reflected his personal views about political change and his department's continuing sensitivity about having this subject made subordinate to the needs of international negotiation:

We all know in our heart that most Colonies, especially in Africa, will probably not be fit for complete independence for centuries .... I am responsible for the Colonies. I could not agree to a phrase which is likely to have such deplorable effects, just to placate the Americans, who do not understand the conditions under which we have to work.

Eden was understandably angry with his department for having failed to alert him to the potential explosive in what he thought a completely innocuous draft. If Law's methods were a little crude, he was able to claim with some justice that his revisions had coaxed out of Cranborne further amendments which gave the Foreign Office most of what it wanted in the way of 'a little harmless icing on the cake which ... would appeal to the untrained palates of those to whom it was offered, without at the same time making us actually vomit'.[57]

By the beginning of November 1942 the three ministers were at last in agreement about the main lines of the draft declaration to be presented to the Americans. The rest of the month was spent putting on the finishing touches, such as when it was decided to accept Halifax's idea of splitting the telegram into two parts, the first outlining general principles, and the second describing the machinery by which these could be realised.[58] Such was Cranborne's association with the evolution of the draft declaration that even after he had been replaced by Stanley there could be no question of his being excluded from the circle of ministers concerned with its progress.

Stanley adapted quickly to the requirements of his new role, using a recent talk with the Prime Minister to advantage in requesting an urgent meeting with him on the form of the joint declaration. Churchill's blessing of the draft prior to its coming before the Cabinet was of critical importance, and this was achieved on 1 December at the cost of only relatively minor changes. Stanley also managed to impress on his ministerial colleagues the advisability of making a more explicit reference in the draft to Hull's conception of 'Parent States, the origin of the whole idea'.[59]

On 9 December 1942, after more than two months of intensive interdepartmental negotiation, a memorandum submitted jointly by Attlee, Cranborne, Eden, and Stanley was considered in Cabinet.[60] Its first two stated priorities of American participation in defence schemes and American recognition of Britain's sole right to administer her own colonies, including those under enemy occupation, reflected the main lines of argument employed from the beginning by the Foreign and Colonial Offices respectively. The aim of the joint declaration was characterised as a 'crystallization in a form not unfavourable to ourselves of the existing vague but widely held theories regarding the colonies'. In the draft telegrams for Halifax, which accompanied the memorandum, the awkwardness involved in dealing with the colonial relationship was overcome by the liberal use of Hull's concept of parent states. In this way recognition was given to the right of the United States to contribute to the articulation of future policy without the suggestion that such policy would go beyond the accepted boundaries of the partnership ideal. Pride of place was given in the declaration to the obligation of parent states to cooperate in effective defence arrangements. Only when this had been achieved would they be in a position to turn their attention to the duty they shared of 'moulding and extending the social and political institutions' of their territories. There was no mention of time-tables or independence; the goal was to help the colonies to become 'capable of discharging in due course the full responsibilities of government'. In recognition of those who attacked the economic aspects of colonial rule, a passage was inserted stating that the natural resources of the colonies were to be organised and marketed in the best interests of the peoples as a whole. If American consciences could not be ignored, neither could their pocketbooks.

If Hull had agreed to a joint declaration on these lines, Halifax would have informed him of Britain's plan for regional commissions to provide for consultation and collaboration between parent states and the nations with defence or economic interests in the areas concerned. Responsibility for administration, which in effect covered all questions of internal policy, remained the exclusive right of the parent state. The whole edifice was supported by the twin pillars of material betterment and Allied cooperation. What Cranborne had sensed from the beginning was that, by linking progressive thinking about social and economic development with the trend towards larger units, it would be possible to forge a viable position which avoided the rocks of international administration on the one hand, and the whirlpool of political independence on the other.

It was an approach that the Cabinet had no difficulty approving.[61] Nor is it hard to understand why. The draft had recognised the need to relate existing policy to the questions of international accountability and political progress. But 'regionalism' excluded outside interference, and political progress, if given greater recognition, was bureaucratised by being made subject to pre-conditions of social and economic development for which the metropolitan authority took direct responsibility. The underlying assumption was that in the post-war world the ideas of technical interchange and material improvement would displace old-fashioned, inherently disruptive notions based on national exclusiveness.

While the high-policy-makers had been refashioning the official language of colonial policy, a renewed bout of American criticism had given a fresh sense of urgency to those already concerned with improving Britain's image.[62] Harold Butler told London that it was 'very important to do what can be done to explain our imperial and colonial policy'.[63] The Prime Minister, however, only made things worse when he told his Mansion House audience on 10 November that he had 'not become the King's First Minister in order to preside over the liquidation of the British Empire'. In the words of a *Times* leader, again written by Margery Perham, 'to deprecate the "liquidation" of the British Empire is surely a false approach'; rather, American criticism should act as 'an encouragement to all in this country who are seeking to grasp the opportunities that the war has offered for a fresh and rapid advance towards wider political freedom and enhanced economic well-being for colonial peoples'.[64] Cranborne had already told Amery of his determination to enlarge and strengthen the Colonial Office's 'propaganda' staff.[65] During November, D. M. MacDougall, a 'beachcomber' with Far Eastern experience, was sent to Washington to join Butler's staff as a temporary adviser on colonial affairs. This provided the Office for the first time with its own representative inside the American-based publicity operation. In London, meanwhile, preparations were being made, in response to a suggestion by the Director-General of the Ministry of Information, to form an interdepartmental committee under Richard Law to examine 'American opinion and the British Empire'.[66]

The formation of this committee gave a new prominence to the question of how to define the role of public relations. Gater had told the Director-General of the Ministry of Information: 'I believe that the Colonial Empire is so important to the world influence of the mother country that expense and materials should not be spared.'[67] Even Churchill, who had earlier dismissed Halifax's suggestion that a full statement be delivered on the aims and achievements of colonial policy, had by this time come round sufficiently to accept the proposal that Cranborne should use a debate in the Lords on 3 December for this purpose.[68] When it came to deciding on terms of reference for the Law Committee, however, an important difference of interpretation emerged. The Office simply wanted more widespread publicity given to existing commitments; the Foreign Office (undoubtedly with the backing of the Ministry of Information) felt this was much too narrow. In the end the Colonial Office agreed that the committee should not be confined to propaganda or publicity, but should take an interest in all forms of action and debate which exerted some influence on opinion.[69] That the Office did not apparently make a fight on this issue is probably explained by a realisation that such grandiose terms of reference lay beyond the competence of the new body.

For one thing, it was well understood that nothing very much could be done until the outcome of the joint declaration was clearer. Also, the establishment of the Law Committee coincided with the period in late 1942 and early 1943 when the Colonial Office began to regain its confidence and poise. Talks with high ranking American authorities in Washington and London did much to reassure officials, Gater in particular, about the moderateness of the United States government's intentions. As seen earlier, the experience of working with American representatives on the Anglo-American Caribbean Commission and cooperating with them in the operations of the British Colonies Supply Mission in Washington had also done much to break down the Office's sense of isolation and provide it with a more sophisticated view of international affairs.[70] Vocal criticism remained a problem, but the difference between phrases and plans was appreciated far more than it had been earlier: 'I favour a sturdier attitude than we have sometimes adopted in the past', Cranborne told Amery in early November.[71] A month later British representatives met some of their critics in the flesh during the Institute of Pacific Relations Conference held at Mont Tremblant, near Montreal.[72] Lord Hailey and his fellow delegates found anti-colonial sentiment running high, among Canadians as well as Americans. This 'scholarly bunch of handpicked liberals', as MacDougall described them, pressed hard for explanations about the Atlantic Charter's application to the colonies.

Yet even here there was room for optimism. The British took heart from the fact that their critics appeared to possess no very clear idea about the future. Hailey, on the other hand, spent time during and after the conference (on a brief speaking tour of the United States) flying the kite of regional councils. He had been well briefed before leaving, and his special position allowed him to act as the publicist of British government thinking without overtly proclaiming himself as such. Though critics were not disarmed at the conference, the British came away feeling that they were on the right track. The fading of party differences at home reinforced this belief: indeed, it was noted with satisfaction that no one had exceeded Creech Jones in his efforts, both at Mont Tremblant and during a subsequent tour of the United States, to defend Britain's recent colonial record.[73]

The Law Committee found itself forced to wait on events and thus operated in a kind of vacuum. All it could really do on its own was commission reports, take soundings, collate information, establish priorities, prepare pamphlets, and dispatch an investigator to the United States to observe events firsthand. Gater informed the committee in February that he favoured taking the offensive with a three-pronged attack consisting of the joint declaration, the forthcoming report by the Development Comptroller for the West Indies, and the latest proposals about the form of the Jamaican constitution.[74] The critical prong was clearly the first. By now, however, unknown to the Law Committee, there had been a subtle shift of emphasis detectable in 'high policy' deliberations on the joint declaration.

Comments by the Dominion governments on the first draft had been mixed and there was growing uncertainty in London about what the

United States government's view of the colonial question really was.[75] Great play was made in Cabinet discussions of the need to avoid any appearance of yielding to American pressure. There seemed to be a growing appreciation of the draft's value as a policy instrument independent of its diplomatic context. The members of the Cabinet had 'learned much from the successful experiment of setting up a Resident Minister in West Africa' about the usefulness of larger units in colonial administration. The declaration would have 'a reassuring effect' on British public opinion; and, although it would naturally be an advantage if it could be issued bilaterally, rejection by the United States would not necessarily.mark the end of the venture. This was one of the first signs at the highest level of an acceptance of regionalism as a doctrine with applications extending beyond the context of Anglo-American negotiations into the embryonic activity of post-war planning.[76]

The final version of the British draft declaration was handed to Hull by Halifax in early February, and the American response, received in London in April, effectively ruled out the possibility of a joint declaration.[77] The high-flown rhetoric and the references to timetables, 'independence', and international administration appeared to confirm the popular British notion that Americans took an ideological approach to colonial questions. 'After reading the American draft two or three times', commented Gater, 'I am left with feeling of complete hopelessness.'[78] Yet the feeling of 'hopelessness' referred to the collapse of a diplomatic initiative, not to the morale of the Colonial Office generally. No longer was pressure being exerted by the Foreign Office and others to make the accommodation of American opinion the determining factor in the framing and projection of broad policy. Unlike a year earlier, the British had a coherent set of proposals of their own. Even Hailey could not prevail against this shift of mood. His suggestion, made after his return from the United States, that the inclusion of 'resounding statements of principle on which America insists' might yet save the joint declaration, was dismissed abruptly by Stanley.[79] To reject the American style did not mean that mutual understanding and cooperation were impossible.

No response was forthcoming from the Americans to an *aide-mémoire*, containing British objections to the draft declaration, which Eden had delivered to Winant, the American Ambassador, at the end of May: there was not even any certain knowledge that it had been transmitted to Washington. As a result, British ministers and officials now began to consider seriously the alternative of a unilateral statement based on the British draft.[80] Those responsible for public relations continued to be kept at arms length, however. Sabine was himself only too conscious of the need to avoid trespassing on forbidden territory. But it was not easy. 'The dividing line between public relations and policy may be at times dangerously obscure', he pointed out in a note drawn up to help prepare the Office for a forthcoming meeting of the Law Committee.[81] He remained convinced that not enough was being done in Britain or the United States 'to explain and expound Colonial policy', and to his request for more speakers and printed material he added the recommendation that the Secretary of State deliver a full public statement, covering the entire range of policy, which could provide the basis for a major publicity campaign on both sides of the Atlantic. Sabine was obviously finding it hard to achieve much, especially since he had not yet been granted permission to make a trip to the United States. There was still no inclination by his superiors to authorise such a trip, however, and his suggestion for a major speech was received coolly, even though Stanley was already thinking of using the forthcoming Supply debate in the Commons to make just such a pronouncement.[82]

The episode illustrates two things about Sabine's position. The first concerns the impact of his activities on Office routines. Parkinson observed that the Public Relations Department sometimes seemed 'to make extra work', that they wanted 'to be "in" on everything of importance and to be there before things [came] to a head'. He gives the strong impression that Sabine was regarded as something of a nuisance by other office departments, an impression confirmed by the tone of some of the minutes written by officials. There were also complaints about the failure of the Public Relations Department to keep others sufficiently well informed about its discussions with the Ministry of Information and about events in the United States.[83] The Public Relations Officer, with his unusual role, his numerous outside 'contacts', and his direct access to the Secretary of State, was bound to experience difficulties when it came to finding support among his colleagues. In the second place, Sabine was faced with overcoming the pervasive doctrine that public relations should not be a source of policy initiatives. The Law Committee would be certain to demand participation in framing any declaration whose admitted function was to influence public opinion. Stanley and his senior officials were obviously keen to demonstrate that their organisation had not been standing still; but they resisted without second thoughts any suggestion that ministerial pronouncements should be shaped by propaganda specialists. It was accepted that the Secretary of State would use the occasion of his Commons speech to impress Parliament and 'as a means of publicity for the Colonial Empire and in the Colonies'; it was accepted at the same time that, when deciding on the contents, *priority* should never be given to the effect on American opinion.[84]

Stanley's speech of 13 July 1943 was a key wartime statement covering the full range of colonial policy, and as such it will be considered in detail in the next chapter. What is of concern here are his references during the debate to international regional cooperation. The final decision on inclusion of this aspect was not made until a few days before the Secretary of State was due to address the House. In a minute to the Prime Minister of 8 July 1943, Stanley asked permission to say something 'if pressed' about international regional cooperation on the lines previously agreed by the War Cabinet. Stanley made a good deal of his passing references to this approach in earlier speeches and writings, and of the likelihood of his being asked for further elaboration in the Commons. He made no mention of the joint declaration's uncertain fate, and a significant amendment in the drafting of the minute removed any impression that it was opportunism rather than self-protection that had prompted this request.[85] In the end it would seem that Stanley felt the gains from appearing responsive to the reconstruction mood outweighted the possible losses of taking the Americans and the colonies by surprise. As Roger Louis notes, 'Stanley saw no chance whatever of bringing the Americans round to his point of view' and hence 'felt it would be better to make a firm but ambiguous stand lest the Americans try to force unacceptable commitments'.[86] The last-minute timing of the exercise made it impossible for the Office to consider its consequences or the possibility of a follow-up. The assent of the Prime Minister and the Foreign Secretary came only just in time for the vital debate.

As no reference to international regionalism was included in the speech itself, Stanley was able to claim that what he said in favour of greater regional cooperation later in the debate was the result of his being pressed by Members' questions. Yet, though some questions did touch on the international dimension of colonial policy, it is arguable whether they actually forced Stanley to deliver his extensive supplementary statement outlining the main features of the government's plan for regional commissions.[87]

Not surprisingly, Stanley's references to this plan took virtually everyone but his officials by surprise. Halifax telegraphed from Washington to ask whether the statement was intended as a substitute for the joint declaration, and senior Foreign Office officials, who had only learned about Stanley's intention to touch on regionalism hours before he did so, found it difficult to frame a reply.[88] None found the episode more galling than those involved with the Law Committee. Its secretary, noting that the American press had hardly noticed the speech, advocated using the occasion to insist that the committee be informed well in advance of all important speeches in order to forewarn representatives abroad and arrange suitable publicity.[89] The head of the Foreign Office's North American Department made no attempt to conceal his anger:

The failure of the Colonial Office to cooperate with us in this and other matters is really exceedingly disheartening. . . . Whether the statement of policy was to be in international form or unilateral, it was to be a foundation for our publicity on the subject in the United States, and the Colonial Office should unquestionably have concerted it with the Ministry of Information and ourselves, and allowed the former to handle it scientifically through the B.I.S. in America.

The Office's behaviour had been 'amateurish' and 'uncooperative'. It marked the culmination of a trend visible for some time: 'It is extraordinary to record that since the Law Committee was constituted there have been about six cases in which the Colonial Office have ignored this [I.e. prior consultation].'[90]

During the autumn of 1943 the Law Committee did make a final attempt to adopt the kind of dynamic role suggested by its terms of reference.[91] Law himself still believed that a joint declaration was possible if the British government made the appropriate overtures, and he saw his committee as the logical sponsor of such an enterprise. The Ministry of Information backed up the Foreign Office in its campaign to give the Law Committee more teeth. Its secretary summed up the objective by noting that 'in order that U.S. opinion will not develop unfavourably and so become an obstacle to success it will often be necessary to make decisions on matters of policy earlier than other considerations might demand.' When matters came

141

to a head during the committee's meeting of 26 November, however, Gater effectively blocked any expansion of its authority by demonstrating that almost everything that pertained to future action on the joint declaration or regionalism was the proper preserve of ministers of the War Cabinet. The Law Committee might resent the Colonial Office's attitude, but it could not escape the force of this argument. In the months that followed the committee appears gradually to have fizzled out.

By the middle of 1943, therefore, events seem to have been running in the Colonial Office's favour. American criticism had been dying away since the end of the previous year, and because of this and the improving fortunes of the war generally, the Office came to take a more narrowly defined view of its needs so far as a public relations effort in the United States was concerned. Increasingly, this was understood as the task of informing a relatively small, articulate group of educators and opinion-makers. For this reason the Colonial Office agreed during the latter half of 1943 to support the establishment of a colonial research library attached to the British Library of Information in New York, and a chair in British colonial history (sponsored by the British Council) at a leading American university. For the same reason the Office did not think it worthwhile to replace MacDougall, whose tour of duty ended in the summer, with a colonial attaché seconded to the staff of Harold Butler in Washington or an adviser to work with the British Information Services in New York.[92]

The Colonial Office was no longer an organisation under attack. Many problems relating to post-war planning and creating the new international order lay ahead, but they could be approached with the assurance that things were never likely to be as harrowing as they had been between summer of 1941 and that of 1943. The obvious irony about the Office's response to external pressure during this period is that, while it always denied that high policy should be shaped by public relations considerations, the driving force throughout its deliberations had been a concern with its public image. This is underlined by the fact that the formulae adopted were chosen precisely because they would convey a sense of change without interfering with established lines of policy. Perhaps, to begin with, the Secretary of State had hoped that effective propaganda could obviate entirely the need to say anything new, but this did not last long. The restructured terminology of 'partnership' and 'regionalism' assumed its authority and acceptability through a process of interaction between what the organisation had experienced in war and what it perceived in current opinion as posing a substantial challenge to the viability. of its existing position.

THE MEANING OF CHANGE

5

FROM MOBILISATION TO RECONSTRUCTION

THE 'turn of the tide' in November 1942 and the publication of the Beveridge Report shortly afterwards ushered in what one historian has christened the 'White Paper chase' when 'the period of discussion and controversy gave place to a period of concrete government proposals'.[1] This shift of emphasis from fighting for survival to preparing for peace influenced the mood and agenda of the Colonial Office, as it did all government departments. The Office was different from most departments in one important respect: it already had a reformist policy on the statute book. But no organisation can expect tangible results from such a new departure without tackling and overcoming the problems of implementation. In this regard, the Colonial Office, with its traditional dilemma of the 'two-way pull' resulting from the Secretary of State's 'dual role', faced difficulties more formidable than those of a domestic department.

The crux of the problem, as has been seen, was how to manage the transformation from a supervisory body, concerned mostly with regulatory measures, into an interventionist body concerned mostly with constructive ones. This raised a number of sensitive questions: how to seize the initiative without trampling on local jurisdictions; how to persuade the institutions of metropolitan science and social science to take an interest in specifically colonial issues; how to develop a broader functional competence within the central organisation. Whatever progress had been achieved by 1939 in defining progressive aims, the Office had only begun to explore the enlargement of its own capability. When consideration could be given in earnest once more to the way ahead, during and after 1943, the setting had changed radically.

It was hardly likely that the Office would be untouched by its wartime experience in the way it approached this task. The shape of the organisation and its 'official' language had been remoulded by the adaptations of the mobilisation phase. These acquisitions were easy to recognise. Others, such as the knowledge gained from undertaking new responsibilities, and the changing pattern of internal and external relationsips, were less obvious but no less important. This leads one to make an essential though easily missed point: that the framework for the Office's post-war planning was provided by pre-war policy goals and dilemmas filtered through the management of the war effort and animated by the British reconstruction mood, characterised as it was by idealism, a sense of urgency, and a faith in planning. The close link between wartime necessity and permanent social change had been recognised by many, including Attlee in a memorandum he wrote at about this time to Churchill:

It is not that persons of particular political views are seeking to make vast changes. These changes have taken place already. The changes from peacetime to wartime industry, the alterations in trade relations with foreign countries and with the empire, to mention only a few factors, necessitate great readjustments and new departures in the economic and industrial life of the nation.[2]

This chapter and the ones that follow are concerned with the implications of wartime change for the Colonial Office, both as they were made explicit at the time and as they may be revealed by the use of more indirect evidence. Our illusive quarry is a process of cross-fertilisation. It did not follow any tidy pattern. It occurred in various forms, on various fronts and at various times. As Keith Hancock pointed out at the time, the developments which had acted to 'strengthen the will and brain of the Colonial Office itself', though 'far more important than many more tangible matters', were anything but 'easy to handle in a history'.[3] Organisational learning could be conscious or unconscious. Some lessons might be emphasised because of their relevance to the shoring up of established positions; others less obvious, perhaps less welcome, in their ramifications might receive less overt recognition. A bureaucratic instrument could have a short life-span, but the enlargement of understanding gained through its operation might make a permanent difference. The distinction between welcome and unwelcome acquisitions was recognised by Caine as early as 1941, when he observed that 'in some cases the war may have given opportunities to start desirable developments ... or pointed the way to new techniques of administration, [while] in others it may have set the clock back for time being.'[4]

War provided the Colonial Office with a more coherent, elaborated set of policy instruments for the realisation of a development initiative, while at the same time deepening the inherent tension between central and local activity. This led to a style of forward thinking which sought a balance between what the war had revealed as effective, on the one hand, and what colonial relationships would bear, on the other. During the war, development policy came to acquire a new meaning, not because the Colonial Office sought this but because the changing climate of domestic and international opinion compelled it. Colonial Development and Welfare had to bear all the weight of heightened expectations about metropolitan responsibility. What had been described in 1940 as an expression of the trusteeship concept was three years later made the symbol of a commitment to the modernisation of colonial society achieved through 'partnership' and resulting in self-government.

The wartime experience conditioned the post-war response. To make sense of the approach to the problems of the dependent Empire shared by the Labour and Conservative front benches after 1945, one must be aware of what happened at the centre, as well as in the colonies or within the 'Grand Alliance', during the war. It is tempting, with hindsight, to accuse London of failing to learn that colonial peoples would want democracy before 'progress', that they would demand not 'economics first' but independence. This suggests metropolitan complacency. In fact, the Colonial Office did appreciate that during the war the desire for change and for improvement had grown and would continue to grow stronger. But it found the shape of those expectations hard to predict. The premise that those interested in self-government would also be interested in social reform and modernisation was not ill-founded: a strong interest was shown by many colonies in the Beveridge Report, for example, with the Office being asked in a number of instances to supply extra copies.[5] What was not so straightforward was the extent to which all parties concerned could work together within the boundaries and assumptions of the British colonial system. 'It is idle to think', Dawe minuted in February 1943, 'that we are going to satisfy political aspirations entirely by schemes of social welfare.' But the hope remained that by the end of the war British prestige would have increased and that it might therefore be possible to look forward to the application of a 'sound progressive policy without having too many hand-to-mouth expedients forced on us by ephemeral agitation'.[6]

A proper understanding of the Office's wartime goals may be obstructed by a knowledge of post-war developments, and particularly of the fact that the colonies found the experience of continued dependence too galling to be offset by promises of future material benefit. As Albert Hirschman has observed:

Curiously, the intended but unrealized effects of social decisions stand in need of being discovered even more than those effects that were unintended but turn out to be all too real: the latter are at least *there,* whereas the intended but unrealized effects are only to be found in the expressed expectations of social actors at a certain, often fleeting, moment of time. Moreover, once these desired effects fail to happen and refuse to come into the world, the fact that they were originally counted on is likely to be not only forgotten but actively repressed.[7]

The partnership doctrine sought to make dependence more palatable by portraying the colonial Empire as a system of cooperation animated by a desire for social and economic reform, rather than a system of rule animated by a desire for good government. War, however, forced the Office to develop the theory of partnership ahead of the practice of cooperative development. This was due to the peculiarly distorted way in which post-war reconstruction occurred. The paradox, therefore, was that the central machine increased both its potential and its vulnerability. The welcome acquisitions of war, such as the stress on the large unit, the trend towards planning and technical cooperation, the enlargement of functional capacity, and Allied pledges to ensure 'freedom from want', allowed the Office to anticipate that, with better communications and the better use of applied science, the centre would be able to interfere more closely in the development of the periphery. At the same time the less welcome acquisitions, notably the disruption of central-local relations, the greater deference paid to local initiative, and the spur given to anti-colonialism, made the Office conscious of its extreme vulnerability in the post-war climate to criticism of empire and charges of centralisation.

Since the nature of these ramifications only began to be explored after 1942, the bulk of what follows is devoted to the reconstruction phase. The rest of this chapter considers the legacy of the mobilisation period, using the Secretary of State's important speech of July 1943 as a focal point. The following two chapters then go on to look at the way in which the Office sought to map out its paths for future action, considering in turn the major problems and the major areas of planning. The concern throughout will be to try to cast light on the workings and results of the process of wartime cross-fertilisation.

The legacy of mobilisation

By the spring of 1943 the Colonial Office was in a position for the first time to examine the main lines of its future policy in the light of all that had happened since 1939. The change of mood is well illustrated in the shifting outlook of A. J. Dawe. In April 1942 he had stated that 'in the actualities of the present grim situation, nobody here has any time for any effective attempts at constructing the brave new world': by February of the following year, however, he thought war pressures and uncertainties had subsided to a degree where it was necessary to start serious post-war planning for West Africa.[8]

Yet the Office did not start with an entirely clean slate in 1943. Indeed, given the strength of post-Dunkirk sentiments, it would have been virtually impossible not to make some gesture towards reconstruction earlier in the war.[9] The Colonial Office was as subject as any other organ of government to the intellectual climate of wartime Britain. To begin with it had done its best to resist the pressures for making special provision for reconstruction planning. But the pressures, official and unofficial, proved too strong. They came in part from the office of Arthur Greenwood, who in January 1941 had been given special responsibilities for post-war problems. Greenwood's appointment had been largely a public relations exercise, and the fact that his Reconstruction Committee met on only four occasions in the year following January 1941 indicates 'that reconstruction had a very low priority in Whitehall in the second winter of the war'.[10] But, even so, Greenwood's ability to call on other departments for information and proposals suggested the need at the Colonial Office for some kind of coordinating machinery to handle post-war questions.

At the same time, pressure for reconstruction planning was exerted directly by colonial experts and scholars wishing to undertake research that might be funded through CDW arrangements. In January 1941, Sir William Maclean submitted a memorandum to the Social Services Department, which, as its Assistant Secretary admitted, 'was not staffed to initiate or work out post-war proposals'. This led to a discussion about the possibility of appointing a reconstruction staff.[11] By the early part of 1941 there existed in Britain a 'South Sea Bubble of reconstruction projects', and in February Margery Perham approached the Office for help on behalf of one of the most ambitious of these — the Nuffield College Social Reconstruction Survey.[12] Other

151

outsiders made their influence felt as well, including a number of prominent scientists.[13]

These events formed the background to the creation of the Office committee under Lord Hailey, which was invited in March 1941 to survey 'post-war problems', a phrase Hailey preferred to the term 'reconstruction'.[14] A month later another Office committee was set up to consider proposals for Colonial Service reform.[15] Although it began with a request to consider the payment of passages for officials imported into the West Indies, this committee came forward with an imaginative project for creating a central pool of Colonial Service officers which would be maintained by the British government for service in any part of the Empire. Such a break with tradition was partly inspired by the parallel discussions on the reform of the foreign and home civil services, which were inaugurated in response to a flood of contemporary criticism in newspapers and journals about the effectiveness of bureaucracy.

The key body on the reconstruction front was clearly supposed to be the Hailey Committee though, like its counterpart in the Cabinet Office, it was not taken seriously in view of what was happening elsewhere. The Office was hesitant to use the very term 'reconstruction', as this had political connotations which it feared would be misinterpreted in the Empire. Both the Secretary of State, Lord Moyne, and the Parliamentary Under-Secretary, George Hall, underlined the fact in Parliament that the Hailey Committee was concerned simply with preparing the ground and collecting facts.[16] Its purpose was obviously to keep things quiet rather than stir them up. In July 1941 a request by the Reconstruction Secretariat for the committee's circulated papers was firmly resisted: Moyne minuted that he hoped they would hear no more of this 'impossible suggestion'.[17]

The Hailey Committee was entirely official in its composition, with the membership confined to Lord Hailey and four Assistant Under-Secretaries. Most of its energies went into the commissioning of specialist studies by former colonial officials. The seven memoranda which Lord Hailey himself wrote for the committee all appear to have been composed between December 1941 and March 1942, after he had completed his reports on native administration in Africa.[18] These memoranda were aimed at exploring basic structural limitations which hindered a Colonial Office initiative. He covered Parliament, British public opinion, relations between the Secretary of State and colonial governments, the former's control over the latter, the

Colonial Service, schemes for internationalisation, and the principle of the 'open door'.

Although, unlike his native administration reports, these writings were never published, they show that the Office was aware that public opinion expected a change in the orientation of colonial policy. The Hailey Committee was, however, poorly placed to consider the relationship between pre-war objectives and wartime change. It possessed neither the necessary information nor the clout. When the Governor of Kenya, Sir Henry Moore, expressed concern about enquiries conducted by the Joint East Africa Board at the behest of the Hailey Committee, he was reassured by Dawe that the committee was 'a very "safe" body'.[19] Few pieces of work which Lord Hailey had commissioned were ever actually used in subsequent policy-making. Moreover, with the establishment of the Research Committee in the spring of 1942, Lord Hailey was given a more pressing and relevant focus for his interests. By the summer of 1942 the Post-War Problems Committee had outlived its usefulness.

The 'turn of the tide' later in the year compelled the Office to consider creating more effective machinery for future planning. Its sense of unpreparedness for the task ahead is well illustrated by the reaction to a request, sent by Baster of the Reconstruction Secretariat, for a list of all post-war commitments. 'This is a vague letter, not very easy to answer effectively', commented an official in the General Department, adding that it was not necessary to 'take it too seriously'. A colleague with African responsibilities reacted more angrily: 'Who is this Baster, at whose demand on half a sheet of note paper we are expected to draw up our post-war programme?' Clauson's reply to Baster was understandably thin and cautious. The nearest thing that could be found to a commitment, he wrote, concerned the constitutional future of Ceylon, while most statements of policy, for example CDW, were already operative. Perhaps nothing says so much about the Office's hesitant, defensive attitude at this time as its rejection of Baster's suggestion that the creation of the Anglo-American Caribbean Commission was connected in a significant way with the prosecution of the war.[20]

When the Colonial Office finally took steps, early in 1943, to meet the growing pressures for full-fledged reconstruction planning, it proceeded very differently from its first foray into the field two years earlier. This time responsibility for general coordination was given to a senior official rather than to an adviser, and, as will be seen, the activity of planning was not confined to any single branch or sub-division of the organisation.[21] The Office could no longer afford to wait on events. The prospect of peace and the need to satisfy external demands for blueprints and timetables, brought home the importance of clarifying objectives and preparing strategies.

To appreciate the framework within which this activity took place, it is necessary to take account of various acquisitions of the mobilisation phase, conscious and unconscious, structural and intellectual. Central management of the colonial war effort had provided the Office with a number of lessons directly relevant to the task of planning social and economic development.[22] A broader and closer knowledge of Whitehall; a more sophisticated understanding of commodity marketing, productive potential, and the application of controls; habits of generalisation and central direction — all these constituted a fund of experience of some value in framing any future initiative. It has been seen already that the improvement and expansion of regional coordinating machinery gave a new meaning to the question of closer union, as well as to the implementation of a forward policy. The 1940 White Paper on Colonial Development and Welfare had pointed to the need for greater coordination, yet it is hard to imagine that innovations which took place in the West Indies, in West, East, and Central Africa, and (on paper at least) in Malaya, would have occurred at anything like the same pace had it not been for the spur of war.

The doctrine of the larger unit, given substance by these developments, was a war lesson the Colonial Office found it useful to stress. Harold Macmillan, addressing the Commons in June 1942, put it as follows:

The war has shown us certain inescapable facts of which we will learn the lesson. Self-government without security means nothing. Independence without defence is vain. The future of the world is in larger organizations and not in breaking it up into a number of small countries. It is in the light of these events that we should think of our future relationship with the colonies as a permanent and not a transitory thing.[23]

The practice of active cooperation with the Americans, particularly in Washington and the West Indies, constituted another kind of education for the colonial Office, one which forced it to relate to one another the hitherto separate concerns of Allied collaboration and regional development. In coming to terms with this kind of wartime pressure, the Office acquired a much more sophisticated appreciation of the possibilities of working with other powers towards a common goal.

The question of war aims and accountability raised by the Atlantic Charter and American criticism of empire had the effect, as was noted in the last chapter, of compelling the Office to examine its methods of constitutional policy-making and to devise a different kind of terminology appropriate for statements about political progress. Bureaucratic innovation in formulating doctrine not only accompanied innovation in devising administrative instruments for the war effort: it drew from it as well. The concept of 'partnership', accorded an official blessing in 1942, had an appropriateness derived not merely from its suggestion of a greater colonial initiative, but also from its associations with the wartime spirit of Allied cooperation. Proposals for international regional bodies, drawn up in response to the American proposals for a joint declaration, were kept under wraps until the middle of 1943, but most of the essential thinking on this question had been completed by the end of the previous year.

By the early part of 1943, then, the Colonial Office had learned that, by emphasising partnership, the larger unit, and international cooperation, it could meet demands for greater accountability and more rapid political progress without abandoning its major commitment to social and economic development. The war, indeed, had encouraged a tendency to portray the colonial Empire increasingly as a network for the transmission of knowledge rather than as a structure for the maintenance of sound administration.

Yet perhaps even more significant than what the Office had done and thought by 1943 was what it had become.[24] The remarkable growth of the subject side since 1939 was a major step forward for the organisation. The rather self-conscious pre-war debate about the proper role of functional departments had been not so much resolved as by-passed. The writing was already on the wall in 1941 when Dawe resisted the proposal to create a separate Finance Department in the Office with the dire prediction that this would be the final blow to the geographical departments. Yet although Parkinson, who shared these sentiments, stated that 'it is essential to maintain the Geographical Departments as the main structure of the Colonial Office',[25] there was no resisting the wartime trend of organisational change. Tensions continued to exist, of course, but few by 1943 were prepared any longer to question the notion of subject departments playing a central part in policy formulation, especially when they had so vividly established their worth in the fulfilment of the Office's new-found responsibilities. The steady increase in the number of advisers and advisory committees also contributed to the shift in the organisation's centre of gravity away from the geographical departments. The Office of 1943 was much better equipped to handle a development initiative than the one at the beginning of the war.

Reconstruction: expectations and intentions

Receptivity to such an initiative had also grown significantly over the same period. The public apathy of the 1930s had been severely shaken by the shocks of the disaster in the Far East and American anti-colonialism. Within educated circles at least, it was recognised that the Empire could no longer be left to take care of itself. The reforming zeal which fuelled the demands for reconstruction at home also supported the notion of a policy of colonial improvement. The ideas of the theoreticians of this approach, such as Lord Hailey or Margery Perham, were much in demand: in fact, scarcely a year went by without the appearance of a new book or pamphlet by Hailey, bearing titles such as A Colonial Charter (1942) and The Future of Colonial Peoples (1944). Hailey's message was the same throughout: recognition of a stronger demand for change; commitment to social and economic development sponsored by the centre; the concept of preparing colonial peoples for self-government through education,. local government, and material advance. One of his favourite images, repeated again and again in his wartime writings, was of the colonies as a great procession, steadily on the move, but with a large gap separating the van from the rear.[26] It was an image designed to reconcile progress with diversity. Hailey drew attention to the links between the development initiative and changing conceptions of the role of the state in domestic life, with the public now able to see the plight of colonial areas as analogous to that of the depressed areas of inter-war Britain. He enlarged the perspective further still to deal with the awkward matter of international accountability: 'the need for improving the economic position of "backward" peoples of the world, and for raising standards of living, stands in the forefront of all the more enlightened schemes for world reconstruction after the war'.[27]

The publicity given to Hailey's views was naturally welcome to the Colonial Office, but his background as high priest of the development idea and his role as official spokesman were so well established by this time that his writings were never likely to be viewed, first and foremost, as documents of the wartime mood. More consciously attuned to the times, in style and content, was W. K. Hancock's *Argument of Empire*, first published as a Penguin Special in June 1943 and reprinted in October. The book was written in January 1943 and its conversational tone and vivid prose were in marked contrast to the cool, rather detached language of Hailey. Hancock's intention was to establish the legitimacy of colonies in the light of everything that had happened since 1939. The essence of his case was that the war constituted a very real challenge, but that its net effect would be to reinforce the trend towards a progressive colonial policy. The new 'sense of urgency' that he recognised was welcome, as was the emergence of a new kind of world order based, he hoped, on cooperation rather than national exclusiveness. 'We have adopted an international programme', he noted, pointing with satisfaction to Sumner Welles's recent reference to the 'frontier of human welfare'.[28]

Hancock's optimism was based on the conviction that those who proposed the goal of colonial self-determination would be forced to recognise that constitutional progress was directly dependent on social and economic progress. What mattered more than anything was that the caution and self-satisfaction of the inter-war years had been wiped away once and for all by the war. Indeed it is significant that Hancock was not willing to see the war simply as an interruption or a diversion: 'no doubt the experience of war is teaching the British Empire and the United States new lessons. We shall not be able after victory to take up the plans of 1938, just as if the war had never been fought.' War had opened the door to economic expansion, and because of the war 'the idea of positive governmental action to ensure basic standards of security and welfare is nowadays in the very forefront of the popular mind.'[29] Nor was the impact of war confined simply to the realm of ideas and attitudes. In a revealing passage, Hancock commented on the links between the administrative instruments of wartime necessity and those with long-term value:

The British Empire and the United States are today mobilizing their resources for victory through the machinery of the Combined Boards.

If human welfare means to them even half as much as victory, they can create appropriate machinery — perhaps they can use the same machinery — to mobilize economic energy for the combat against want.[30]

Hancock had been given the opportunity to see first-hand the extent to which the war had transformed the content and structure of policy in the Colonial Office. He had been impressed by what he found, and this no doubt played a part in giving him the confidence to predict that 'when the war is over, the nations which have saved the world's freedom will have in their hands new war-tested instruments of service to the world's welfare.'[31] Towards the end of the book, he summed up his vision of the future as follows:

.. I feel sure that the progress of self-government in this coming age is closely associated with economic and social progress . . . . I expect to see in the immediate future many new groupings and partnerships of territories which have lain too long in stagnant waters. I expect to see some of these associations taking shape both inside the British Empire and outside. Some of them are taking shape already. They are necessary in war; they will be no less necessary in peace.[32]

There is no publication which charts the shift from mobilisation to reconstruction more effectively, in colonial terms, than *Argument of Empire*. Hancock's choice of the three major 'targets' as 'welfare', 'freedom', and 'peace' expressed the current desire to discuss Empire primarily in the context of living standards, potential nationhood, and security. The achievement of these targets depended on a number of variables which were difficult to predict: the terms of international economic collaboration; the need for local consent to and participation in development schemes; the pitfalls of communal tension; the question of whether the job could be done sufficiently quickly (the last chapter was entitled 'The Time Factor'). The attraction of the 'partnership' approach for Hancock, as for others, was that it provided a theoretical reconciliation between central and local initiative: 'In this way', he wrote on the concluding page, 'the campaign for social advancement will merge into the march of self-government. This will be its greatest vindication and the final proof of its success.'[33]

The Colonial Office found Hancock's book timely and reassuring.[34] Nor was this the only source of outside support at home, for, as Hancock had pointed out, there had 'never before been so great a unity of opinion on imperial affairs as that which now manifests itself in every parliamentary debate and every newspaper discussion'.[35] Coalition government and the manipulation of the war machine provided a form of practical education in the bi-partisan spirit of future colonial policy. Labour and Conservative views about the dependent Empire began to appear much less distinct and opposed than they had in the previous decade. The Labour Party pamphlet *The Colonies*, originally drafted by Leonard Woolf in 1941 and prepared for publication by Labour's Reconstruction Committee under the guiding hand of Creech Jones, was publicly unveiled in March 1943.[36] It presented no doctrines which were repugnant to their political opponents or to the Colonial Office itself. Its importance lay in the fact that it was 'the first detailed party statement— by any party—to take full account of the new concepts of dynamic development and metropolitan financial responsibility embodied in the 1940 Act'. Political advance would be determined by progress in tackling social and economic problems: 'no longer was even lip-service paid to the notion of capitalistic exploitation' and the document was 'virtually silent' on the subject of political development. As David Goldsworthy points out, 'of all Labour's pronouncements, this one seemed most deliberately to aim at "realism" and "practicality"'.[37]

It was precisely the 'realism' of the pamphlet which so forcibly struck Colonial Office officials. For Sidney Caine, as for others, *The Colonies* came as a pleasant contrast to previous statements of general policy: 'considering that the Labour Party's plan is naturally inspired by a wider conception of the possibilities of planning of the socialistic kind, whereas we are still tending to look a good deal more to private enterprise, it is remarkable how extensive is the area of agreement.'[38] The leaders of the two major parties might disagree about tariff preference and international supervision, but they were by 1943 agreed on the need for a progressive colonial policy which would bring the individual territories along the road of self-government. The Fabian Colonial Bureau, which did so much to canalise Labour Party thinking in this field, had been established in October 1940 as a direct response to the CDW Act. It tended to attribute the liberalism of the Coalition government's colonial programme to the influence of Labour's humanitarian interests which had been so vociferous in the inter-war years, and to explain the 'conversion' of official opinion by reference to the same long-term process.[39] In fact the Labour Party had itself really been 'converted' to a development approach, as their humanitarian spokesmen between the wars had been particularly suspicious of any form of economic development run from the centre.[40]

Given the domestic mood of early 1943, it is hardly surprising that the Secretary of State felt the time was ripe for a major policy pronouncement. In mid-May officials were informed that Stanley wanted a 'great deal of time and trouble' devoted to preparing a speech to be delivered during the July Supply Debate, intended to impress the Commons and publicise colonial policy. On the one hand, the speech would look forward to the end of the war; on the other, it would embody the experience of almost four years of war administration. In the two months that followed, the minister and his officials reviewed together the many changes of mood and opinion through which the department had passed. It was a collective enterprise which contained traces of the manner in which the experience gained was going to be applied to reconstruction thinking. As such, it was one of the very few occasions when the Office could take the time to consider how the experience of its constituent parts was related to its central priorities. For this reason, it is worth looking fairly closely at the speech's preparation and contents.[41]

The task of coordination was given to the General Department, headed by Eastwood and supervised by his Assistant Under-Secretary, Lloyd. These two officials betwen them drew up a list of subjects which established the pattern of the whole exercise. They did this prior to consultation with other Office departments. The wartime development which both saw as most significant was the growth of regionalism, with its 'material', constitutional, and international implications. This was something that provided opportunities but also raised problems, as demonstrated by the uncertain fate of the British draft for a joint declaration with the Unitd States, and by the 'closer union' question in Africa. 'Partnership' was another theme identified by Eastwood and Lloyd, as were education, publicity, and constitutional progress in central and local government. More specific reference was made to the two projected commissions into higher education in the colonies, constitutional planning for Jamaica and Ceylon, the appointment of an economic adviser to the Resident Minister in West Africa, the work of the Research and Social Welfare Advisory Committees, the decision to create an Economic Advisory Committee, staff shortages, and tours in the colonies by officials and advisers. Lloyd commentd on the fact that the Secretary of State would shortly have available to him 'a network of advisory bodies which between them cover all the more important aspects and fields of colonial administration'.

The purpose of focusing on subjects such as these was clearly to convey the impression of a central organisation gearing up for a big burst of activity. But the transition from mobilisation to reconstruction made officials aware for the first time of certain problems to be encountered again and again in the next two years. Eastwood, suggesting that 'something probably ought to be said about post-war planning', admitted that 'the line between "war" and "post-war" is not a clear one'. Much would depend on decisions taken elsewhere, and on the Office's ability to keep pace with such crucial developments as the formulation of new trade and currency arrangements. 'We are very much alive to all this and have our finger in all the post-war pies', he commented optimistically. But post-war reconstruction was only just beginning, and the Office would discover quickly enough how hard it was to stay abreast of, let alone influence, planning by other departments. Shortage of men and materials presented another obstacle: as Lloyd observed, 'in many branches, particularly social services, where the Secretary of State would like Colonial Governments to take more active measures, it is not possible at present to do more than look ahead by collecting expert advice, planning etc.'

Stanley was given the Eastwood/Lloyd list towards the end of May. Early in June he came forward with his general plan for the speech. It was based to a considerable extent on the labours of his officials. The first of the four parts into which it was divided was a reaffirmation of the argument that colonies were to be prepared for political advance by 'our taking active steps to fit them' for such through education and economic development. The second part considered the question of education in its widest sense, from mass literacy to university provision; while in the third part, on economics, emphasis was placed on the interdependence of policy on currency management, commodity control, and trade regulation. The fourth and final part explained the role of the Colonial Development and Welfare Act in providing the principal instruments of advancement. The war was portrayed as something which both hampered activity and 'stimulate[d] progress in other directions'. At this stage, however, the question of including a reference to the future of regionalism was left open.

For the next month Eastwood collected material from almost every part of the Office to flesh out the draft plan. In a minute written two weeks before the speech was due to be delivered, he drew the attention of Stanley's private secretary to the similarity between the speech's central theme and that found in Hancock's *Argument of Empire*: that 'constitutional advance requires a basis of education and sound economics'. What remained to be resolved was the question of what to include about regionalism. And, as was seen in the last chapter, Stanley's decision to include a reference to international regional commissions was taken very much at the last minute.[42]

The speech which the Secretary of State delivered on 13 July 1943[43] was widely regarded at the time as evidence of a more vigorous approach to colonial policy. *The Times* welcomed the main body of the speech as 'liberal and forward-looking', while the later statement about regional commissions was described as 'an important declaration of policy upon a subject of urgent and controversial interest'.[44] 'One felt, listening to Colonel Stanley's statement as a whole', commented the Fabian Colonial Bureau's journal *Empire*, 'that things have certainly travelled far in these last years.'[45] The content of the speech, with its unequivocally progressive ring, spelled out the meaning of metropolitan responsibility in the light of war aims and war lessons. The opening invocation of the 'partnership' model, with its stress on social and economic development as the essential preparation for self-government, was the outward and visible sign of the Office's recognition that expectations had undergone a powerful change since the early days of the war. The draft plan of early June was followed fairly carefully, with education and economic development remaining the two key themes. A good deal was said about the training ground of local government, the promotion of trade unionism, Colonial Service reform, improved air communications, more secondary industries, and the establishment of an Economic Advisory Committee. Economic self-sufficiency was no longer simply a wish, but the goal of an active central policy.

Most of the ideas and proposals in the speech were not in themselves new. But what was striking was the comprehensiveness of the programme itself, the readiness to relate economic and social to political change, and the improvement of planning capacities at the centre. Economic planning could be emphasised not simply because it had become fashionable in the domestic context but also because the Office now had the experience and instruments necessary to address the matter seriously. Stanley's statement that 'we are pledged to guide Colonial peoples along the road to self-government within the framework of the British Empire' presented a sharp contrast to what officials had said two years earlier about being 'careful not to commit ourselves to fully responsible government as the goal for the whole Colonial Empire'.[46] Another reflection of Office learning was Stanley's espousal of his albeit mild form of international regional cooperation. It was obviously in his interest to make it appear that he was not forcing the pace on regionalism, but, as has been seen in the previous chapter, he and his officials had been considering the inclusion of this aspect of wartime change for some time.

The speech of 13 July contained the fullest expression to date of the development vision. But along with hope and optimism there was also impatience and frustration about the inevitable delay in implementing this vision in wartime conditions: 'this time', Stanley observed, 'which we should so much like to be a time of action, has essentially to be a time of preparation'.[47] The Colonial Office by 1943 had acquired both 'brain and muscle' in mobilising resources for the war effort and in proclaiming the purposes of colonial policy to an international audience concerned with Allied war aims. It was now time to start considering what bearing this acquisition would have, and could have, in determining action to be taken as soon as peace was declared.

6

THE DIMENSIONS OF PLANNING

THE Colonial Office spent the last two years of the war planning for peace, partly as a direct response to the reconstruction initiative of the government, partly as a preparation of its own machinery for demobilisation and rehabilitation. The uncertain length of the period of transition provided an opportunity for a more self-conscious consideration of its position as a central policy organisation whose existing structure had been reinforced by the war. During the mobilisation phase, innovation, both physical and conceptual, was primarily a function of the fight for survival: learning was geared to the defensive purpose of reconciling external demands with internal resources. In the reconstruction phase innovation became a function of planning: learning was exploratory, and designed to measure internal resources against post-war needs. It was a process characterised from the beginning by a search for a new balance in colonial administration; a balance between tradition and change, the centre and the periphery, geographical and subject specialisations, the general and the specific.

The potential which relationships between different parts of the Office carried had to be explored against a background which combined the obligation to join in post-war reconstuction discussions, with the frustration of having no opportunity to put ideas into practice until the war was over. This experience underlined the contrast between what could be achieved by taking various forms of action at the centre and what might be necessary in order to bring these into harmony with local expectations. Officials in London knew they were very ignorant of the impact of the war on the colonies themselves. All the fashionable discussions in London about planning provided a vocabulary and an idiom in which the consequences of war could be examined but they were a poor substitute for developing central-local cooperation through regular practice.

The need for such cooperation added a new dimension to a fundamental question: how to prepare a central development policy in an administrative system that gave such prominence to local initiative. Any satisfactory answer had to cover at least two aspects of the problem. In the first place, it was important to decide more precisely what the content of work should be at the centre. Were there any principles which would help in establishing what the centre could do best? Secondly, it was useful to have some impression of the changes necessary in the balance between central and local initiative as plans were implemented. Was there any optimal method for determining where the balance might be struck in any given circumstances?

The centre always ran the risk of falling between two stools. On the one hand, it could become so devoted to the abstraction of general principles for colonial governments to follow that none of its pronouncements would carry sufficient weight to impress responsible administrators. On the other hand, the Office might be so responsive to individual territorial demands that no set of general metropolitan commitments could be defined. If representative functions were stressed too much, the centre would be swamped by a series of hasty submissions to pressure from local interests: if generalising functions became too broad, its products would never be applied in the field. The dilemma was nicely expressed by Dawe, who complained of too much 'philosophising' about planning in early 1943, yet at the same time attributed lack of progress in planning for West Africa to an ignorance about techniques.[1]

Post-war planning in the Colonial Office had relevance for three broad areas of policy. To begin with, of course, there was social and economic development, which entailed finding concrete courses of action to achieve the results envisaged in the CDW Act and the Secretary of State's speech of 13 July 1943. In the second place, there was the question of constitutional change, which comprised not simply overseeing the progress of colonies through a recognised series of stages towards self-government, but also the creation of regional bodies, preparing for the reconquest of Japanese-occupied areas of the Far East, and framing programmes for training in local government and native administration. Finally, there was the international aspect, which entailed defining the conditions for British entry into a new world organisation, and anticipating, so far as this was possible, changes in international arrangements for trade, communications and security.

While each of these areas presented special problems of its own, all to some degree drew attention to three major dimensions of the planning process itself. These were concerned with (i) machinery (what instruments were available, what could be invented, how change might impinge on existing routine); (ii) information (what kinds of intelligence were available, what forms of knowledge were relevant or applicable, how expertise outside the organisation could be tapped); and (iii) control (how Office interests were to be represented and protected within government as a whole, how advisory functions could be managed, how effective guidance might be exercised over colonial opinion and colonial initiative). Obviously, it would be a mistake to view these as mutually exclusive categories: one depends upon and shades into another. Nevertheless, by plotting these three dimensions against the three major areas of planning (social/economic, political/constitutional, and international) one is provided with a kind of crude grid which is helpful in bringing some clarity and unity to an understanding of what was a highly complex, fragmentary process.

Before considering this process in greater detail, it is important to be aware of the steps taken by the Office to exercise some kind of coordination over everything that could be subsumed under the heading of post-war planning. As was seen in the previous chapter, the Secretary of State, in his speech of 13 July 1943, expounded a comprehensive, integrated policy of material, political, and international development sewn together with the interlocking concepts of progress, partnership, and regional cooperation. It was always a good deal easier to frame an integrated policy, however, than to create the conditions for integrated policy-making. When applied to the General Department, the traditional means for ensuring coherence — a reference to 'higher authority' or the weekly meeting of Assistant Under-Secretaries — had clear limitations. The General Department, for example, had its own functions to perform, while 'higher authority' acted as a kind of adjudication agency, reconciling conflicts and inconsistencies between different branches of the organisation, often well after the work of policy formation had begun. The reconstruction phase called for improved coordinating machinery, as senior officials and ministers recognised. The Office was now expected to take the initiative on a wide variety of fronts rather than simply supervise administration. It was necessary to provide a focal point to monitor internal deliberations, collate information, and act as a link with the rest of Whitehall. The war had already done much to break down a sense of isolation and emphasise the interrelatedness of all aspects of Office activity.

The first steps in the direction of coordinated planning came early in

1943. Battershill, Cranborne's choice as Deputy Under-Secretary, who had originally been intended to return to a governorship after a two-year stint in the Office, was designated by Stanley in March to take charge of the handling of post-war problems. At the same time another 'beachcomber', Benson, who had been seconded to the Cabinet Office[2], was brought back as a Principal in the General Department with special responsibility for coordinating activity on post-war planning in the Office, working directly under Battershill.[3] The latter was subsequently given proper Deputy Under-Secretary status. Until October 1944, Battershill, like all his predecessors as Deputy, acted as an Under-Secretary supervising a number of divisions but, from that date until he went to be Governor of Tanganyika in April 1945, he shared direct responsibility for the whole organisation with the Permanent Under-Secretary, as did Dawe, his successor. Post-war planning was therefore firmly tied to the post of Deputy Under-Secretary.

The implementation of the new coordinating machinery did not begin in earnest until June 1943, when Benson began to collect the basic material of reconstruction planning.[4] At about the same time the Permanent and Assistant Under-Secretaries began to meet for the purpose of agreeing on an internal directive outlining the reporting procedures and allocation of duties for post-war planning.[5] The result was Establishment Branch Notice (EBN) number 97 of 10 August 1943, which provided a list of relevant subjects, with the reassurance that 'there will be no change in the responsibility of the Departments in the Office for the subjects which at present fall within their sphere'. It would be Battershill's job to keep in touch with all major developments, while Benson would create a repository of information at the General Department. One result was that the Reference Section, recently established in the Public Relations Department, was now incorporated into the General Department.[6]

Coordination was necessary, as already noted, for internal and external purposes. But what the Office supplied to Whitehall did not necessarily reflect its own interests and priorities. This may be seen in the difference beteen EBN 97 of 10 August and a return made in November to the Cabinet Office, providing a detailed statement in reply to the Prime Minister's directive of late October on reconstruction.[7] The thirty-three headings of the Office notice were grouped according to areas of policy interest — constitutions, regionalism, and social questions — with many references to the work of advisory committees which revealed the true inspirations of the centre. The fifty items of the Cabinet Office return, on the other hand, followed instructions to distinguish the stage reached from the work required, and the expected date of completion. The only part of this schedule of work in which the Office had some freedom of manoeuvre was the section on development policy and staffing; all the other parts were dependent to a greater or lesser extent on the conditions of peace which the Allies thought fit to impose. The international negotiations which were covered by five or six headings in August appeared under almost every item in the November schedule, which separated the political from the security aspects, and the financial from the economic. Nearly all the questions for political settlement depended on the course of Anglo-American discussions on the United Nations and the future of the mandates system; and the economic questions had to be related to the future of Lend-Lease and the run-down of the Combined Boards in supplies and marketing. When the Office indicated the expected date of completion as 'possibly within the transition' or 'at the end of the transition', it was usually expressing the hope that other authorities would have made arrangements which it could safely follow. Apart from a few emergency items such as the future of the bauxite concession in the Gold Coast, the major parts in the schedule of work for which the Office accepted full responsibility to complete plans before the defeat of Germany were those dealing with the reorganisation and training of the Colonial Services, the demobilisation and resettlement of colonial forces, and the review of wartime controls in the colonies.

The Caine memorandum

There can be no question that when most officials and informed outsiders considered the relevance of post-war planning for the Colonial Office, they did so in the light of its commitment to a policy of social and economic development. Whether there had been a war or not, much thought would have had to be devoted to the Office's capacities for planning such a policy. What the war contributed, aside from a general boost for planners everywhere, was a particular set of experiences and structural innovations which shaped the way in which development planning could and did take place. Here, as with overall coordinating machinery, the first significant stirrings took place in the early months of 1943. The major restructuring of the Office, which gave rise to two new Under-Secretary posts, also brought about the further expansion of the Economic Division: a Production Department was established, and Caine, in his role as Financial Adviser, was given responsibility for the supervision of Colonial Development and Welfare policy. In August, just after the Office notice on post-war planning had been issued, Caine presented his colleagues with a major memorandum on the fundamental problems involved in the task of development planning.[8]

Caine's memorandum, more than three thousand words long, is a key document for understanding the wartime Colonial Office and the process of cross-fertilisation. Caine had by this time established his reputation as the Office's leading economic expert, the administrator chosen as Financial Adviser in 1942, the one most able to maintain personal as well as professional links with economists such as Robbins, Keynes, and Henderson.[9] Caine's remarkable rise since 1939 had been closely bound up with the organisation's need for officials more fluent in the language of economic management and less constrained by a narrow specialisation in colonial administration. As early as 1941, in a paper written for the Hailey Committee on Post War Problems and entitled 'Thoughts on reconstruction in the Colonial Empire'[10], Caine had demonstrated his penchant for identifying 'developments . . . which will give opportunities for further growth after the war'. These ranged from increased local production (be it of food or Gold Coast bauxite) and wartime measures of colonial taxation, to new uses and marketing arrangements for colonial products. Even at this stage Caine anticipated that the United Kingdom was 'likely to be financially a great deal worse off after the war' and that international cooperation would be 'a major issue of Colonial post war policy'. It was typical of his whole approach in seeking advantages in such a rapidly changing context that he suggested providing much broader access to colonial government contracts and giving 'foreigners' the opportunity as well of using their scientific and technical expertise to further the work of colonial development:

Clearly any scheme of this kind would mean a big break with the past and would meet with much opposition in many circles in this country . . . I suggest, however, that our duty to the Colonies requires us to use this method of development if it will really help us in attaining our ideals more quickly, and that if we can help to quieten the quarrels of Europe by diverting the surplus energy of European peoples to a cooperative task we should not allow considerations of national advantage to stand in our way.

By 1943 Caine had a considerably fuller understanding of the 'tasks of war', and his memorandum of that year was the *cri de coeur* of one whose day-to-day experience of the mobilisation phase had made him impatient with the Office's outdated machinery and limited horizons. Indeed, the impact of war may be detected everywhere in the document: in its emphasis on long-range planning, its sense of urgency, its evidence of increased contact with outside interests and increased pressure of public opinion, its stress on the distinction between what was necessary for good administration and what was necessary for effective planning. Reading the memorandum, one is made aware of two worlds within the Office of 1943. One is the traditional, supervisory world of the geographical department; the other is the burgeoning, activist world of the subject department. Caine, as a leading representative — perhaps the leading representative — of the latter, was spokesman not just for one part of the organisation chart but for a distinctive style of administration, characterised by a zest for innovation, the language of economic efficiency, and the habits of centralisation: qualities that, taken together, were so intrinsic a part of managing the colonial war effort.

Caine's memorandum was wide-ranging, exploratory, and concerned with addressing the essential problems of machinery, information, and control. In a covering note to his Permanent Under-Secretary, Caine admitted that the subject of colonial development policy had been troubling him for some time, and that:

ever since assuming nominal charge of the subject in April, I have been more and more impressed by the absence of any opportunities for constructive work upon it under the present set-up, and also of my own inadequate equipment for such constructive work in time, knowledge, staff and in powers.

The point he wanted to press home was that though the Office was already familiar with the machinery required for the promotion of social services in the colonies (because of the numerous pre-war precedents in those fields), there was little or no experience of the role of the state in economic planning. In this sense, the slow pace of action under the CDW Act, about which he sensed a 'general uneasiness', could be blamed only in part on the war: 'We have an alibi, becoming a little worn with use, in war conditions'. Speeding up the processing of claims for grant money would not be much of a solution on its own, because the essence of the problem was that not enough schemes were being produced in the first place. The fact that there was so little 'original and coherent thinking' about development possibilities taking place in the colonies reflected a lack of local machinery for this purpose. In the absence of any really constructive activity by colonial governments, the centre would be obliged to improvise mechanisms which would go beyond the established forms of advice, guidance, and control. The record to date had not been inspiring: the Colonial Development and Welfare Advisory Committee, 'which might have grown into an originating body, had almost disappeared even as a screening organ; and the Colonial Office retains its purely passive function'.

Caine saw that the major barrier was 'a fundamental reluctance to take the initiative out of local hands'. The Colonial Office might claim in public that it was devoting its energies to forward planning, but very little was being originated. Yet public expectations would not be satisfied with excuses about the inadequacies of existing machinery and prevailing conventions: 'When the war is over, we shall be asked where our plans are, and the answer is likely to be somewhat embarrassing.' What Caine wanted to stress was that fundamental changes had taken place in metropolitan thinking during the war and that the Office could not afford to ignore them. This meant that it was necessary 'to face today a new concept of the place the State must take in planning'. The conditions which had formerly allowed officials to look to private enterprise to lead the way had disappeared and were not likely to return at the end of the war. A new framework was being erected, in which state regulation would be 'imposed by "priority" requirements, by wide-spreading international economic agreements and by the difficulties of securing private finance even if it is not desired for internal reasons'. Future conditions of taxation and control of capital markets would discourage private investors and force the state to become involved on a much wider scale.

In colonial terms, this required the centre to adopt a much more forceful role in what Caine described as the work of 'economic prospecting'. It was unrealistic to expect colonial governments to find the time or expertise necessary, as it was 'a job needing specialised qualities different from those of ordinary administration and needing

171

continuous thought, not odd half-hours snatched from a busy day of current work'. Caine pointed to the examples of Russia and the Tennessee Valley Authority to support his case. The manner in which he framed his argument revealed how far matters had progressed from the tentative, rather limited pre-war explorations of a central initiative. Development was now to be regarded as a specialisation in its own right, for experience inside the Office had emphasised 'the difficulty of trying to frame large constructive proposals in the intervals of dealing with the multitudinous details of current business'. The priorities of development were also changing to reflect shifts in metropolitan thinking and in the allocation of responsibilities within the central organisation. Caine defined his own priorities as follows:

In all this I am thinking mainly of development of an economic character or new capital developments of the character of social improvements, e.g. slum clearing, extensive re-planning of urban areas etc., and not of the *mere* extension of welfare services, education, health, and so on. I hope the educationalists and medical men will forgive me if I suggest that the latter consist primarily of the multiplication of processes and facilities which are essentially already familiar to us and do not involve new constructive planning of the same character as major economic developments or improvement work.[11]

Caine felt there was no dispute within the Office about the fact that 'the machinery of Colonial Administration needs supplementing to carry out the task of planning development'. The question was how. Adding special development staff to the large secretariats would not go nearly far enough. Regional bodies obviously had a very important part to play, but even here there seemed to be a danger in assuming that adequate regional organisation would itself transform procedures with sufficient effectiveness. The example of Sir Frank Stockdale's organisation in the West Indies was instructive here: it had unquestionably brought about a considerable improvement, yet its work was 'handicapped and slowed up' because it was 'merely acting as a projection of the Colonial Office in the examination of schemes initiated locally'. Regional organisations were always likely to be too dependent on local governments and too pregnant with 'political implications' to take the lead in planning development.

The only way forward, in Caine's opinion, lay through a strengthening of the centre. What he looked forward to was a 'strong organisation in or attached to the Colonial Office, with considerably more powers or at any rate habit of initiation than exists at present'. The only existing example of the kind of approach he had in mind was provided by the Colonial Research Committee, which was not content to behave simply as a vetting agency, but made suggestions of its own and stirred up responsible authorities. Was not something similar possible for economic development? There were a number of options to be considered: a strengthening of the Colonial Office itself; a Colonial Development Board; or a government-controlled commercial enterprise like the Imperial Development Agency recently advocated by H. W. Foster and E. F. Bacon in *Wealth for Welfare.*

Such suggestions automatically touched on the Office's traditional central/local dilemma, for any major change of administrative method in London would clearly raise fears about infringements on the jurisdiction of colonial governments. For his part, Caine was not in the least reluctant to modify time-worn traditions if this was the necessary price of progress. The danger was in being 'too nervous' to break with the past:

I cannot avoid the feeling that sometimes when we speak of avoiding offence to the susceptibility of local opinion nothing more is really involved than the susceptibility of the official group. There is a real danger that the privilege of Colonial officials to have the sole right to deal with matters of development may be as great an obstacle as the privileges of private property are sometimes alleged to be.

Such outspokenness about the realities of colonial administration can only be explained in the context of wartime experience, both in the erosion of the sanctity of local administration and in the strangthened practice of centralisation. War had stressed the urgent need for metro politan activism It had stressed the rights of colonial peoples. But it had not given any psychological or material boost to the intervening layer of colonial government; indeed, confidence here had been badly shattered by what had happened in the Far East. Without question it was important for the Colonial Office to rebuild its day-to-day, peacetime relationships with local governments, but forces at work in the centre would ensure that the working of such relationships would be altered in a number of ways. Caine's final words reiterated his conviction that the time was ripe for bold innovation: regional organisations were called for in certain areas, but what was necessary for the future of social and economic development in the colonial empire as a whole was a 'strong central organisation for general

173

supervision and assistance, and particularly with a much greater development of initiatory power at the centre'.

The Caine memorandum was soon being carefully examined by Benson as part of his new coordinating functions at the General Department.[12] His reaction was warm, in part because his own experience in the field bore out Caine's point about the inadequacy of resources for planning at the local level. Benson also agreed that 'the practical implementation of education and health plans must . . . depend on plans for economic development.' His reasoning was expressed in somewhat more ITMAish language than Caine's:

Just as it is futile to build a road for the sake of building a road, so it is absurd to plan a school or a hospital at Mumbo Jumbo, if economic development is going to draw the population away to Pingo Pongo.

On 20 August 1943, four days after the submission of the Caine memorandum, an important meeting took place between Gater, Battershill, Eastwood, Caine, and Benson to consider the whole subject of development planning in the light of that document's recommendations.[13] The essence of Caine's argument was accepted, even if his strictures on the role of local governments were toned down. It was agreed that staff caught up with day-to-day administration could not reasonably be expected to get down to serious 'forward planning', and that 'the stimulus of outside ideas and access to non-official expertise', only fully available at the centre, were 'very valuable'. Those present recognised that under existing arrangements the Office was constrained by insufficient local information and a lack of planning machinery. In other words, each end of the colonial system possessed significant elements of machinery, information, and control but neither had enough or could have enough to proceed on its own. The objective, therefore, was to devise a new balance which would ensure the fruitful interplay of central initiative and local participation:

Both Colonial Governments and Whitehall must . . . play their full parts: the former contributing local knowledge and technicians and ensuring local support; the latter providing stimulus, experts and — most important — money.

The devices seen as necessary to make this work were by now familiar — planning sections for the larger secretariats; regional bodies (though with more executive authority in planning matters than

Stockdale's); and special tours and visits by Office staff. The work of modern development missionaries would be to export or 'project' the Colonial Office in such a way as to disturb settled patterns of thinking and overcome older jealousies and suspicions. But once again this raised the question of how well equipped the metropolis was to seize this kind of opportunity. Caine's chief concern had been with the facilities for forward planning at the centre, and the meeting came out in favour of seeking a solution within the Colonial Office framework. A separate 'planning section' should be created, and 'wider discretion' should be obtained from the Treasury to arrange visits by officials and experts to all colonies, great and small. In the task that lay ahead there 'would be constant need for the stimulus of outside ideas'. And it was no time for timidity or half-measures: 'The organisation should not be afraid of putting forward projects for the expenditure of big sums.' Altogether, the meeting appeared to endorse the more active approach to development policy advocated by Caine.

The summer of 1943 was a time when things began to move, when it became possible to look beyond the immediate frustrations caused by wartime delays and distractions. Caine, Battershill, and Benson were busy with their new assignments. Clauson had been relieved of his duties as Assistant Under-Secretary in charge of the Economic Division in order to allow at least one senior member of the Office to specialise in science and technical cooperation.[14] The Economic Advisory Committee was about to start its work, while the Research Committee was already in full stride. And now there was talk of establishing a special 'planning section'. If one is to understand what was and was not achieved during the next two years, however, it is important to flesh out the administrative framework against which planning took place. This raises a number of questions. How far was the Office as a whole geared for the change of emphasis in and after 1943? What were the constraints and advantages of the central machine as it had evolved during the mobilisation phase? How much room for manoeuvre did those pressing for greater metropolitan initiative actually possess?

Development planning

In seeking answers for these questions it is useful to consider each of the major dimensions of planning in turn, starting with machinery.

In conducting its reconstruction duties the Office was left to explore the scope of the administrative structure to which it was committed. The latent tensions, which had been recognised as part of the price to be paid for a 'forward policy' in 1940, in due course became the overt expressions of organisational strain. The geographical departments were sensitive to the expansion of the subject side; the administrators were suspicious of advisory committee activity in the rather opinionated atmosphere of pressure-group propaganda. While the subject side might be given general supervision of development planning, it was made clear from the outset that geographical departments would have a major part to play as well. Gater stated that West African planning should be centred in the West Africa Department under the watchful eye of Dawe, with subject departments and advisers being consulted where appropriate. No sooner had Caine been given his new CDW responsibilities, than he was complaining that no member of the Economic Division had been invited to a meeting held under the auspices of the West Africa Department to consider a draft plan for development and welfare in that region.[15]

The knowledge required for formulating specific proposals required a geographical expertise which could not be supplied by an Office organised on a strictly subject basis. Whenever the question of balancing central and local programmes was raised, the corresponding issue at the centre was to find new forms of exchange between geographical and subject departments. At the time of Benson's appointment his Assistant Under-Secretary, Lloyd, referred approvingly to a suggestion by Jeffries that subject departments should as a general rule prepare statements of policy which were phrased in a manner suitable for transmission to all colonies, under the cover of separate despatches which geographical departments would draft. But Lloyd admitted at the same time that this would necessitate major changes in the registration system.[16] The difficulty about planning as a self-conscious activity was that it always ran the risk of causing geographical and subject departments to compete for control over the main papers 'in action'.

Advisers and advisory committees presented their own special kinds of problems. The idea that an adviser to the Secretary of State could both channel the best advice through his advisory committee and manage the careers of specialists serving in the field was not pursued as the universal mechanism for providing central support. The character of the association of the Colonial

Office with metropolitan net-works required a number of different combinations between advisers, committees, and subject departments, as well as the flexibility to effect a quick change of emphasis. The debate at home on post-war reconstruction introduced new combinations. Although some tried to build up the adviser's office as 'mayor of the palace' in his own field of expertise, there was little opportunity to lay down special rules of general application on the manner in which technical advice could be deployed. Advisory committees tended to value their 'independence' from Colonial Office control, and to prefer to appoint their own secretaries rather than rely on subject department officials.[17]

There was a hierarchy of advisory positions arranged by salary according to the prestige and importance of the networks involved. The post of Legal Adviser was always treated as an exceptional position, which with its three or four assistants constituted almost a separate executive department. In the field of Advisers on development, however, senior status was awarded only to agriculture, medicine, education, and labour; the second rank included geology and colonial products research; and the third covered areas which were complementary to agricultural work, such as animal health, forestry, fisheries, and cooperatives.[18] Some appointments which were not regarded as long-term advisory positions, such as the Adviser on Demography in 1944 and the Adviser on Engineering Appointments in 1945, came into an even lower salary range. Any proposal to establish a new advisory post had to be related to this existing order of priorities. Special appointments were made to assist the Office in wartime arrangements for food supplies in 1942 and civil aviation in 1944;[19] part-time appointments were made to strengthen its coverage of natural resources in forestry in 1942 and fisheries in 1943.[20] Finally, as will be seen, there was the appointment of Stockdale at the highest possible salary in November 1944 to be Adviser on Development Planning, as well as chairman of the Economic Advisory Committee.[21] The main areas which had been discussed at the time of the 1940 Act—surveying, public works, physical planning, and architecture—were not, however, provided with special staff.[22] The post of Adviser in Planning and Architecture, approved in 1942 and offered to William Holford, Professor of Civic Design at Liverpool University, was never brought into being. The appointment of assistant advisers was confined to the fields of agriculture and education. Although some established Advisers

177

were given additional staff during the war, the bulk of applications to the Treasury for advisory posts did not come until 1946-47.

A great deal of the initiative in the alliance with home institutions was left to the entrepreneurial skills of individual advisers and their professional associates, through either Office committees or outside bodies. In each major field of policy there was a number of interlocking groups to which the adviser could appeal, and with which the Office might be linked in different ways. Some individuals held a variety of positions which they used to bring together related topics. Lord Hailey presided over both the Post-War Problems Committee and the Research Committee, as well as chairing the councils of the School of Oriental and African Studies and Chatham House.[23] Carr-Saunders was not only a member of three advisory committees (Research, Social Welfare, and Social Science Research), but also ran a coordinating committee on research questions for universities and institutes. Each adviser learnt how to work through the organs which defined the science of his subject.

The complexity of these arrangements was apparent whenever the management of advice had to be related to the execution of policy. The administrative staff of the Office, as has been seen, recognised their dependence on outside enthusiasms, but obviously felt there came a point at which they should intervene to limit the excesses of Advisers and their committees. An Office discussion in the autumn and winter of 1942 led to the printing of a directive on the 'Functions of Colonial Office Advisers' in April 1943: it defined their position as 'to assist with their special knowledge the Secretary of State and the officers to whom his authority is delegated'.[24] This document made it clear that action which followed advice could only be authorised by the appropriate administrative officer, not by the Advisers themselves; and it also tried to regulate the channels of communication with both advisory committees and officers in the field. It was categorically stated that no advisory committee resolution could bind the Secretary of State, and that he was not obliged to refer any matter to a committee or to accept its advice. The approval of the appropriate administrative officer was to be sought before any question was sent to an advisory committee for discussion. Jeffries, in a paper about the reform of the Office which he prepared in November 1942,[25] even went so far as to suggest that research and advice functions should be incorporated into subject departments.

Caine, in his memorandum, had commented on the disappointing performance of the advisory committee set up to oversee the commitment to development and welfare. Certainly, the Colonial Development and Welfare Advisory Committee (CDWAC) had not lived up to the high hopes generated before its creation in 1941.[26] For one thing, it had remained a purely official body throughout; for another, it was seen as part of a procedure which lacked initiative, was marked by delay, and produced meagre results. There had been a spirited attempt in 1942 by Gater and the Secretary of State (Cranborne) to alter the committee's composition to include a large contingent of MPs. For Gater this was worth running a certain risk: ' . . . if we are to obtain from Parliament and from the public in this country the interest and financial support we desire for a forward policy in the Colonies, we must associate a strong advisory committee with the actual work of development and welfare.' Strong resistance from the Assistant Under-Secretaries, concerned with the dangers of centralisation and interference, eventually scuttled the project, however. Dawe, who presented the senior officials' position most forcibly in the minutes, commented that politicians would expect to do real work on a committee which had acted to date largely as a 'rubber stamp'. By 1943, with Caine assuming his new development responsibilities and the Colonial Economic Advisory Committee on the horizon, the CDWAC had entered something of a backwater: indeed, Caine was successful in putting forward proposals to reduce the committee's participation in the vetting procedure for CDW grants.[27]

The failure of the CDWAC was intimately bound up with the wartime shift of activity away from the social services and towards the economic side of the Office. The argument about the welfare element in the 1940 Act was continued in a muted form while the central organisation expanded its participation in the application of economic controls, for the outbreak of war seemed to have deprived the Social Services Department of its basic rationale. Apart from a standing interest in labour conditions, other areas of social policy looked like being neglected for the duration of hostilities. Even if there were no appropriate mechanisms to inspire the development of central activity in economic planning in the colonies, the conduct of war was against any further institutionalisation of social welfare advice without a better understanding of economic forces.

No advisory committee on social services was appointed to monitor progress under the 1940 Act, at least not immediately. When proposals for such a committee were considered in August 1941, the only outcome was the creation of a small Office committee consisting of the principal advisers meeting under the chairmanship of the Assistant Under-Secretary for Social Services, Jeffries, who also had responsibility for Colonial Service reform. Although the minutes of this committee have not survived, it is possible to reach some conclusions about its work and importance.[28] The Central Welfare Coordinating Committee (as it was called) was in part a phenomenon of Office accommodation arrangements, which in August 1941 moved Advisers and the Social Services Department together from Queen Anne's Gate to an annexe in Park Street — 'isolated from the main currents of affairs in Whitehall', as Eastwood told Burns in August 1942.[29] The committee first met in December 1941 and it was hoped it would provide a regular forum for the discussion of development and the examination of specific programmes. The original proposals for such a committee arose from Lord Hailey's request that the agencies used in social welfare work should be reviewed at the territorial level, and recommendations made for effecting better coordination between them. Some advice was transmitted to the colonies in this field, but the principal value of the committee was to provide a meeting place for the advisers to raise any questions of mutual interest. Though Malcolm was asked to become secretary of the committee when he arrived in the Office as a 'beachcomber' in May 1943,[30] it does not appear to have survived the transfer of Advisers from Park Street to Palace Chambers, or the transfer of Social Service responsibilities from Jeffries to Lloyd as Assistant Under-Secretary in March 1943.

To create an advisory committee on labour questions was a more precise objective, for which some priority could be claimed. The Office already had a Labour Adviser and a standing official committee which could be converted into a regular advisory body. A great deal of parliamentarary interest had been focused on the issue of compulsory labour in the colonies. Creech Jones raised the question of the prohibition of the right to strike in the autumn of 1941, a time when labour questions played a prominent part in the debates of both Houses.[31] The Trades Union Congress, which had played an active role in recruiting British trade unionists for work in colonial labour departments, was eager to establish an appropriate advisory committee. The British delegation to the International Labour Organization Conference, which took place in the United States during October-November 1941, provided an opportunity for those interested in colonial labour questions to consult together.[32] Wartime inflation also played its part in heightening sensitivity to labour problems, actual and potential. The Colonial Labour Advisory Committee was formed in April 1942 and held its first meeting in May.[33]

This creation was soon followed by another. In September 1942 the juvenile delinquency sub-committee of the Committee on Penal Administration suggested that its parent body should be renamed the Social Welfare Advisory Committee and that its terms of reference should be widened.[34] This reversal of priorities was quickly accepted. The work of the parent committee, which had been established at the suggestion of the Howard League in 1937, did not justify its status, and it was agreed to demote the subject of penal administration to be the responsibility of a sub-committee of the new welfare committee.

Yet rather than reflecting any revitalisation of the social services side of the Office, these proved to be rather barren exercises which led to a series of jurisdictional wrangles. The setting up of the Social Welfare Advisory Committee was immediately challenged by the Colonial Labour Advisory Committee in a dispute over their respective fields of competence. The latter in March 1943 suggested a joint sub-committee to link the two on questions dealing with housing. Its members seem to have misunderstood the former committee's terms of reference. There had not been any very rigid definition of functions between the two advisory committees, because the Advisers themselves and the Social Services Department could normally find ways of making sure that all those interested in a matter had been consulted. As the Labour Committee had been first in the social services field, it did not take easily to any suggestion of overlapping membership with other committees, or at least the regular exchange of papers. The main areas in dispute were housing, industrial welfare, and social insurance.The administrative staff in the Office stood their ground against any pressures from the Labour Committee.[35]

The absence of any central activity of consequence in the social services field was symbolised most strikingly by the delay in appointing a fully-fledged social welfare adviser. The Social Welfare Advisory Committee, soon after its appointment, had pressed for the establishment of such a post but without success. When the request was repeated in October 1945 it was approved in principle and then agreed that Jack Longland should be approached.[36] But the latter was not prepared to consider the post at the salary offered and no appointment was made until 1947, after the Treasury had insisted that the vacancy should be advertised. Instead, the Office covered the welfare aspects of its work by making a special appointment in the Social Services Department in September 1943. Mary Darlow, a Principal from the Ministry of Labour, acted as a substitute for an Office adviser in social welfare work.[37]

Planning facilities at the regional and local level were, as Caine had observed, uneven and lacking in resources. Preparations for the end of the war were conditioned to no small degree by the strength and character of local interests. Many of the larger and richer colonies appointed their own reconstruction committees or reconstruction officers. Occasionally, as in the Gambia, where the Governor was personally interested in development, even a small colony could find it possible to draw up an extensive plan.[38] As a general rule, however, there was in most of the smaller colonies a sense of neglect and sometimes a sense of bitterness which was not easily overcome. The work of regional planning, in those areas where such an approach was feasible, was still in its infancy. The most conspicuous example, that of Stockdale in the West Indies, was hampered by lack of information and the difficulties of being caught between the poles of local and central authority.[39] Such problems were to arise in one form or another for all regional bodies. Yet the possibility still existed for definite progress in the realm of forward planning, and, besides Stockdale, the key figures were Noel Hall, Development Adviser to the Resident Minister in West Africa, Sir Charles Lockhart, Chief Secretary of the East African Governors' Conference, and Sir Douglas Harris, the Reconstruction Commissioner in Palestine.

Turning from the dimension of machinery to that of information, it may be argued that the most pressing question was how to foster the growth of a specifically colonial development expertise. The established system of advisers and advisory committees reinforced a tendency to work with the organisation of established science at home. The Office was tied closely to the intellectual community of Britain through its network of contacts, and, through this, to the course of the debate about reconstruction. The role of the state envisaged for post-war Britain was not all that different from that which the Colonial Office contemplated in developing its own machinery. The basic shape of the Office's organisation met the requirements of constitutional doctrine better than any new public corporation for development would. Wartime experience encouraged an elaboration of the existing system of contacts and reaffirmed confidence in the transforming power of metropolitan learning and technology. The prevailing attitude was that opportunities which already existed to apply scientific knowledge to colonial conditions could at last be developed.

The reconstruction debate in Britain induced a faith in the potential for scientific development and economic growth and aroused opinion in scientific circles in favour of technical cooperation between the great powers. Meetings of scientists held in 1941, such as the British Association and the gathering on Science and World Order, had stressed the importance of international cooperation. Prominent scientists such as Huxley and Boyd Orr were pressing the Office to develop its plans for the promotion of the natural sciences in the colonies.[40] The combined planning for war, as Hancock had noted, could be transferred to the cause of peace, if there was sufficient political will to join scientists in a series of common enterprises which transcended national boundaries, particularly on a regional basis.[41] The first major task faced by Clauson, after he had assumed responsibility for science and technical cooperation, was to attend the international conference on food and agriculture held at Hot Springs, Virginia, in the summer of 1943, and to apply its conclusions to the formulation of colonial policy.[42] After a meeting of the Colonial Survey Geophysical Committee in March 1943 Clauson was invited to preside over a number of small sub-committees which investigated research organisation in these and allied fields. His committee on the scheme for a central organisation on colonial surveys reported in April,[43] and that on geological needs in July 1944.[44] The sub-committee on agriculture, animal health, and forestry, which he was also invited to chair, was requested to consider the appointment of an agricultural research council and the creation of an appropriate research service.[45] Much of the consideration of general principles in which Clauson came to specialise involved basic questions of relating Colonial Service organisation to the appropriate professions at home. He acquired an expertise which was itself an expression of the new capacity which the Office saw fit to cultivate. In many cases colonial studies had to be deliberately encouraged in fields which metropolitan professions had hitherto neglected. Those who had been first in the field found their knowledge at a premium.

Applied science seemed to offer the central policy organisation a major escape from the embarrassment of issuing empty generalisations, if a sufficient number of talented home institutions could be recruited to encompass colonial studies. An alliance with metropolitan professionals might provide the strongest guarantee that opportunities would be created for regular scientific careers in the service of colonial governments. The reconstruction debate attracted considerable emphasis to the training and deployment of skilled manpower. Whatever the field of endeavour, the empire would be helped with sympathetic contributions from the metropole if the normal careers of scientists and other specialists included a period in the colonies.

The association with established science was seen most clearly in the creation and composition of the Office's Research Committee. The advisers to the Secretary of State had been anxious to have implemented the proposals for a research committee which had been envisaged in the 1940 Act, even before the loss of Singapore which had exposed all officials to violent criticism. The Research Committee, which was finally appointed in March 1942, consisted of the Scientific Advisory Committee of the Cabinet meeting 'under another hat', with the addition of representatives from the social sciences. That Cabinet Committee drew its membership from the Medical Research Council, the Agricultural Research Council, the Nature Conservancy, and the Royal Society. The intellectual climate of early 1942, when the Research Committee began its work, was very different from that of March 1940, when its functions were first discussed, and the formulations which it accepted were a reflection of this change. In the debates in Parliament on the role of science in public life and the importance of securing further applied scientific research, the Colonial Office enjoyed a certain reputation for having begun an enlightened policy of encouragement which other departments might emulate.[46] It published its own White Paper in November 1943 on its first year of research work, when some other departments had hardly begun to consider how they might proceed.[47]

The White Paper summarised the 'fields of research' which the Committee had surveyed to date — land surveys, the magnetic and meteorological services, forestry, fisheries, agriculture, animal health, medicine, and the social sciences. More interesting, however, was its discussion of the major problems encountered in initiating and sponsoring colonial research. They were treated under headings such as 'the need for an extended range of research', 'continuity of research', 'research affected by shortage of technical staff', 'isolation and restricted opportunities for Colonial research workers', 'the need for central and regional organisation of research', and 'the question of Government control in relation to Colonial Research'. The effect was to underline, as Caine's memorandum had done, the difficulties involved in transmitting knowledge and expertise from the centre to the periphery:

While the Committee has been impressed with the efforts that have been made by research workers in the Colonies, often in the face of great difficulties, and with the value of many of the results achieved, it is convinced that scientific facilities and terms of service must be improved, and new or additional methods of recruitment and organisation devised, if research is to play an effective part in colonial development. Under existing conditions scientists and research workers in the Colonies frequently have to work in isolation, and with relatively inferior equipment . . . . Even if they are freed from the pressure of routine [administration] there is a tendency for research problems to be dictated too exclusively by local and temporary interests, without due regard to scientific possibilities, or to the scale on which a given investigation must be planned if it is to have any reasonable hope of success.

Some way would have to be found of keeping the long-term interests of science alive amid the short-term pressures of administration.

One possible solution, touched on by the White Paper, was the strategy of seeking alliance with self-governing professions. Yet, although this was helpful in reducing the spectre of Colonial Office centralisation, it contained one very real weakness: the existence of a difference between what the metropolitan knowledge industry was designed to tackle, on the one hand, and certain specifically colonial problems requiring a solution, on the other. It was indeed possible from time to time to encourage disciplines which had hitherto neglected colonial phenomena to extend their horizons; or to promote new areas of research in largely colonial subjects. Tropical medicine and tropical agriculture were long-established subjects with their own systems of promotion and reward. But what about colonial administration or colonial economics? Where 'home industries' had not been set up for the study of key aspects of colonial development, the alliance with established science was of little avail. It seemed extremely ineffectual to be preaching the virtues of colonial responsibility for real economic growth if there were no research of a high standard into the problems which the colonies faced.

This question of applicability, of finding parallels, was very much part of the Colonial Office's experience of refining its approach to development planning. Action taken through a variety of initiatives at the centre during the period of reconstruction was strongly influenced by developments taking place in the reform of home institutions. The advisory network drew the Office into extensive talks on higher education, research, and Colonial Service reform, which were all easy to relate to metropolitan interests. But it was unable to provide any parallel activity on the institutions of economic planning. The most important aspect of 'forward policy' raised all the questions on which it was most difficult to secure agreement and called for a series of government contacts which had scarcely been satisfactorily made for the metropolitan economy itself. The management of the war effort provoked an extensive debate on economic theory in intellectual circles which was awkward to extend to the colonial context.

Thus the war might have given a boost to the notion of planning, but it did not, as Caine had emphasised in his memorandum, supply the knowlede of how best to exploit these new enthusiasms for the purpose of realising CDW objectives. This was left for administrative innovation; yet the administrative system was not accomplished in taking over new theories and devising new administrative methods from them. The business of controlling economic forces had no peacetime precedents to which the Office could refer, and any adviser or official taking initiatives in this field could not easily identify a comparable context in discussions taking place at home. Raymond Firth's proposal[48] for a colonial economic research service in 1941 or Caine's suggestion for an 'economic prospecting service',[49] possibly operating under aegis of a government-inspired private company, were not taken from metropolitan examples but from the diagnosis they had made of the empire's needs in real economic growth. The post of Development Adviser, hinted at in the summer of 1943 and brought into being the following year, could not be readily linked with all that was being said in Britain about the role of economic departments in the central government machine.

Higher education and research were already subjects of concern to the Colonial Office at the outbreak of the war. The Advisory Committee on Education in the Colonies (ACEC), for instance, had set up in 1940 its own sub-committee on higher education in West Africa; and its consultative committee on the University of London Institute of Education provided regular reports on the progress made in colonial studies for teacher training. But fundamental questions about the structure of the universities and research institutes had to be asked while the war was still in progress. The short-term necessities of demobilisation compelled decision and promoted a degree of certainty in this field which was not found elsewhere, as may be seen by the choice of education as the keynote for Stanley's speech of 13 July 1943. The coalition government reached agreement on nearly all major educational matters. The University Grants Committee was reconstituted in November 1943; the Education Bill passed through all its stages in 1944; and the privileges to be granted to ex-servicemen were determined in the same year.

Similarly, Colonial Service reform was already being adumbrated in the discussions on the 1940 Act. The principle of unification for the specialised branches of the Colonial Service could not prevail against the obscurantism of local legislatures or a bias in favour of local candidates.[50] When Jeffries in 1941 took up Lord Moyne's suggestion that the Office should consider paying from a central fund the passages of officials brought into the West Indies, he was responding to his own doubts about the basis of promotion and posting, and the current criticism at home of the foreign and home civil services. Sir Percival Waterfield, the Civil Service Commissioner who was asked in 1941 to put forward proposals for the reform of the home civil service and to act as mediator between the Treasury and the Foreign Office on foreign service reform, was kept in touch with Office thinking in the committee on Colonial Service reform which Jeffries chaired.[51] Although the whole subject by 1943 had become overlaid with detailed plans for demobilisation, the treatment it received reflected the degree to which the Colonial Office was involved in domestic discussions. Jeffries himself held strong views on the future of the administrative class of the home civil service.[52] One difference between the approach to education and that adopted for Colonial Service reform was the absence in the latter area of any advisory committee network. Such outside experience as was recruited to help on these questions was kept firmly under administrative control.

One part of the dimension of information in development planning entailed establishing links with the institutions and practitioners of metropolitan learning, especially its scientific branches. Another part was concerned with the collection of data for creation of practicable plans. The two aspects were naturally tied together; and the stronger the ties became the more systematic would be the research involved. The methods used for collecting and analysing data from the colonies before the war seemed too haphazard, and the continued practice of commissioning specific pieces of research from individuals on special contract particularly inefficient. In the early stages of the war the habit of recruiting temporary or part-time assistants was continued. Dr Platt, for instance, of the Medical Research Council, was engaged in 1941 to analyse the results of the nutrition survey and to attend the Office every Monday to give advice. His work was then made the basis for a department of human nutrition at the London School of Hygiene, and the Colonial Office remained extremely dependent upon the services of this single researcher, who was not given an assistant until March 1942.[53] Similarly, Lord Hailey in 1941 had used nine different workers drawn largely from retired officials. In September 1941 Arthur Lewis was recruited from the London School of Economics to write about the flow of capital to the colonies, and for a second assignment in October 1942 he was given the assistance of F. V. Meyer, who was appointed as a research assistant.[54] Sometimes tasks were duplicated through the accidents of posting and promotion. For example, the subject of cooperatives was dealt with by both J. S. Smith, a district officer on leave, in February and March 1943, and by W. K. Campbell a few months later, when he found he was no longer able to take up his post as economic adviser in West Africa.[55]

But as the debate on reconstruction at home progressed, it induced considerable dissatisfaction with this continued dependence upon *ad hoc* initiatives. Advisers and advisory committees came to accept that administrative officers should look more closely at the way in which expert opinion was sought and utilised. By 1945 it was possible to make a formal distinction between advisory committees on policy and advisory committees on research.[56] The latter were particularly encouraged to sponsor surveys of the work required. The Secretary of State himself appeared in person to give an inaugural address to each new committee, and to provide some guidelines on the state of official thinking. It was assumed that there would be plenty of opportunity after the war to explore individual problems, as the appropriate manpower became available. The Research Committee itself set an example, by examining all the principal areas of academic research covered by its terms of reference and surveying their institutions with a view to deciding where special research councils were required for colonial purposes. This achievement meant that the Research Committee denied itself the authority to spend CDW research funds and set up a series of specialist bodies in the appropriate fields. This work was completed between November 1943 and February 1945.

It was the Research Committee, also, which opened up discussion of the social sciences. The Office was fortunate in having secured the services of an anthropologist, Audrey Richards, as a temporary Principal in the summer of 1941, after she had decided not to take up the post she had been offered as Director of the Rhodes-Livingstone Institute in Northern Rhodesia. She wrote a memorandum for the Hailey Committee on Post-War Problems on the requirements of colonial research in the social sciences, which was circulated in January 1942. She was close to many social science discussions, such as those conducted by the British Association in the summer of that year. Carr-Saunders, Director of the London School of Economics, who had reported to her on the latter meeting, put forward the suggestion that the Research Committee should sponsor a number of working parties to survey the needs of the colonies in social research. Eight groups were appointed in May 1943 and by October six had reported. The surveys they produced helped to define the scope of colonial interests in the social sciences: demography, sociology and anthropology, economics, law, colonial administration, education, psychology, and linguistics.[57] All these fields were recognised by the sociology working party, which Carr-Saunders himself chaired, when it put forward the recommendation that a separate research council should be established for the social sciences alone. This recommendation was accepted by the Research Committee and the new Colonial Social Science Research Council (CSSRC) began work in July 1944.[58]

A parallel activity to that of the Research Committee was the first venture into scientific development which was secured with the support of the Scientific Advisory Committee of the Cabinet. The creation of the Tropical Products Institute was inspired largely by the anxieties expressed in organising the war effort on the need

189

to secure alternative sources of supply of and alternative uses for raw materials; the delay in setting it up was an expression of the difficulties which were always likely to be met in appointing scientists in wartime. But once established the Institute provided a precedent for the argument that special executive bodies could be created under the Colonial Office 'umbrella'. It was supervised by a form of advisory committee which could act as a committee of management.[59] The Colonial Products Research Council, under the chairmanship of Lord Hankey, the former ministerial chairman of the Scientific Advisory Committee, did not hold its first meeting until January 1943; but the debate which preceded its conception provided the Office with an excellent introduction to the delicate problems of government-sponsored scientific research. Not only were improved colonial products a vital element in helping the war effort, but they were also the key to economic growth and social development. The consequences of cash crop economies were fully recognised as an area of interest which had to be tackled.[60]

Lastly, there was the question of disseminating development policy information in a way which would involve the 'man on the spot' more immediately in the framing and realisation of forward policy. If far more direct government intervention was to be contemplated at the territorial level, the Office had to search for a more flexible instrument than the formal dispatch. Colonial governments had to be persuaded to examine their basic options more thoroughly. The difficulty with sponsoring journals or news sheets was that they required an editor. The Secretary of State accepted in April 1942 Jeffries' proposal to start a bulletin for distribution to colonial governments but it was never implemented.[61] The journal *Oversea Education* was taken over by the Office in 1943 and provided with an editor in association with the advisory committee. More important was a new series of special circular memoranda to handle the major reconstruction questions which was inaugurated in November 1943 and ran until 1945. This series provided the colonial governments with their best guide to the conduct of discussions in London.[62]

The dimension of control was, in essence, about the degree of certainty, of predictability, that could be built into the process of planning for development. The aim of encouraging regional machinery or of reforming the Colonial Service or in stressing the virtues of applied science was to increase the leverage of the centre. But awkward questions always arose: what resources would be available, what would be the effect of decisions taken elsewhere, how could local participation be ensured and channelled in the 'right' direction? Control was a function of power and it must be recalled that, whatever else had happened since 1939, there had been no changes made to the Secretary of State's formal authority. What the Colonial Office had to depend on, therefore, was an *informal* shift in the balance of authority between the centre and the periphery, a hope that the lessons of war would help to break down the barriers, geographical and psychological, which separated the two worlds. London did possess one recently-acquired advantage: the right to vet applications for CDW funds. But this would be of little value unless the terms by which the money was made available encouraged the formulation of truly comprehensive plans. It was this recognition, borne of a more sophisticated appreciation of the planning process, that lay behind the efforts to revise the 1940 Act.[63]

Like all other enterprises in reconstruction, the work of the Colonial Office was subject to the elaborate game of bluff and manoeuvre which the belligerents conducted in order to try and secure their expected peacetime advantages. The business of planning also suffered during 1944 from the increasing signs of strain in the coalition government, as well as the diversion of effort introduced by the American presidential campaign. There was considerable delay in securing agreement on the appropriate machinery for civil administration as Allied armies advanced and occupied enemy territory. It was not until the summer of 1943 that the main lines of rehabilitation and relief organisation were settled.[64] There was also difficulty in securing the continuation of bilateral talks on the post-war economic order which had been agreed between the British and Americans under Article VII of the Mutual Aid Agreement signed in February 1942. The main talks had taken place in Washington in September and October 1943, and the questions of imperial preference which they raised were placed before representatives of the Dominions and India in February and March 1944. But the coalition government was unable to agree on a common approach, and officials were inhibited from talking to their American opposite numbers on subjects which aroused such passion.[65] Apart from the Bretton Woods discussions on monetary questions, many important areas in which decisions were required that affected the colonies could not be handled until after British ministers had settled their differences. There were also difficulties in getting international agreement on several issues of technological cooperation, particularly civil aviation. In reaching an agreement on air route licensing, the British had to find a compromise between the opposing remedies of full internationalisation or an all-empire system of control. Members of the Commonwealth met separately before and after going on to the international convention in Chicago in October 1944.[66]

Internal uncertainties were no less real. Behind the informal alliance with the development sciences lay the cloven hoof of political power. The debate at home encouraged a way of thinking about giving help to the colonies from the centre which avoided the appearance of concentrating too much authority in the hands of the Colonial Office. The dependent Empire was seen in terms which emphasised the benefit of extending home institutions to meet the needs of colonial territories, but not in any doctrinaire or systematic way. The central role was conceived in large measure as an alliance with the self-governing professions in Britain which controlled the production and diffusion of knowledge. British concepts of the state and its functions allowed a range of public services to be performed through associations of private people, such as universities, learned societies, research institutes, and professional examination boards, as the same bodies were geared to promote learning.

All that the administrative staff could do was to follow the character of existing relationships, adding here and there particular emphases for colonial benefit. They learnt to tolerate variety, as long as they could maintain a general supervision, and were ambivalent about the development of any career systems for 'colonial scientists' which were based on the assumption that cooperation in the field was not enforced through administrative authority but through voluntary association of allied professions. While the Office and the Governors in the field continued to embody British sovereignty, they had to recognise a proper distance between the natural community of development assistance personnel and the political authority of the administrative service. In some subjects such as agriculture and medicine it was easier to envisage cooperative links persisting, regardless of political ties, than in others such as social welfare and economic assistance. The debate on reconstruction at home underlined the puzzles which arise when economic and social development is related to political progress.

It was easy enough to talk about the accumulation and transfer of expertise, but there were formidable difficulties in marrying a system of dissemination, based on conveying information from the centre to the periphery, to the necessity for consultation with those in the field. Colonial governments sometimes called for more information on items noticed in the press, or complained about the degree of confidentiality surrounding some key negotiations. Advisory Committee papers, which occasionally strayed into the hands of people working in the colonies, enjoyed a peculiar status: suggestions for action without formal commitment. The Office was from time to time embarrassed by advisory committee activity which gave some impression to colonial governments of forthcoming events. A fundamental principle of the advisory system was that it was essentially metropolitan. When the Comptroller's office was set up in Barbados, and the Resident Minister's in Achimota, arrangements were made to send them copies of advisory committee papers, but colonial governors were not normally granted this privilege.[67] They were expected to refrain from interfering directly in the Secretary of State's network of advice.[68]

The domestic debate on reconstruction exposed the Office to the danger of paying too much attention to metropolitan interests and thereby tipping the balance of the system of administrative supervision away from the needs of colonial authorities. While an alliance with 'home institutions' carried the benefits of metropolitan prestige, it also brought the disadvantages of investing great amounts of energy in demarcation disputes between rival bodies, or in obscure theoretical debates which were not easy to relate to practice. The more entrepreneurial the adviser and his associates, the more administrative tangles there were to unravel in taking up the major proposals for implementation. Laboratories competed for special recognition; professors placed bids for their own universities; research associations expected contracts. After the winter of 1941-42 the Office was caught up in making its own treaties with those parties in Britain which had an interest in colonial development.

Constitutional and international planning

Neither constitutional policy nor international affairs received anything like the same investment of time and manpower for forward planning that was devoted by the Office to development and welfare.

It is not hard to see why. The very idea of planning, as it was popularised during the reconstruction debate, was closely bound up with problems of fostering economic growth and providing social services. Constitutional progress, though a central responsibility, was itself seen to be dependent on the pace of social and economic advance. Also, it was the traditional preserve of the geographical departments, and was governed to a high degree by the state of communications between the Governors and London. International planning, for its part, was essentially adaptive; a matter of preparing bargaining positions which would protect the organisation against threats to its traditional freedom of manoeuvre.

Yet if the Office did less in these areas than it did in that of development planning, what it did do was none the less significant; and the problems it faced in the three dimensions of machinery, information, and control are worthy of some consideration. Constitutional change was naturally linked very directly with shifts in colonial opinion, and finding an appropriate balance between central and local initiative in these circumstances involved an exploration of organisation and policy which was more closely associated with the older administrative tradition than was necessary in an alliance with metropolitan science. The geographical department in London was the acknowledged interpreter of local opinion in the area it supervised, and the Legal Adviser was employed to translate specific purposes into instruments that would fit the law. Changes in the administrative structure at the centre were considered, but little more, for the reason that proposals to create special planning machinery flew in the face of geographical department privilege. Just before Hailey's return from Africa in June 1940 Parkinson suggested that the Office should examine the desirability of creating a post to coordinate progress made in constitutional development but was attacked by Dawe for daring to suggest an innovation which would place an extra level between the geographical departments and the 'top of the office'.[69] Yet the lack of any central repository of information and the consequences this could have in policy-making were revealed all too starkly in 1942 during the preparation of the abortive White Paper on 'Constitutional Policy'.[70]

The only conscious examination of constitutional alternatives was undertaken not by the Legal Adviser, whose office until 1949 remained curiously compartmentalised in different specialisations, but by the research assistants recruited by Lord Hailey for his

Post-War Problems Committee. While Hailey wrote up his Africa reports in 1941, his assistants concentrated on smaller colonies, fortresses, and islands.[71] Martin Wight in the Nuffield Social Reconstruction Survey at the same time began work on what Margery Perham called a 'stock-taking' of colonial constitutions;[72] the Fabian Colonial Bureau appointed a colonial constitutions committee.[73]

From time to time the Secretary of State and senior officials toyed with the idea of creating a 'planning staff', but Stanley in the spring of 1943 looked primarily towards the geographical departments when he called for plans for constitutional development. It was the geographical departments which had the responsibility for formulating proposals about the extent to which wartime regional machinery could be carried into the post-war period, and, in the case of Malaya, the extent to which new regional arrangements were feasible. Benson's appointment in the General Department was the only gesture made to establish a central point for general intelligence in political questions. The idea was later mooted of creating a small secretariat attached to the private office of the Permanent Under-Secretary on the lines of the committee secretariat at the Foreign Office or the central secretariat at the Ministry of Food.[74] Even after 1948, when ministers became worried about the increasing incidence of subversion, the creation of a political intelligence section was delayed until 1953.

The organisational arrangements for constitutional planning reflected the prevailing view that the geographical departments possessed or had access to most of the necessary information. The ferment of discussion in the colonies seemed less articulate, more remote than the reconstruction debate at home, but it was at least acknowledgeable. By comparison with India, the dependent Empire seemed remarkably free from serious political violence. Apart from the activities of the Malayan Communist party in fomenting strikes during 1940-41, the majority of colonial labour disputes seemed to have been provoked by genuine economic grievances which were not closely linked to political activity. The most dangerous industrial action in terms of the war effort was in fact brought on by the action of European workers who in May 1940 brought the copper mines in Northern Rhodesia to a standstill.[75] They were alleged to have created a situation in which the African workers were mobilised to withdraw their labour, and were again accused of provoking unnecessary violence in 1942 when the army was called in to compel a return to work.[76] The peculiar political situations in Palestine and Cyprus tended to turn all industrial disputes in those countries into political gestures and some problems were created, as in the Bahamas, simply because the presence of imported labourers for war work aroused local resentment. The Colonial Office listened to its Adviser on Labour Affairs, and received petitions and deputations which from time to time provided the flavour of local debate. Its main concern was to improve the quality of communications between London and the territories. In 1943 it had no difficulty believing that the educated elements in the native population in the majority of colonies were capable of being recruited to help further the cause of colonial development.

But how far could the Colonial Office hope to exercise control over the pace of change demanded by colonial opinion? Colonial opinion was in fact so multifarious that it would hardly be regarded as a single phenomenon which could find expression at the centre, and British interests in the colonies were not always easily identifiable while the character of the peace settlement was in doubt. Pressure from the colonies came in at least two forms: Governors offering their interpretation of the situation they faced, and colonial peoples submitting petitions either through the established institutions or directly. The fashion of reconstruction planning led Governors to take the initiative in issuing development proposals which by their very territorial origin were not always reconcileable with regional planning. Some Governors liked to stress the political character of their office, and drew the distinction between their own 'governing' and the Colonial Secretary's 'administering' of a colony. While the Colonial Secretary's secretariat remained in no way a substitute for Cabinet government, the person of the Governor had to be directly involved if the 'government' were to be engaged. It was easier to regard the governor as a kind of Tudor sovereign rather than as his own Prime Minister, and no reconstruction committee at the colonial level could be very effective without his personal support.[77] Reconstruction issues revealed the inadequacy of the machinery of central government in each colony, but, apart from a little desultory note-taking in the Colonial Service Department, the subject was not studied at the centre. Those indigenous elements in the colonies which could articulate political demands were accustomed to operate on a local stage in which regionalism was not attractive and progress self-defined.

Nevertheless, the centre had to formulate some concepts of order and progress to satisfy its own peace of mind if it were to avoid making *ad hoc* responses to individual demands, either from Governors or from Legislative Councils and other representative institutions. The war had at least taught the Office to be prepared to take the initiative itself. An approach based on regionalism, education, and orderly evolution through a series of recognised stages employed generalisations which could accommodate the wide variety of constitutions and social structures which the geographical departments had in their charge. These ideas could be adapted to any eventuality, and they left open the fundamental questions about the international order which could only be answered after the fighting had stopped.

Not surprisingly, planning for the international order itself was the most constricted and ultimately frustrating of the three major areas. The only significant change in machinery came about with the dissolution of the General Department and its incorporation into the restyled Defence and General Department under Poynton in July 1944. It had become clear by this point that the old General Department's post-war planning functions had become too onerous, and, with Benson set to leave shortly for Northern Rhodesia, it was necessary to find another official to act as Poynton's deputy. The description, supplied in a minute by Gent to Gater, of the qualities required for this post, provides an excellent illustration of the character of the Office's role in international planning:

(a) He must be able to do his own thinking—constructive as well as destructive. A 'dogsbody' who will merely do drafting and other routine work as directed from above would be no relief to Mr. Poynton.

(b) He must be the sort of person who can meet the Foreign Office and other Departments and the academic 'volunteers' in F.O.R.D. [Foreign Office Research Department] on equal terms, hold his own in discussion by telephone or at meetings, and have their confidence. The Colonial Office function on many of these problems is to act as a brake and it is easy to gain a reputation for obstructiveness and narrowmindedness, and it takes a man of proved merit to make headway in such circumstances.

(c) He must be fully familiar with the internal organisation of the Colonial Office and the general system of Whitehall machinery.[78]

With the Colonial Office so dependent on the outcome of negotiations conducted elsewhere, information was understandably patchy and irregular. The only kind of control the Office exercised in a situation such as this came through the personal clout exercised by the Secretary of State, and the ability to anticipate demands by preparing proposals for which support would be forthcoming from within the British government and from the Dominions. Regionalism and technical cooperation had emerged as the favoured concepts for this purpose, the main lines of which had been worked out before 1943 in the context of meeting demands for a Colonial Charter and American criticism in general. After the Secretary of State's speech of 13 July 1943 it became more and more urgent to adapt earlier formulations to fit the requirements of a world organisation whose shape was to be hammered out in a series of multilateral negotiations in 1944 and 1945.

This shift meant that the question of trusteeship began to assume real weight, alongside that of accountability. The Colonial Office, opposed to the creation of a new mandates system, occupied itself in devising machinery which would allow the world organisation to discuss colonial problems without granting to it the right to direct participation in administration or policy-making. As will be seen in the next chapter, however, plans that had taken months to assemble could be set aside at a moment's notice as the result of what happened in top-level Allied negotiations. The permanent officials were much more at the mercy of their ministers here than they were in the areas of constitutional or development policy, where various counterweights were available to them. The whole exercise of international planning was a dramatic illustration of the Office's continuing inability, in spite of the expansion of its representative functions, to influence the course of external negotiations, even where they directly affected the shape of British colonial policy.

The business of reconstruction planning therefore embraced a range of activities which brought into play to a greater or lesser extent the contrast between what the centre could initiate and what it could only anticipate. Much of what was formally defined under the heading of reconstruction duties consisted, in large part, of appearing ready to respond to the action of other authorities. The most serious practical task was the preparation for the return of British sovereignty to the Far East.[79] This was a 'high policy' question which had to be handled in conjunction with the military authorities, because whatever the Colonial Office did it could only follow in the wake of the occupying armies. In general, apart from the Foreign Office, other central departments in Whitehall were not pressing the Office to join in the debate on reconstruction questions. The latter found that it had to keep its own eyes and ears open in order to discover what kind of developments were taking place in other policy areas, so that it could continue to fulfil its traditional representative function and guard those colonial interests which might be affected.[80]

Those ministers interested in maintaining an imperial system seem to have been a minority in the coalition government, and other Whitehall departments were not on the whole concerned with the exploitation of the resources of the Empire for British post-war purposes—at least not until after the war. Unlike the reconstruction debates of the First World War, discussion tended to shy away from the idea of imperial self-sufficiency and to stress instead the importance of technical cooperation between the great powers. The definition of the means for realising central objectives in the Colonial Office took place against a background of domestic discussions about economic and physical planning for the United Kingdom. The critical problem, as Caine pointed out in his memorandum of August 1943, was finding an appropriate balance between central and local activity; and consideration of this problem took place while a number of different local groups were making their feelings known. No side in the debate had the satisfaction of direct negotiation, free from all emergency wartime restraint, except perhaps in a few specific constitutional adjustments. But the planning continued all the same, though all the participants realised their vulnerability to forces outside the colonial system. The context and dimensions of the planning process in the Colonial Office during the reconstruction phase have been discussed; what remains to be seen is what that process actually produced.

7

THE WORK OF RECONSTRUCTION

CONSIDERING the restraints on the planning process discussed in the previous chapter, the achievements of the Colonial Office in post-war reconstruction were far from negligible. Plans were prepared for education, social science research, future policy in the Far East, new regional structures (for both internal and external purposes), and, perhaps most significantly, for a revised and greatly strengthened Colonial Development and Welfare Act. There were setbacks and disappointments, especially in the areas of economic planning and Colonial Service reform. Yet in spite of the fact that achievements were largely in the form of 'paper exercises', what was done was significant. It marked the first stage in the exploration by a newly strengthened Office of its major policy objectives and methods for the postwar period; by 1945 it was far better prepared to go into action than it had been at the beginning of the war. Whether the climate of international and colonial opinion would also become more favourable was, of course, another question entirely.

Educational and colonial service reform

The basis of the changes proposed for higher education in the colonies was an improved system of cooperation between British universities and institutions of comparable standing overseas. Professor H. J. Channon had presented a memorandum on this subject to the Advisory Committee on Education (ACEC) in the context of their enquiry into West Africa in 1940-41.[1] The discussion then moved forward at different levels. In the spring of 1942 administrative staff advised the Secretary of State to invite Lord Harlech to head a West African commission, but the latter declined,[2] and the advisory committee had in the meantime set up its own sub-committee to consider what Channon had proposed. In April 1943 the committee recommended the appointment of two bodies — a general commission for the whole Empire and one for West Africa alone.[3]

The result was a classic example of an advisory committee imbued with reconstruction fervour — the Commission on Higher

Education in the Colonies appointed in August 1943 under Mr Justice Asquith to consider 'the principles which should guide the promotion of higher education, learning, and research and the development of universities in the colonies'. The Commission not only included two members who were to serve on the enquiry into West Africa, but also decided to create its own regional enquiry by sending three members to the West Indies.[4]

The Asquith Commission recommended the establishment of residential university colleges which included all the principal disciplines in their range of studies and whose staffs enjoyed salaries related to those of universities at home. These colleges, which would be autonomous and independent of the colonial governments, could enter into a special relationship with London University for an interim period until they gained sufficient experience for full university status to be granted. The commission also proposed the creation of an Inter-University Council, on which home and colonial universities would be represented, to provide common services and a continuity of regular advice in the formulation of policies for academic development; and suggested that the provision of United Kingdom funds to maintain such universities should be undertaken on the advice of a specially constituted Colonial University Grants Advisory Committee, on the lines of the University Grants Committee at home.[5] The Asquith report, which was published as a White Paper just before British voters went to the polls in the 1945 general election, became the basis of post-war policy.

No equivalent set of institutions could be worked out for the different branches of the Colonial Service, which at the end of the war remained in roughly the same position as at the beginning, in spite of many attempts to follow up an agreement in principle to the reform sanctioned by the Cabinet in June 1942. Civil servants were directly responsible to territorial governments, not to autonomous bodies such as university colleges. The Inter-University Council was designed to provide a basis for the metropolitan recognition of colonial degrees, but there were no 'home institutions' to be persuaded into providing the appropriate support to officers serving overseas who were technically in the pay of another government, except for the existing recruitment, posting, and pension arrangements of the Colonial Office Personnel Department. The University Grants Advisory Committee was designed to provide the British government with control over financial incentives that could influence the course of academic policy in each college. But there was no willingness at home to extend this method to the employment of civil servants. Indeed, there were strong prejudices against using the system of providing grants-in-aid to the colonies for establishments purposes. The instruments which might guarantee a healthy growth in colonial higher education could not be widely applied in other fields.

Senior administrators saw that any proposals for Colonial Service reform which involved creating a 'General List' of officers paid by the British government ran the risk of tempting colonial governments to transfer their costs to the centre.[6] The idea of a 'central pool' in Britain proposed by the Colonial Service Committee in October 1941, with a general list of specialists available for service wherever they were required and no posts specially reserved for members of the unified Service, entailed a great deal of careful planning to provide for the very delicate system of personnel management. When the proposals were put to Governors and senior officials in the colonies in December 1942, they were not universally well received. Some Governors in Africa thought they were designed to meet a West Indian situation — an indigenous civil service scattered over many small islands requiring only a small number of expatriate advisers and experts — and not to fit the more usual colonial arrangements — white expatriate administrative and technical services above a large local clerical staff. In certain 'more politically advanced territories' there was the fear of local objections to any label like 'General List' which would be associated with expatriate officers: Governors here 'urged that any scheme which would command acceptance from political leaders would have to be so framed as to show at least as much concern for developing the opportunities open to local staff as for improving the lot of European officers'.[7]

Replies from the colonies were analysed in the Office during the Spring of 1943, and between May and August the Colonial Service Reform Committee produced a second report.[8] This modified the 'General List' idea, stressed the formulation of standard conditions of service for all expatriate officers, and raised the whole question of placing part if not all of the Colonial Office staff in the Colonial Service. This proposed 'fusion' of the field service with the London administrators normally recruited into the home civil service created a difference of opinion which was not easily resolved.

While the home government was working out the details of its demobilisation policy for the United Kingdom, the Colonial Office was locked into its own private battle on the implications of Colonial Service reform. So great was the internal resistance to the idea of 'fusion' that this feature of the revised plan was eventually dropped by the committee. What remained was a draft White Paper which gave first priority to developing local services, and which proposed a minimum standard of service to be funded by a central subvention in cases where the local legislature could not or would not provide for such a guaranteed minimum.[9]

The manner in which the Office's deliberations on this matter were resolved remains obscure, because the file dealing with the question seems defective.[10] It looks as if the Secretary of State was persuaded to call a halt to the uncertainties which the debate had produced by pronouncing against any fundamental change in July 1944. The most important meeting took place on the day before Jeffries, the Assistant Under-Secretary responsible, returned home from West Africa where he had been on a special tour to gather views and news on the proposals which the Personnel Division was making. His colleagues may have decided that the pressure of events at home, particularly in Parliament where demobilisation was an important issue, called for an end to the internal Office debate. In his own version of this episode,[11] Jeffries suggests that Stanley and Gater were much less interested in this measure than were their immediate predecessors; Stanley apparently told Jeffries and other senior officials shortly afterwards that 'whatever its administrative advantages', any scheme which subsidised expatriate officials would not be 'politically practicable' in Parliament:

From the colonial point of view, he considered, such a move would be contrary to the way the tide was running. It was not a time to be taking a step which would be represented as an attempt to tighten central control.

The dilemmas of central planning in a colonial system could hardly have been more clearly put. As Jeffries points out, the scuttled measure 'could have been interpreted by ill-wishers as an "imperialist" device', though he adds in defence of his pet project that 'it could with equal or greater force have been presented as a genuine intervention by the British government aimed at providing the territories with skilled staffs needed for the implementation, for the benefit of the colonial peoples, of the Development and Welfare policy'.

In due course the Secretary of State announced his plans for post-war recruitment into the Colonial Service to be in line with the general release from the armed forces. But for almost the whole of the year before this announcement (September 1944), the Colonial Office had discussed the merits of two major alternatives in institutional reform. On the one hand, as has been seen, considerable interest had been shown in the possibility of managing a 'central pool', at least for certain technical services. The division of opinion provoked by the issue of 'fusion' did not prevent serious consideration of the problems of management involved. On the other hand, there was strong pressure from the field to consider forms of regionalisation. The 'central pool' idea could be applied with more effect perhaps at the intermediate level between London and the colonies, if a method of payment could be devised. Those who saw the 1942 proposals as a reflection of West Indian interests thought that they could easily be confined to a scheme covering that area.

The whole vexed subject of Colonial Service reform was not submitted to an advisory committee, but dealt with through the normal channels of internal consultation. The Colonial Service Reform Committee was entirely official in composition; Governors were addressed by circular despatch to elicit their views on the 1942 proposals; Assistant Secretaries were circularised and asked to state what position they took on the issue of 'fusion'; and all the advisers were given a chance to air their views. There was naturally a tendency for the advisers and the 'beachcombers' to be more sympathetic to 'fusion' than the permanent administrative staff.

Nor was the task of defining the general principles of training submitted to an advisory committee. The Devonshire Committee, appointed in March 1944 under the chairmanship of the Parliamentary Under-Secretary, was asked to work out the details of a scheme which had already been decided. In February 1943 Sir Ralph Furse had presented a memorandum outlining a number of alternative methods for providing Colonial Service courses at British universities.[12] He suggested that the Office should use a combination of the resources of the three major universities — Oxford, Cambridge, and London — and not commit itself to one institution or establish its own staff college. After a series of internal discussions, this principle was accepted and the Devonshire Committee, which reported in February 1945, was composed largely of representatives from the three universities already designated.[13]

As Jeffries later admitted, the 1946 White Paper on the

organisation of the Colonial Service 'contained nothing that was startling and little that was really new'.[14] The agonies of the debate on the 'General List' and regionalism were hidden from public gaze. The central services announced for biological research, surveying, geological, and meteorological services were a vestigial element to survive the 'General List' — 'central pool' plans. The principal decisions taken were to set aside special allocations from CDW funds over the next ten years to provide professional and vocational training to candidates for higher grade posts — the 'Devonshire Courses' — and to support general and technical training schemes.

The 'General List' — 'central pool' idea was pursued in a series of long-drawn-out negotiations with the Treasury which in 1949-50 led to the creation of the research service, modelled on the Scientific Civil Service at home.[15] But the proposal to regionalise staffing was never taken beyond the creation of common services organisations. Discussion on the future of the Comptroller's organisation in the West Indies and the Resident Minister's office in West Africa was centred in part upon the value of providing advisory staff at an intermediate level between London and the territories. The West African Council which replaced the Resident Minister provided a base from which to continue the examination of problems which interested all four territories.

The encouragement of social research also kept alive the regional ideal. It seemed important in recruiting research workers to provide them with a regional field of operations in which common problems could be studied, and where career prospects were improved by opportunities for movement across territories. Some administrators felt the need to develop a mechanism which would improve the distribution of knowledge gained in one colony for use in another. Existing academic arrangements such as the Bantu Studies Departments in South African universities demonstrated one method; the Rhodes-Livingstone Institute another. The proposal to set up a Caribbean research council provided yet another example of genuine regionalism which involved the United States and the major colonial powers. When the Colonial Social Science Research Council came to consider its interests in research organisation, it was faced with the example of the West African Institute of Arts and Crafts established in 1942. Even before the CSSRC had begun to consider the general lines of policy, Audrey Richards was despatched to East Africa from July to September 1944 to report on the feasibility of founding a institute of social research in association with Makerere College.[16]

Economic development

Important though the questions of education, Colonial Service reform, and research were, the heart of the development initiative lay in the economic transformation of colonial society. The interest in managing social change at home drew attention to the importance of understanding whether economic development was compatible with traditional social structures. Some thought that the war would transform British society; Harold Laski preached a doctrine of revolution by consent, in which the middle classes would voluntarily surrender their predominant position.[17] Others believed that the war would inspire the colonial peoples to question the pace of social and political development; native affairs and colonial anthropology had to be replaced by technical cooperation and economic planning.

Caine had touched on most of the major problems to be faced in this area in his memorandum of August 1943.[18] It was clearly easier to recognise standards of attainment in education than to standardise public service duties or economic planning goals. And it remained to be seen what progress could actually be made in tapping metropolitan expertise, formulating general guidelines, and finding a workable balance between the conceptual world of economic theory and the political realities of the British colonial system. The exercise was made that much more difficult by the additional restraints of wartime shortages of men and material, and uncertainties about the international order.

But no one doubted that the exercise had to be undertaken. Between the summer of 1943 and the spring of 1945 there were two major sets of activities on this front: (i) experimenting with central planning machinery and (ii) negotiating for changes in the provisions of CDW legislation. The two areas were closely intertwined, as Caine demonstrated when commenting on a memorandum being sent to West African Governors about post-war planning. It was not clear, he pointed out, whether £5 million a year was really sufficient and, if not, how much more to ask for, since colonial governments had been reluctant to frame their plans without knowing how much help they could expect: 'We have got to break that vicious circle somewhere and the present [central planning initiative] seems the best method of doing it'.[19] To make long-term planning a reality, the periphery had to be aroused to take action, and for this the centre had to become a powerhouse of ideas, techniques, and information. But none of this would be to much avail if the centre's trump card, its power to dispense funds, was offset by misgivings within colonial governments about the conditions by which funding was made available. The patient had no wish to take advantage of a new wonderdrug if it might not be potent enough to ensure a rapid improvement, yet was capable of causing harmful side-effects. The activities of economic planning and revision of the CDW Act ran in parallel, and both came to a head in late 1944. The progress in each will be considered in turn before attention is devoted to the series of resolutions concerning both which emerged at the end of that year.

It will be recalled from the previous chapter that the meeting chaired by Gater to consider Caine's memorandum of August 1943 had favoured the establishment of a proper planning section in the Office.[20] What this amounted to before the appointment of a Development Adviser the following year, was the sum total of the work done by those recently given special development resposibilities — Caine, Clauson, and members of the Colonial Economic Advisory Committee (CEAC). The problem of mobilising the central organisation to effect any method of economic planning for the colonies proved particularly intractable, in spite of the tremendous boost that the debate at home had given to an understanding of the crucial importance of a growth of real resources. The Colonial Office was about to discover the pitfalls of seeking expert economic advice, as the Cabinet and Treasury had discovered them in the early 1930s after the creation of the Economic Advisory Council.[21]

The CEAC, which began its work in October 1943, was without doubt the most distinguished advisory committee on social science questions. It tried to cover all the major fields of interest by setting up sub-committees on communications, industry, marketing, minerals agriculture, finance, and research. With such a broad definition of functions a number of questions were raised about the overlap between the activities of different advisory committees. 'Economics' tended to claim the right of entry into all other subjects. For example, in May 1944 the industry sub-committee wished to discuss the training of native personnel, and after a meeting with the Education Adviser agreed that some of its members should meet the Advisory Committee on Education. Similarly, the minerals sub-committee, in deciding to examine the possibility of a policy for mineral development on lines suggested by the Fabian Colonial Bureau, found that it had to trespass into the technical knowledge of the Colonial Surveys and Geophysical Committee. The research sub-committee was bound to take note of the Colonial Social Science Research Committee's interest in economics.[22] The line between academic research and policy research was always difficult to draw.

Coordination was another problem. The agenda sub-committee of the CEAC was designed to supervise the division of work among the various sub-committees, but at this stage there was no adviser in development planning to provide the proper links with the administrative staff. Caine, who in April 1944 was promoted to Assistant Under-Secretary in charge of the Economic Division, tied the committee to this section of the Office through Arthur Lewis, the distinguished West Indian economist who had already been commissioned to undertake research and who agreed to join the Office staff to become the committee's secretary.[23] At the beginning the CEAC included three other professional economists: Hubert Henderson, Evan Durbin, and Lionel Robbins. Arnold Plant was added at a later date. Other members were mostly ex-colonial administrators and businessmen.

Although economists only constituted about a third of the committee's membership, they supplied most of its driving force. It was obviously necessary to establish some balance between different schools of economic thought, but this was not a means of avoiding the tensions that were bound to arise from questions which went beyond the restricted bounds imposed on Office deliberations by the Coalition government, a Conservative Secretary of State, and the natural caution of most permanent officials. Stanley himself probably contributed to the confusion by suggesting a 'double approach' in his address to the committee of late 1943. The first approach was the rendering of advice on particular matters as they were referred to the committee by officials. The second, longer-term approach entailed a survey of the field as a whole and the creation of a programme of work into which particular aspects could be fitted.[24]

The Secretary of State did not want to condemn the CEAC to nothing more than a series of *ad hoc* responses. It was intended for more than that. But just how open-ended the second approach could be was never defined, at least not before the committee had ground to a halt as a result of confusion and bickering. Problems started to appear as soon as the sub-committees began to settle down to their tasks.[25] Henderson suggested that the CEAC should consider the whole question of imperial preference and the future of commodity regulation in the autumn of 1943, just when the report of the Law mission to the United States on Article VII questions was beginning to polarise opinion in the Cabinet. Sir Bernard Bourdillon, as chairman of the sub-committee on finance, sought to discuss the colonial public debt and the division of taxation between the colonies and the United Kingdom. The chairman of the marketing sub-committee wanted to move ahead with an examination of bulk-purchasing arrangements. The industry sub-committee started to raise general questions about planning machinery, the securing of capital, and regional concentration in industrial development. In each case objections were raised by permanent officials and action was curbed. Henderson was apparently told that Stanley's decision not to refer the specific matters of commodity control and imperial preference to the CEAC should be interpreted as meaning that these lay beyond the committee's competence. Raising the colonial public debt and the division of taxation resulted in objections because both subjects involved the Office's relationship with the Treasury; while a broad investigation of industrial development had serious political and social ramifications.

By the summer of 1944 frustration within the committee about lack of progress was becoming intense. Only the minerals sub-committee had made significant headway in preparing a survey. The rest had either been largely dormant or had been occupied with relatively specific questions such as the Uganda cotton industry, about which the marketing sub-committee was asked to give advice for a letter to be sent to producers' associations regarding the possible continuance of marketing controls. Three leading critics of Office attitudes towards the work of the CEAC—Bourdillon, Durbin, and in particular Lewis—decided by this point that the time had arrived to come off the defensive by using the agenda sub-committee to force the whole question of planning machinery into the open. An Office paper on this subject, which was produced for information only and not for discussion, was given an airing by Durbin during the agenda sub-committee's deliberations about post-war personnel requirements, on the pretext that the sub-committee could not advise on this matter without knowing the uses for which personnel were envisaged. This led, as it was undoubtedly meant to, to a broad discussion about economic policy. The three 'rebels' apparently recognised the unconstitutionality of this procedure, but by this time did not seem to have been unduly concerned about such niceties. The result of this discussion was a memorandum, largely written by Lewis,[26] which defined agricultural units in Africa as uneconomically small and recommended that (i) more expert advice be provided in the colonies to remedy the situation; (ii) industrial development proceed on a regional basis; and (iii) 'industrial experts' be despatched with executive powers to oversee projects first hand.

The reaction of officials, most prominently of Caine and Clauson, was anything but warm. By September the smell of battle was in the air. Lewis produced a long minute whose purpose was to document the degree of obstruction which various sub-committees had experienced. Total deadlock appeared to have been reached, and, as a way out, it was agreed to accept the agenda sub-committee's suggestion that five key 'political' questions, which it had subsequently formulated, be referred directly to the Secretary of State. By this means it was hoped that the way would be cleared for the sub-committees to get down to serious work.

The five questions were sent forward to Stanley in a memorandum from the CEAC of 31 October 1944.[27] It explained that the committee had been faced with 'certain suggestions [Lewis's memorandum] raising wide questions about the speed of economic development in the Colonies, the sort of measures which must be adopted in order to secure such development, and the machinery required for planning development'. The questions themselves, which the accompanying memorandum admitted would not prove easy to answer with precision, were to dominate Office discussions until Christmas. They are worth considering in some detail.

The first question concerned the speed of social change and the extent to which the maintenance of 'native institutions' could or should serve as the basis for economic policy-making. In the second question the committee addressed the issue of the economic structure of agriculture by asking about the degree to which the Secretary of State would be willing to devote money and manpower to the adoption of new methods and larger working units.[28] The third question was equally predictable in the light of the agenda sub-committee's memorandum: whether industrial policy would be 'primarily directed towards the creation of a limited number of planned and balanced industrial centres, situated in the main regions of the

Colonial Empire . . . rather than towards the grant of equal facilities for the encouragement of factories in every Colony'. This led to the fourth question, which asked for Stanley's reaction to 'new instruments for both planning and execution', such as teams of industrial experts sent into the field and the creation of public corporations, both possibly with executive powers independent of colonial governments. The fifth and last question asked whether all foreign capital for economic development must take the form of private investment, or whether it was possible to contemplate the United Kingdom government approaching foreign governments or a future international investment fund.

The CEAC's questions got to the Secretary of State within a week, but even such a comparatively short journey along the official route gave senior administrators enough time to clarify their thoughts and start preparing a common front on the shape of the draft answers.[29] The critical role was to be taken, not surprisingly, by Caine, who as will be seen, was identified by Lewis as the chief antagonist in the official camp.[30] Caine's minute accompanying the CEAC's questions was measured and circumspect. But he had no hesitation in stating that the proposals for economic development put forward by some members of the committee could 'without exaggeration, be called revolutionary'. It was not a question of their economic merit as such, but of their social and political implications. The questions had been framed in a way calculated to 'prevent a temporising or evasive answer', and he hoped that Stanley would 'not find it too embarrassing' to have to provide his views about them. On the other hand, Caine emphasised that without some clear indication from above the committee would feel unable to prepare any realistic general plans: 'I make no attempt here to suggest what the answers should be, because in any event I think they must be determined by political and social rather than economic policy.'

In the event, however, Caine was himself given the job of drafting the answers, once Stanley had accepted Gater's suggestion that this be done by 'the Department'. Caine circulated his draft replies[31] among the Assistant Under-Secretaries with the qualification that they were 'very much of the character of cockshies, as the issues involved are more political than economic'. His answers consisted of a qualified approval for rapid change in native institutions, where there was substantial economic benefit; a willingness to push ahead in the area of agricultural modernisation; an unwillingness to exclude any colony from economic development (with the observation that there was bound to be a 'natural concentration'); approval of new planning instruments, including public corporations, but with powers determined by colonial governments; and a preference for foreign capital to come in the form of private investment.

Only the first and last answers attracted much comment from Caine's colleagues, and even here the differences were not large. The general consensus was that the first answer suggested too rapid a pace of change, while the last was not definite enough in its rejection of the notion that Britain approach foreign governments for loan capital. One point, made by Dawe, caught the attention of Gater and was eventually incorporated into the final draft. 'The trouble about these questions and the proposed answers,' Dawe had minuted, 'is that they appear to assume to too great a degree that these matters will be determined by consciously directed government policy. But I feel that the determining forces will lie largely outside any government control'.[32] He also stressed that time factors were very hard to predict, and that the only acceptable generalisation was that 'gradual evolution' would occur in a way not too rapid to produce sudden social dislocation.

By 27 November the draft was back with Caine, who noted that he was relieved the comments had not been more critical. Further discussion with the Secretary of State was still required, yet it was clear, given the relative unanimity at the Under-Secretary level, that the main core of the replies had been determined. It is not hard to understand why Lewis chose this moment to hand in his resignation as secretary of the CEAC and retire to academic life. In a long, sometimes bitter minute written on 30 November, the day after he discussed his resignation with Stanley, Lewis gave his reasons for leaving.[33] In his view, the good intentions of the Secretary of State to make the CEAC a wide-ranging and significant body had been sabotaged again and again by timid, conservative officials:

Broadly speaking, the permanent officials took the view that the Committee should not be taken very seriously for some time. 'Give it a few small matters,' said Sir George Gater, 'and if it handles these competently we can gradually increase its scope.'

Caine was portrayed as the chief obstructer, throwing political and procedural logs in the path of bolder spirits like Lewis, Durbin, and Bourdillon.

Lewis admitted that some members of the CEAC were not as active as they could have been, and that the membership of the agenda sub-committee had been 'badly selected'. But for all this he had no hesitation about pointing to 'the attitude of the office' as the single most important reason for the CEAC's failure to make progress. His description of the reaction to the agenda sub-committee's memorandum was especially scathing:

The attitude of the office to these platitudes was unbelievable. At first they attacked their economic soundness. Mr. Clauson denied to the sub-committee that the smallness of existing units created a problem; and Mr. Caine attacked the underlying theory that administrative action is necessary for, or can make a substantial difference to economic development, quoting Britain and the U.S.A. as countries which developed rapidly without serious prodding. As these views were not taken seriously, the attack was shifted to political grounds, and an attempt made to suppress the memorandum on the ground that acceptance of these economic policies would raise political questions outside the Committee's terms of reference.

Lewis provided a long list of subjects that had been excluded from consideration by the CEAC including trade relations, currency systems, population policies, local authority finance, internal air transport, and shipping facilities. Other subjects, like colonial taxation, banking policy, land tenure, marketing, and what was contained in the CEAC's questions to Stanley remained to be settled. Aside from particular crises and disputes, there was the general atmosphere in which the committee functioned:

Now I cannot prove that the atmosphere was unfavourable to this survey; I can only assert that I have consistently found it to be so, and am consequently resigning; that various members have commented on it; and that the record of the committee itself shows unwillingness on the part of the Office to use the sub-committees. The Committee was welcomed as a means of shelving on to others responsibility for unpleasant 'political' decisions . . . . But the idea that it should 'poke its nose' into others matters is resented, especially if administrative arrangements in the colonies are involved, or discussions impinging on the policies of other United Kingdom Departments.

There can be no doubt that Lewis wanted to make as much as possible of the differences between his views and those of Caine. But it is clear all the same that in a number of instances Caine seemed to be resisting arguments which he himself had made with some force in the summer of 1943. It had been Caine, after all, who had talked about the 'new concept of the place the State must take in planning', about the need for the state to become the major source of capital, about the usefulness of an economic prospecting service and a public development corporation.[34] As was noted earlier, it was Caine more than any other official who chafed against the restrictions imposed by traditional routines and thinking, who could speak to economists on equal terms, who wanted the Office to adopt a bold and experimental approach to development planning.

The difference between Caine's stance in the summer of 1943 and his response to men like Lewis in CEAC was due more to change of context than to change of heart. It was one thing for an official with administrative responsibilities to press for change, but quite another for an advisory body (or a group within it) to call major principles into question. Caine's frame of reference was informed by a sensitivity to the 'dual role' of the Secretary of State and to the subject/geographical tensions within the Office. His chances of achieving anything depended upon the creation of a working balance within the organisation and the colonial system, something only attained by a continuing process of negotiation and exchange. An awareness of the Office's social system, added to the desire to retain control of the central planning initiative, is sufficient to explain Caine's determination to see that the CEAC operated within carefully defined boundaries. An aggressive, high-powered advisory committee which sought to participate in the making of economic policy could produce a backlash capable of weakening the prospects for any effective central initiative of the kind Caine favoured. In other words, the whole question of economic planning was too fraught with danger to be entrusted to those who were not acutely aware of the complexities and uncertainties of the colonial reconstruction phase. Expert advice was essential, but the very process of formalising it raised certain threats and made its management vital.

Another professional, Evan Durbin, also offered his resignation from the CEAC in December, and suggested that Lewis should be appointed a full committee member in his stead.[35] Both were Labour Party supporters whose declarations stem partly from the strains induced in the Coalition by the prospect of a looming election. There was no better illustration of the weakness of the centre to provide a satisfactory conception of policy knowledge for dissemination throughout the Empire than the collapse of morale in this committee. For all the well-meaning objectives laid out in its principal memoranda on economic and social planning which proclaimed the duty to promote the true independence of colonial peoples and their material welfare, the network of contacts which the committee could exploit was of little help in defining what kind of work should be performed at the centre. Apart from commissioning research, the Office was largely confining its duties to a criticism of submissions from colonial governments. Any specific economic policy required the political will to discriminate between territories and in favour of certain industries or types of investment.

To offset the sad plight of the CEAC, however, there was by the autumn of 1944 considerable progress to report in the framing of a revised CDW Act. The Treasury had been warned in 1943 that the Colonial Office would apply for an extension of the CDW system to cover the immediate post-war period beyond 1951 and to remedy the loss of unspent balances in the fund which Parliament had voted.[36] Actual grants between the spring of 1940 and October 1942 only amounted to slightly over £2 million, less than half the sum available for a single year. Money tended to be spent largely on minor projects, particularly agricultural improvement schemes and those covering health services, education, communications, and transport. The White Paper of February 1943, which contained this information, was not, as Gater told Harold Macmillan, a 'very inspiring document'.[37]

By the middle of 1943 it was agreed that new procedures were required to avoid unnecessary delays. The CDW Advisory Committee was, as seen earlier,[38] given a less active role and from October onwards regular weekly meetings were held by Treasury and Colonial Office officials to expedite CDW procedures: the application to renew the Act was preceded by a rush of activity to spend the remaining balances.[39] The really tough bargaining about the new legislation took place between September and November, and, while some attention was given to economic return, the major argument employed by the Colonial Office concerned the need, in Stanley's words, 'to demonstrate our faith and our ability to make proper use of our wide Colonial possessions'. The Treasury could haggle about the terms but found it hard to resist the case for a revised bill. One Treasury letter included the statement: 'we are conscious that we must justify ourselves before the world as a great Colonial power'. This was, as Roger Louis observes, 'remarkable language for a Treasury official'. Louis also demonstrates convincingly that there was no American pressure to use Britain's mounting debt as a lever to control colonial development policy. The moving force lay rather in the fact that 'the Second World War witnessed a moral regeneration of British purpose in the colonial world'.[40]

In November 1944 Cabinet approved a Bill which extended the period of assistance by five years to 1956, and provided a sum of £120 million for the ten-year period (1946-56) as a whole. Money allocated but not spent in one year could be carried forward into the next. Stanley came armed with news of these provisions when he addressed the CEAC on 19 December.[41] In fact before dealing with the committee's questions he outlined the main features of the new Bill as agreed in Cabinet. He stressed the degree to which 'coherent long term planning' would 'be possible for the first time'; no longer would priority be given in the colonies to projects that could be done easily and quickly.

The Bill was subsequently passed without a division in 1945, the only piece of formal legislation which the Office submitted for inclusion in the Coalition Government's reconstruction programme.[42] It was to make a considerable difference to territorial planning, as the Office hoped, since it became possible to tell each colony what it might expect to receive as an overall total for the entire ten-year period; the administrative secretary to the Comptroller in the West Indies pointed out later that it was now feasible to embark on 'comprehensive development'.[43] It is usual to portray the 1945 Act as a somewhat unexciting, straightforward supplement to its predecessor of 1940. But it can be argued that the second CDW Act, with its 'colossal increase' of funding, was 'truly the turning point in British commitment to improving economic efficiency and production, and to raising the standards of health, education and welfare in the colonies'.[44]

Stanley had another announcement of some moment for the CEAC. To meet the 'greater strain upon the machine in London', Sir Frank Stockdale would be assuming the post of Development Adviser starting the following spring. No new machinery was contemplated, but in an obvious attempt to boost the morale of the committee Stanley laid considerable stress upon the fact that the CEAC was regarded 'as being on a different footing from any of the other Committees'. Stockdale would himself become chairman of the CEAC and would 'be able to thrash out with members the best way of obtaining . . .

[their] advice'. Stanley was keen to revive sagging spirits, but he did not misrepresent the broad trend of opinion in the Office when he stated a wish 'in all these plans to emphasise the particular importance of economic development as distinct from welfare'. It was the same point that Caine had made in August 1943 and it expressed once more the wartime shift of interest from social services to economic modernisation. Stanley by 1944 sounded rather like the Treasury in 1940:

Nothing could be worse than to give Colonial peoples the impression that the Colonial Development and Welfare Act was a permanent subsidy to their social services which the tax-payer of this country would undertake to pay without thought either of return, or indeed supervision.[45]

The difference lay in the fact that unlike the case four years earlier, planning for economic growth no longer seemed the dangerous, untested panacea of a few intellectuals.

Stanley was attempting, both in his general remarks and in the answers he circulated to the CEAC's five questions, to educate outside experts in the art of marrying their theoretical skills with a closer understanding of and sympathy for the political realities of his constitutional position. There were too many competing jurisdictions, too many voices to be heeded, too many uncertainties, and too many differing sets of conditions to allow an approach which was wholly comprehensive or centralised. Thus the answer 'yes' to the first question in what Stanley called his 'examination paper' was qualified by the observation that the speed of social change would not be determined solely by official policy. The second question was the only one which received unqualified assent, but then it did not refer to the time-scale for agricultural modernisation, the need for compulsion, or any specific areas. The third answer was the one most obviously shaped by the Secretary of State's own hand: Caine's somewhat mixed reply was replaced by a 'no', to which was added a much stronger reference to the 'desirability of developing a balanced and diversified economy in each individual territory', something that should be accorded as much weight as 'any advantages of convenience in the concentration of development in selected areas'. This answer made the fourth question somewhat academic, but Caine's original answer to it was included all the same. The fifth and final question was met, in accordance with the views expressed

217

by senior officials, with a more strongly worded reply equating foreign investment with equity capital and rejecting any approach to foreign countries or international investment funds.

The discussion which followed[46] revealed that some committee members' uncertainty about their role had by no means disappeared. Henderson, for example, pointed out that the CEAC 'never seemed to get to grips with the actual concrete problems of development and policy which lay ahead of all Colonies'. Only Durbin, however, called into question the possible usefulness of the committee or indeed of the CDW approach itself. He attempted to re-open the question of foreign borrowing and regional concentration, but apparently received no support from his fellow members. Stanley's response was shrewdly aimed at placing the Lewis/Durbin viewpoint in the worst possible light:

... one difficulty about limited areas of development was that if, for instance, it was decided to develop one part of Nigeria as the industrial area for West Africa, it was almost the German 'herrenvolk' idea. . . . It might offer economic advantages but it would also have very great social disadvantages.

Henderson was equally critical of concentration, and tended to agree with Hailey about the dangers of seeing development entirely in terms of industrialisation.

In general Stanley offered the committee the prospect of being able to discuss matters such as future tariff schemes on the clear understanding that these questions were bound up with wider issues which though not beyond the knowledge, were beyond the official cognisance, of the committee. The corollary was that the Office would in no way be bound to follow or even wait for a recommendation from the committee. As far as differences within the CEAC were concerned, Stanley hoped they 'could agree to disagree'. This compromise was tacitly accepted by members of the committee. Bourdillon, who had been so active as a critic of the Office during the earlier phase, limited himself to proposing the overhaul of colonial secretariats and agreeing that development would be the result of more than official policy. The great hope dangled before the CEAC was that of a steady inflow of development plans from the colonies resulting from the new Act, plans which could give the committee something worthwhile to chew on at last. There was no question of imposing economic solutions on Governors, however correct they might appear in 'pure economics'. But Stanley did suggest that the CEAC could operate within a kind of middle range: 'when the programmes under the new Act came in and Sir Frank Stockdale was asking the advice of the Committee, they would get away both from abstract considerations and from small detail.'

Thus ended the unhappy first chapter of the CEAC's existence. The episode had been instructive in a number of ways for the Office, especially regarding the dangers of having an advisory committee without a recognised coordinator of its activities. Stanley had shown considerable deftness and tact in dealing with the episode of late 1944, and the final outcome says much for his acumen and agility. He was conscious all the time of the great uncertainty which still hung over the future of the world trading system.[47] In practice, the function of the centre was defined after the war largely in terms laid down by the role anticipated for colonial development in the British 'economic survey', for which a trial run was made in 1946 and a White Paper published in 1947. The Colonial Economic Advisory and the Colonial Development and Welfare Committees were abolished in 1946 and replaced by the Colonial Economic Development Council, which prepared the way for the creation of the Colonial Development Corporation in 1947. Only in the post-war setting could consideration be given in earnest to the kind of basic questions thrown up in 1944 by the more radical members of the CEAC.

Regionalism and constitutional change

The Colonial Office had long recognised that a 'forward policy' based on regionalism and the concept of planned progress meant bridging the gap between two sets of relationships which its own existence had tended to accentuate — from Britain and the Dominions to Britain and the Colonies. A more definite time-scale in transforming 'dependent' into 'self-governing' territories implied some blurring of the line between the Dominions and the Colonial Offices which the prospect of common services or cooperative ventures under a regional authority made it easier to contemplate.

The Colonial Office was never very successful in associating any of the existing Dominions with its schemes for regional groupings or planned development. Canada's interest in the Caribbean was intermittent; Australia and New Zealand saw colonial problems in the Pacific from a different point of view; and South Africa was always treated with suspicion for having claims on 'the north' in any proposals for closer association in East and Central Africa. Meetings held by the Dominions and Colonial Offices between January and April 1943 in connection with the idea of a 'Commonwealth Charter' for the colonial peoples were inconclusive, and did not lead to any major step forward involving the Dominions.[48] The Colonial Office decided not to be represented at the daily tea meetings held by the Secretary of State for Dominion Affairs for Commonwealth High Commissioners in London.[49]

Regionalism may have solved certain problems for the planning of social and economic development, but it created others as well. So long as intermediate authorities were confined to coordination duties for external purposes, such as supplying information or providing services in communications — aviation, shipping, telecommunications — which were important in international relations, then they could be handled through interdepartmental cooperation at the local level and subject departments at the centre. But as soon as regionalism was considered as a vehicle for internal purposes, such as providing better qualified civil servants or securing economies of scale in services, it began to touch on constitutional questions which required adjustments both at the centre and in the territories concerned. A geographical department could not always pursue the idea of creating a regional authority in its own area of responsibility with full confidence, precisely because it was difficult to conceive how the creation of any intermediate level of activity might alter central-local relationships. Whoever was posted to a regional role had to recognise that the constitutional structure of the Empire gave precedence to the point 'above and below' where the authority of the Crown was embodied. Parkinson said in 1941 that the office of Comptroller in the West Indies 'needed an archangel'[50]; Stockdale often felt 'left out' by both the Governors — to whom his office was 'the circus'—and by the West Indies Department of the Colonial Office.[51]

Part of the inspiration behind internal regionalism was the desire to encourage the devolution of advisory services. The Comptroller's office in the West Indies supplied a precedent for providing a centre where specialists could be employed.[52] Governments which asked the Office for permission to appoint advisers were directed to consider this example. Economists were in great demand by 'advanced' colonies. Bermuda's request for an economic adviser in 1941, when coupled with American expectations for the Anglo-American Caribbean Commission, led to the suggestion that the Comptroller should be assisted by an economist.[53] The Gold Coast's interest in appointing a development adviser was satisfied on a West African level through the Resident Minister's office.[54] Northern Rhodesia's request for a development adviser was also met by an appointment which associated the territory with Nyasaland.[55] Towards the end of the war the Colonial Office had come to rely on a number of key advisers in different regions, like Hall, Lockhart, and Harris, when it wished to take a rapid survey of the general scene.

Paradoxically, the most extensive regional planning undertaken by a geographical department at the centre for internal purposes in the territories was carried out without any possibility of consulting the locality. The Eastern Department under Gent considered the whole question of the return of British sovereignty to the Far East in association with the Foreign Office, the defence departments, and other appropriate metropolitan interests, from 1943 to 1945.[56] Its proposals were embodied in what came to be known as the Malayan Union Plan. This was a deliberate attempt to take advantage of the usages of war to proclaim authority for British jurisdiction over the Malay rulers which had hitherto been lacking, and to make new constitutional arrangements which would join the Malays and the non-Malay communities in a number of common institutions. The South East Asia Command, itself a regional authority in military affairs, saw great propaganda value in publicising a plan which would accompany the returning armies, and perhaps bring the Chinese communities on to the British side. The Colonial Office saw advantages in a form of regionalism which would provide the basis of social and economic development. After undertaking its own post mortem on the loss of Malaya by appointing a small office committee in 1942, the Eastern Department pressed for special arrangements which would constitute a shadow administration or a 'colonial government in exile'.[57] It had to recognise that the return to the Far East was in the first place a military operation which would be followed by a period of military administration. The War Office eventually agreed to set up the Malayan Planning Unit in its Directorate of Civil Administration in London in July 1943.

It had already been agreed at the official level that the plan should proceed on the assumption that the new regional authority would be a Governor-General. Unlike the former Governor of the Straits Settlements, who had also to act as High Commissioner for the Malay States and British Agent for Borneo, the new Governor-General was to have no direct administrative functions, but would exercise general supervisory control over all British territories in South East Asia. One of these would be Singapore, which was to be separated from the Straits Settlements and established as a colony in its own right. The idea of joining the other Straits Settlements to the Malay States meant designing a form of constitution which would please the Malay rulers by being less centralised than the previous arrangements for the four Federated Malay States, but sufficiently strong to provide a general protection and legal status for people in communities of non-Malay origin. The Cabinet Committee which considered the plan from March to May 1944 agreed to issue directives to those planning for civil administration, and to open negotiations with the British North Borneo Company and the Raja of Sarawak. The Coalition Cabinet hesitated to give a final seal of approval in January 1945, and the scheme was only passed by the caretaker government a few days before the general election. It had been intended to send Sir Harold MacMichael to negotiate with the Sultans at the same time as a statement was made by the Secretary of State to the House of Commons in October 1945, but the scheme became embroiled in differences between the Colonial Office's conception of a Governor-General and the Foreign Office's proposal for a special commissioner. Gent, the Colonial Office's Assistant Secretary who had piloted the first moves for Malayan Union in 1942-43 and then supervised the Eastern Department as Assistant Under-Secretary in 1943-45, became Governor-designate of the proposed Malayan Union in January 1946. Malcolm MacDonald, the former Secretary of State, became the first Governor-General in April.

Elsewhere planning by geographical departments to promote regionalism for internal purposes could be undertaken only after some consultation with local interests while the war was being fought. The Office acknowledged the importance of local opinion in its sharp reactions to proposals which the presence of white settlers in the colonies had provoked. Each essay in internal regionalism was an experiment with constitutional structures and geographical constraints which respected the effects of wartime cooperation on local political initiative. The centre saw that some territorial governments of East and Central Africa had been moved in the direction of advocating a constitutional reform which would satisfy settler aspirations for Dominion status. The administrative officers, 'men on the spot', were always under pressure from settler opinion. In the West Indies and West Africa constitutional change was a means of strengthening other local interests. Each region was therefore considered according to the possibilities which the centre envisaged. For the West Indies these were concentrated on an exploration of the viability of a genuine federal constitution which would encompass all the major colonies. In West Africa they were directed towards a reconstitution of the Governors' Conference after the post of Resident Minister had been abolished. In East and Central Africa they were centred on a way of retaining the advantages of interterritorial cooperation without giving way to settler interpretations of 'closer union'.

Each exercise in geographical department planning for regionalism and political development became a statement about local political interests and the view taken of them in London. The balance between the centre and the locality was a negotiated arrangement in which many different purposes were pursued. In the West Indies the benefits of a limited association for war supplies had been so thoroughly discussed at the formation of the Anglo-American Caribbean Commission that the obstacles to furthering internal purposes were not fully exposed. The autonomy enjoyed by West Indian governments provided a strong element of resistance to central management at the local level. Neither the Governors nor the representative assemblies could easily be brought to a general agreement about the advantages to be gained by bringing the territories closer together. There were still strong feelings locally about the negotiations with the Americans to provide bases in the Caribbean. One of the major purposes of sending Parkinson on tour in the Caribbean was to take proper soundings of local opinion.[58] The Royal Commission in 1939 had concluded that the time was not ripe for federation, but had recommended that steps should first be taken to join together the Windward and Leeward Islands. This recommendation, which was not taken up until March 1943, involved securing the approval of the Treasury which supervised several grants-in-aid to the smaller islands, and overcoming local opposition, particularly in Dominica.[59] A specific proposal to amalgamate all the islands into a single colony was not made until March 1946. In the meantime, the Fabian

Colonial Bureau had in 1942 pressed the Colonial Office to consider the conclusions of the Royal Commission, including its suggestion that executive councils should be more representative, and in April 1943 the Secretary of State authorised the drafting of a statement which declared that federation for the West Indies was a desirable objective to discuss.[60] Many officials, including Stockdale, thought that federation was at that time impracticable, and no draft statement was sent for the Governors to consider until July 1944 after a local conference had been held.[61] Although the West Indies had enjoyed the benefit of Stockdale's organisation, the state of local opinion was not particularly favourable to any movement for closer union. The Secretary of State's announcement in favour of federation in March 1945 was couched in cautious language, and invited colonial legislators to send delegates to a conference.[62]

In West Africa the idea of joining four territories in some kind of federation could not be contemplated against the strong indigenous territorial organisations to promote constitutional advance which had been established in Nigeria and the Gold Coast, while Sierra Leone and the Gambia lacked an equivalent source of drive. The four colonies were also separated by French administered territory. Federal instruments were considered instead as possible solutions to the problem of holding together the different regions of the two richer countries. The promotion of West African cooperation was confined to finding a replacement for the Resident Minister's office which was itself extremely active in preparing reconstruction policies. It was generally agreed that it would be a retrograde step to revert to pre-war arrangements for a governors' conference, because the great value of the Resident Minister had been his role as a coordinator between the Colonial Office and the actions of the four governments concerned.[63] An attempt was made to conceive a post-war organisation which would in some sense be a projection of the Colonial Office in West Africa, and as such be financed from central funds. It was agreed in London in May 1944 to go ahead with plans to replace the conference with a West African Council of which the Secretary of State would be chairman and a Colonial Office official secretary, but such an agreement was not easily accepted by the four Governors concerned,[64] who were extremely sensitive about any infringement of their privileges. The West African Council was not created until November 1945, and its first secretary was Creasy, the Assistant Under-Secretary in charge of the Africa Departments.

Any possibility of a gap between the geographical department and its regional extension was thus narrowed.

From East and Central Africa the Colonial Office was under considerable pressure to accede to constitutional innovations for closer union which had been inspired by wartime expedients. Moore, the Governor of Kenya who had served for two years as an Assistant Under-Secretary, favoured some kind of federation for East Africa; and Huggins, the Prime Minister of Southern Rhodesia, pressed for a further consideration of closer union in Central Africa where his own self-governing Dominion was adjacent to the dependent territories of Northern Rhodesia and Nyasaland. In both cases the Colonial Office feared the creation of any institutions in which a powerful caucus of European settlers might be created.[65]

In May 1943 Moore submitted a plan for the complete fusion of Kenya, Uganda, and Tanganyika under a Governor-General with an executive council and a legislative assembly enjoying an unofficial majority, and was asked to discuss it with his fellow Governors beside alternative plans for a federation or a high commission with control over certain specified services. In March 1944 all three Governors agreed to support plans for creating a high commission that would take over the major functions of the governors' conference after the wartime emergency powers had elapsed.[66] Without creating a regional projection of the Colonial Office like the West African Council, the proposal for a high commission had the merit of providing a separate executive body which was independent of the Governors. But suspicions in London that any scheme might give the impression that Europeans would predominate led to long and complicated discussions, which centred partly on the proposal that the commission should be governed by an East African legislature. The final announcement which was not made until December 1945 emphasised that the proposed machinery was in no sense a step towards political union, but was primarily intended to promote economic coordination.

In Central Africa the pressure from local interests in favour of closer union was resisted even more strongly. The invitation issued to Huggins in October 1941 was not taken up until the summer of 1944.[67] The solution proposed for prolonging the benefits of wartime cooperation was the creation of a Central African Council, announced in October 1944, a consultative body with a permanent secretariat but under the chairmanship of the Governor of Southern Rhodesia. Even this form of organisation — extremely traditional, without any devolved part of the centre or any separate executive authority — was regarded by some as a step towards amalgamation.

Wherever regionalisation was not carried to the extent of a formal amalgamation of territories to make fresh constitutional forms, the work of a geographical department in planning for post-war developments was largely a matter of comparing the different territories in its charge, and noting the precedents which could be used on future occasions. The structure of the Empire encouraged *ad hoc* concessions to local demands or specifically territorial arrangements for the balance between central and local activity, both of which might handicap any consideration of larger units. The fundamental expression of central-local relationships was the balance between officials and unofficials in local institutions, as the power of the centre lay largely through its retention of a majority of officials in the executive and legislative councils. During the debate on reconstruction some argued that the traditional distinction between official and unofficial should be abolished, and that metropolitan control should be expressed only through the reserve powers of the Governor. But the practice of granting unofficial majorities as a mark of confidence in orderly progress was sufficiently ingrained to prevail over suggestions for reform.

Discounting the fact that Hong Kong, the Straits Settlements, the Malay States, Sarawak, and North Borneo were all in Japanese hands, the dependent Empire consisted of fifty-one territories which could be ranked according to their constitutional status. Seven had neither executive nor legislative councils, nine had executive but no legislative councils, but thirty-five had both. The most important category were those twenty-nine colonies in which the legislative council formed the single unicameral legislature for the dependency. By the end of the war fifteen of these had official majorities, and ten unofficial majorities but with a minority of their members elected. This group constituted the 'normal type' for which constitutional progress could be envisaged.[68] Self-government was attained when the executive council became responsible to an assembly of unofficials elected on a broad franchise.

The preparation of the appropriate legal instruments for effecting change was the duty of the Legal Adviser on instruction from the geographical departments. Pressure from the colonies led him to anticipate a massive expansion of work, because there was a grave risk that the time which normally elapsed between the Secretary of

State's agreement in principle and the execution of the necessary instruments would be extended to an intolerable degree. In 1943 staffing difficulties delayed the presentation of the reforms promised to Jamaica; in 1944 the Treasury was persuaded to authorise the appointment of a fourth assistant adviser to specialise in the Malayan Union and other Far Eastern work.[69] The Legal Adviser in July 1945 asked to be given some kind of time-table to get through his work in an order of priority which corresponded to questions of political importance, and his successor, whose promotion from first assistant was approved in September, laid plans to improve the Adviser's office organisation. The Secretary of State wanted urgent consideration given to the reinforcement of the Legal Department.[70]

Formal changes in constitutions made by altering the membership of individual councils had different meanings according to the context of local debate, but they were the principal negotiable elements in each situation. The special expertise of the geographical departments lay in their ability to anticipate the consequences of any particular concession. The unofficial element introduced into a colonial constitution could be either nominated or elected, and then only on a specially limited franchise; and nominations could be made from a variety of different sources. A white missionary to represent native interests in one colony might be inappropriate in another; a black lawyer on the executive council might symbolise local participation only in conditions where an indigenous professional class had been created. While the formal structure remained bound to an official/ unofficial distinction, the geographical departments were called upon to interpret the connotations of changing this balance. What interests might capture the unofficial side? What significance would a particular appointment have? The basic dilemma of central supervision was to retain the necessary discretion to make deliberate differences of treatment between territories, while at the same time acknowledging the force of local arguments based on examples drawn from particular precedents. The Colonial Office wanted to design a special combination to meet a specific situation; local opinion called for concessions which could be seen at work in other colonies. Any formal change in the constitution of one colony might have a demonstration effect on opinion in another.

The added dilemma induced by the reconstruction debate was the conflict between planning a theoretical model of the appropriate stages in development and recognising the growth of political consciousness in wartime conditions. While the centre was elaborating its ideas on political advancement, individual colonial governments were assessing the impact of the war on local opinion. Although the Colonial Office was prepared to consider particular applications for constitutional reform even in war, there was general agreement that it would be unwise to give the impression of making piecemeal concessions to a disturbing variety of demands. During 1941-42 the concept of long-range planning which was so familiar in other reconstruction debates began to be quoted in a colonial context, even outside the preparations for a return to the Far East. But at the same time individual colonial governments wished to respond to the situation as they saw it.

The geographical department's role in interpreting local opinion emphasised the rather special position which the African colonies enjoyed in departmental thinking, particularly those in West Africa. They constituted the only part of the dependent Empire where Britain's influence looked like remaining strong after the war, and the only area where regionalism for external purposes did not involve the interests of the other great powers, except the French. America did not have to be consulted on all African issues; the special claims of South Africa and Southern Rhodesia could be handled within a Commonwealth framework. Dawe, the Assistant Under-Secretary in charge of the three African geographical departments until February 1944, was the only official of that rank who had no subject department responsibilities, except for an interest in education. The Africa Division was the epitome of geographical department style. By encompassing three very different areas of responsibility — West, East, and Central Africa — it was constantly required to juggle with the different meanings of constitutional concessions, insisting on discriminating between territories and trying to avoid the consequences of direct comparisons made at the local level. In 1942 none of the African colonies had been granted an unofficial majority in the legislative council. If the conflict between long-range planning and *ad hoc* response were to be experienced at the centre, it was likely to be felt most strongly on African questions. That continent offered the greatest scope for experiment.

West Africa — or rather Nigeria and the Gold Coast — presented the sharpest picture of political consciousness, at least in the coastal areas where 'educated elements' in the native population aspired to create local governments with Dominion status.[71] As the whole region was brought into the productive side of the war effort in 1942, the Governors were anxious to make a political gesture. Burns, the Governor of the Gold Coast, requested permission to appoint Africans to his executive council and was supported by Bourdillon, the Governor of Nigeria. They were opposed at the centre by Lord Hailey who then argued that such appointments should be regarded as the end of a process in responsible government, not the beginning. He thought that Africans should be introduced first of all into the provincial government and then into the civil service, and urged the Office not to repeat British mistakes in India. Although the Secretary of State originally rejected the Governors' proposal, they repeated it and secured his acceptance in September.[72] This concession to the Governors' appreciation of local opinion was followed by several attempts at long-range planning, which included the suggestion that the Colonial Office should publish a white paper on planned progress in West Africa. During the winter of 1942-43 the West Africa Department thought it could identify the main signposts to follow; the advisers to the Secretary of State produced a memorandum on policy matters; the Governors' meeting under the auspices of the Resident Minister's office prepared a statement on economic policy;[73] and the geographical department itself responded to the Secretary of State's request for a planning document on constitutional development.[74] While a major speech was being prepared for the Secretary of State to deliver in July 1943, the West Africa Department was toiling over its own special area of privileged development. It was announced that the Secretary of State would visit West Africa in the Autumn. Sensing an appropriate time to express their views, the West African newspapers sent a delegation under Nnamdi Azikiwe to London to spell out in detail their demands for planned progress towards Dominion status for Nigeria and the Gold Coast.[75]

As the fortunes of war changed and the greater use of air transport made Governors increasingly available for consultation, the basic doctrines of African development were evolved in a series of meetings. In this situation Lord Hailey's work on native administration came to the fore; the reports which he had written in 1940-41 on the evidence of journeys he made in the spring of 1940 became a primary source for Africa Division memoranda in the spring of 1943. The attraction of Hailey's arguments lay in their avoidance of dilemmas associated with the official/unofficial distinction. All his writings stressed the importance of providing 'education in responsibility', a concept which implied granting real responsibility for a limited range of governmental functions. The unofficial in executive councils was not being trained in responsible administration, unless he was in some way associated with a specific schedule of work, almost as a 'shadow minister'; the unofficial in legislative councils was not being brought to exercise genuine self-government, only a rather unusual form of licensed opposition. The core of planned constitutional development, at least when considered in West Africa, was the evolution of native administration from small authorities into an intermediate system of regional councils — large enough to employ and train indigenous personnel and experienced enough to receive at a later stage the authority to run certain services which had been devolved by the Legislative Council. This form of internal regionalism was an influential concept in the design of the Nigerian and Gold Coast constitutions. It provided a rough time-scale for advance, if not an exact time-table. The colonial government could not devolve its powers until a local or provincial authority system had adequate experience. Such arrangements contrasted strongly with the precise demands of the West African press delegation, which called for the abolition of crown colonies, to be followed by fifteen years of planned tutelage for local personnel — ten of Africanisation and five under expatriate advisers. Part of the appeal of a policy for education in responsibility lay in its emphasis on moving forward tentatively and reaping the benefits of experience, instead of following a set model. The Secretary of State at the end of his West African tour said at a press conference that the Westminster model could not be adopted without insult to Africa's own traditions, and warned against 'slavish imitation' in the process of achieving self-government.[76]

The implication of this doctrine was that the centre should guide the locality into finding its own particular combination of training institutions for self-government. The seeds of the idea that colonial institutions of self-government should begin at the level of village, town, and region were found in pre-war discussions of native administration. Local government could be linked with 'responsible government' in many different ways according to the combination of jurisdictions in question.

The general acceptability of doctrines derived from native administration in Africa sometimes made it hard to remember that other geographical departments had numerous 'special cases' which could not easily be brought into constitutional development planning. The 'front line' colonies of Palestine, Cyprus, and Malta could not produce a sufficiently orthodox body of local opinion to form the basis of cooperation with the colonial power. The threat of partition still dominated Palestine; the idea of *enosis* or union with Greece still captivated many Cypriots; and the Maltese were given assurances that their problems would be considered as soon as peace was attained. The principal colonies where local interests were in a position to conduct protracted negotiations with the Colonial Office throughout the war, Jamaica and Ceylon, were both under anomalous constitutions not of the 'normal' type. Jamaica had a bicameral arrangement — a nominated Legislative Council and an elected House of Representatives — and Ceylon an elected legislature, the State Council, governing through a number of executive committees. Each colony gained concessions from Britain in 1943. The new Jamaican constitution came into force in November 1944, just before the Royal Commission on Ceylon under Lord Soulbury began work.[77]

World organisation

International planning began to have meaning during and after late 1943, when hopes for a joint declaration started to wither away and the emphasis became placed instead on preparing a stance for entry to the new world organisation.[78] It was to be a time of adaptation rather than innovation, as the earlier policy of regionalism was expanded to meet the demand that the British, along with other colonial powers, be made accountable to world opinion as represented by the emerging international body. The importance of the exercise for the Office lay more in the impetus it gave to the amplification and further specialisation of international policy-making than the actual results. In other words, from an organisational point of view, it taught the Office more about the meaning of the war and about the art of reconciling its aims to the demands of world opinion.

The changing mood of Allied diplomacy in the second half of 1943 made the reconsideration of Britain's attitude to a joint declaration of colonial policy with the United States unavoidable. The Four Power Declaration of the Moscow Conference had raised the possibility of international trusteeship being placed on the agenda for discussions of the post-war world order; and the American interest in exploring the possibilities of some form of international supervision had received further confirmation by Roosevelt's remarks at the

Cairo and Teheran meetings of late 1943.[79] The Cairo Declaration of 1 December was especially important: 'for those concerned with dependent territories, trusteeship plans could now be made on the definite assumption that Japan's Empire would be dismembered.'[80]

For the Colonial Office the growing stress on trusteeship resulted in a significant change of context. The chances of reviving the joint declaration appeared very slim indeed by early 1944, and at about the same time it was decided that the question of regionalism should be considered by a new committee under Cranborne specifically charged with preparing the ground for the conference of Dominion Prime Ministers due to take place in London during the spring. The question of regionalism was very much in the air, not only in relation to post-war planning in general, but also in a more limited Commonwealth context. The Australian and New Zealand governments had recently pronounced in favour of a South Seas Regional Council with advisory powers and containing representatives of other countries to secure a common policy for social, economic, and political development; and it was realised that the Canadians and South Africans were likely to press for inclusion in regional bodies functioning in the West Indies and Africa respectively.[81]

By the end of January 1944 it was possible, therefore, for the consideration of regionalism in the Colonial Office to 'proceed independently of the question of a joint Anglo-American declaration'. The content of post-war external policy had become formally detached from the particular initiative which had originally given it form and meaning. The Office's plan for regional commissions emerged from the doldrums in which it had been languishing into a setting which demanded its urgent elaboration. The point had arrived for the Office to relate its experience of internal regionalism, whose development had been accelerated by the demands of war, with the debate about regional cooperation between different nations which the Secretary of State had touched on in the Commons debate of 13 July 1943. In February 1944, therefore, the geographical departments were circularised with a minute from the Permanent Under-Secretary asking them to submit material reviewing the 'purely British' as well as the international 'moves towards regionalism'. They were asked at the same time to make some estimate of future trends.[82]

This represented one of the few occasions during the war when the organisation as a whole consciously examined the manner in which assumptions and categories had been altered by the peculiar circumstances of the emergency. The task was coordinated in the General Department by Benson and Eastwood, whose Middle Eastern responsibilities were removed temporarily so that he could devote his full energies to it. Each geographical department submitted what amounted to a historical record of all steps taken towards regional collaboration in its area, as well as some indication of what was being considered for the post-war period. The exercise certainly demonstrated the degree to which progress had been made in all areas during the war. But the existence of regional bodies for internal purposes did not wholly solve the problem of how to deal with regional cooperation at the international level.

The Anglo-American Caribbean Commission clearly represented the best model for such cooperation in so far as it ruled out any executive functions, while providing a form of permanent machinery and looking forward to the participation of local inhabitants. Yet, as Eastwood pointed out, 'there has been so much confusion of thought about "regionalism" and the word has been used in so many different senses', that it would be necessary to show in detail what was envisaged. The question of 'accountability' to a world organisation was bound to be raised. And regions which made sense and served a useful function for internal purposes might not provide a suitable basis for international cooperation. Indeed, as was to become evident, an East African regional body could actually be seen as dangerous since it could provide South Africa with a means of extending her influence further north. In the end Eastwood decided to eliminate all references to internal regionalism from the draft Cabinet memorandum for the Dominion Prime Ministers' conference.[83]

The main problem which impressed itself on senior officials and Stanley during their deliberations on the memorandum was how to give some recognition to the principle of accountability without in the same breath accepting the need to link regional commissions to an international organisation, which might be staffed with inspectors who toured the colonies and reported on their condition. The solution which was eventually adopted was to introduce the concept of an International Colonial Commission. The creation of such an organ possessing supervisory powers would never be palatable, but if its functions were limited to the collection of reports from colonial governments and the collation of information, its existence might be an acceptable price to pay for the abolition of the inter-war Mandates system and the Congo Basin Treaties, both regarded with little favour in the Office. Nevertheless, as the final version of the memorandum made clear, international regional commissions were still to be regarded as 'our main contribution to the solution of Colonial questions'; and, while defence was no longer thought to be a fit subject for the commissions, they might nevertheless provide a point of entry for world-wide functional bodies such as the International Labour Organization.[84]

The Colonial Office still had little means of knowing how much support it could expect to receive for its approach from other powers, particularly the United States. An American mission to the United Kingdom headed by Edward Stettinius (Under-Secretary of State), in which Isaiah Bowman was given responsibility for dealing with colonial questions, made it clear that, if the stress on 'independence' had by now softened, the spectre of supervisory machinery remained very much in evidence (apparently as an attractive 'camouflage' which the Americans would employ to achieve permanent control of the Japanese Mandated islands). The Foreign Office, for its part, was as keen as ever that the Colonial Office make every effort to accommodate its plans to those of the Americans.[85]

In the end it was felt best to tell Bowman that, while the British government was opposed to any joint declaration at present, it was not against creating machinery 'to promote good Colonial Administration and the material well-being of dependent peoples' along the lines described in the draft memorandum. Indeed it was possible to agree with the American representative that the joint declaration should not be revived, that regional commissions should not assume executive powers, and that reports on colonial territories would not be debated in the general assembly of the new world body. But although there was cordiality and evidence of goodwill, there was still a large gap between American and British conceptions of the proper role for an international body in the colonial area. The spectre of accountability had by no means been exorcised. Discussions at this stage were still at the exploratory stage, and the real value of the talks with Bowman lay in the recognition they evidenced that policy-making had entered a new phase.[86]

The Colonial Office could at least take some satisfaction from the Cabinet's approval of its memorandum and the generally favourable response the Office's regional approach enjoyed at the subsequent meetings of the Dominion Prime Ministers. The only difference in Cabinet had concerned the specific areas where commissions might be created, something also discussed with Dominion representatives. Only New Zealand, however, sought to broaden the definition of accountability being used by the British.[87]

By the early summer of 1944, therefore, the Office appeared to have made a good start in the area of international planning. Regional commissions, besides meeting the demand for accountability, might actually be beneficial in helping to 'diminish local suspicion and increase regional feeling', and in drawing in specialists of various kinds from associated international functional bodies. The idea of an International Colonial Commission could be held in reserve for the time being, with the understanding that such a body with 'limited functions' would be acceptable 'as the price for getting rid of the Mandate system and the obnoxious features of the Congo Basin Treaties'.[88] The new team of Poynton and Robinson were now given charge of international affairs questions in the recently reconstituted Defence and General Department,[89] with the first priority being to prepare for the hard negotiations about the shape and powers of the new world organisation.

It was not yet clear, however, just how these negotiations would actually proceed. While uncertainty persisted about the agenda for the forthcoming Dumbarton Oaks conference, there was a fear in the Office that sending a representative of its own to the United States might create the impression of a desire to have territorial trusteeship brought up. This was the last thing the Office wanted. To leave everything in the hands of the Foreign Office, however, was no less welcome because of the latter's 'propensity . . . to ideas of international supervision'. Once again, especially during July 1944, relations between the two departments became decidedly acrimonious.[90]

As it turned out territorial trusteeship was never discussed at Dumbarton Oaks, mainly because of a major clash between the State Department and the Joint Chiefs of Staff about the future of the Japanese Mandated islands.[91] But Poynton's visit to Washington was not entirely wasted, for while there he was able to have informal conversations with a number of State Department officials, including the very important figure of Leo Pasvolsky, special assistant to the Secretary of State and the American government's chief planner for international organisation. It was still difficult to read the State Department's intentions — not surprisingly, since its plans for a system of territorial trusteeship were by no means assured of success.[92] Nevertheless, although Poynton's conversations did little to penetrate the fog surrounding the treatment of ex-enemy colonies or the machinery for supervision or inspection, sufficient progress was made for Pasvolsky to suggest a preliminary exchange of documents between the two governments covering 'trusteeship machinery', the future of existing Mandates, and the development of regional bodies in relation to the new world organisation.[93]

The time seemed ripe at last for negotiations. According to Lord Halifax, American thinking was still 'in an embryonic stage where we can do much to influence it'.[94] By late October Poynton was back in London and work began in earnest on a revised and expanded version of the April Cabinet paper.[95] Most of the deliberations which attended its progress were concerned with the sections where aspects of the earlier position had to be developed in the light of Pasvolsky's terms of reference. The recognition given to the role of functional agencies at Dumbarton Oaks made it possible to strengthen the case for their cooperation with regional commissions, whose establishment continued to form the core of the British position. The most vital change, however, was that which transformed the earlier, rather tentative mooting of an International Colonial Commission into a firm recommendation for a body restyled the International Colonial Centre. The Centre was put forward as 'a means of ensuring world-wide publicity on colonial affairs, and of providing an opportunity for healthy constructive criticism, without contravening the constitutional principles [of British rule] or giving rise to...local political resentment'. The context of publicity ruled out the necessity of supervisory or executive powers: the Centre's chief function would be as 'an international centre of information and research on colonial affairs', issuing annual general reports.

The exercise of drafting the new paper was important in what it revealed about the Office's perceptions by this stage of the war. While the reception was generally favourable, some officials did express the fear that even the limited type of international collaboration and consultation proposed would be difficult to reconcile with the 'progressive attainment of self-government' and 'may derogate from full sovereignty'. It was felt too that the case against mandates should not be overstated. It is of interest that Caine, whose tussle with Lewis over the CEAC was just coming to a head, took the opportunity of commenting on the draft Cabinet paper to reestablish his credentials as the Office's 'forward thinker'. For him the issue of sovereignty was of less moment than a stress on the colonies' role in world economic development. But in stating this and in pointing to the advantages of international inspection he was adopting what Roger Louis fittingly describes as 'a lonely dissenting view'.[96]

What the Office reaction to the Poynton/Robinson approach signified was an acceptance of the need to meet the demands for accountability and an understanding that, hazardous as this was, it could be done without destroying the ability to take a central initiative after the war was over. An attempt to marry internal and international objectives was made by writing into the document the message expounded by the Secretary of State in July 1943. The shift from 'trusteeship' to 'partnership' was emphasised once again and the aims of 'good colonial administration' were defined as:

(i) the development of self-government within the British Commonwealth in forms appropriate to the varying circumstances of colonial peoples;
(ii) their economic and social advancement; and
(iii) recognition of the responsibilities due from members of the world community one to another.[97]

In this way it was possible to place the argument for British control over her dependencies firmly in the context of a commitment to 'progressive' social and economic improvement (mention was made of the forthcoming legislation to improve and extend the provisions of the 1940 CDW Act). Yet at the same time the paper was careful to add that:

the Parent State must be mindful of its international obligations in such matters as defence and good-neighbourliness in social, economic and commercial policy: it must not, even for the apparent benefit of its colonial peoples, order its colonial policy any more than its home policy to the detriment of good international relations. At the same time proper development of the resources of colonial (and indeed of other) territories is a duty to the world no less than to the inhabitants themselves.

In the course of the deliberations in Whitehall on the draft there was naturally a good deal of discussion among ministers and officials about the status and place of the International Colonial Centre in the permanent machinery established by the United Nations, and particularly the relationship of its operations to the proceedings of the

General Assembly. Eventually a formula was agreed whereby the Centre would be placed under the aegis of a sub-committee of the Economic and Social Council, with the General Assembly able 'to discuss international aspects of questions arising out of the Centre's work'. The new combination of regional commissions, functional agencies, and the Centre was presented as a fitting and necessary replacement of the existing Mandates system, even in the case of ex-enemy territory. By the beginning of December a third draft was ready to proceed to Cabinet via the departments concerned and the Armistice and Post War Committee. The memorandum (entitled 'International Aspects of Colonial Policy') was approved by the War Cabinet on 20 December 1944.[98]

Before the memorandum could be communicated to the Americans, it had first to be sent to the Dominions for comment. As this was bound to necessitate redrafting and resubmission to Cabinet, a considerable delay was unavoidable. It was at this point that the Colonial Office's lack of effective control over the agenda and timing of international negotiations proved most telling. All the work that had been done by Poynton and Robinson during the autumn of 1944 was now effectively to be undermined by a decision reached at the Yalta conference (February 1945) to confine the San Francisco discussions on world organisation to territorial trusteeship in relation to existing League Mandates, ex-enemy territory, and any other territory which might 'voluntarily' be placed under trusteeship.[99]

The effect of the Yalta decision was to throw the Office's international colonial policy once again into the melting pot. It was hard to be certain whether Britain was now committed to preserving the old Mandates system or not. Stanley, who had never been enthusiastic about sponsoring the creation of new collaborative machinery, now began to lean strongly in favour of abandoning the policy contained in the December memorandum. The Yalta decision, added to what he had learned of American intentions during a visit he had paid to Washington in January, convinced him that American consent to the abolition of Mandates was highly unlikely. And this automatically threw into question the viability of the scheme for employing regional commissions, functional agencies, and a central body for publicity. Furthermore, Stanley considered it tactically unwise to proceed on these lines since the original idea had been to go to San Francisco with an agreed Anglo-American Plan. To maintain the broad regional frame of reference without such an agreement would be to risk opening up questions of British colonial administration in a dangerously unpredictable and uncontrollable setting.[100]

In spite of the fact that the Foreign Office and the Prime Minister maintained that Yalta did not mean a commitment to the Mandates system, Stanley continued to press his view that it would be unwise to continue with the original plan. In the end his argument that the best course would be to concentrate on eliminating the worst features of the Mandates system carried the day. The proposal for an International Colonial Centre was dropped completely; that for regional commissions was held in reserve for a more suitable occasion. It had always been accepted in the Office that there were very real dangers in associating regionalism too closely with discussions about trusteeship machinery, especially since this link could produce anxiety within the colonies themselves.[101]

The question of Mandates raised difficulties for the Colonial Office in other ways as well. The matter of the disposal of former Italian colonies in North Africa which might be related to existing British possessions in the Horn of Africa created a nightmare for the Office, as it vainly tried to make plans while at the mercy of the latest idea being advocated by any one of a number of authorities, including the Prime Minister, the Chiefs of Staff, the Foreign Office, and the United States government.[102] There was no greater wish to assume additional responsibilities here than to continue holding that for Palestine, whose fate was once more in the balance. A Cabinet committee, created in the summer of 1943, had carried out its brief in producing a plan for partition in accordance with Churchill's wishes. But persistent Foreign Office opposition, the growth of terrorism resulting in the death of Lord Moyne, and uncertainty over the future of Mandates generally had thrown the feasibility of partition into question by the beginning of 1945. Apprehension grew that the matter would prove troublesome at San Francisco.[103]

Indeed the weeks leading up to the great conference were anxious ones for the Colonial Office. Australia and New Zealand made it plain that their cooperation could not be taken for granted, when they used the occasion of the British Commonwealth meetings in early April to express themselves strongly in favour of a specific provision being made to enable colonies to be placed voluntarily under trusteeship, with the British taking a lead in putting colonies under this form of administration. This was not something the Cabinet found palatable.[104] Meanwhile, hopes that Poynton might achieve some preliminary agreement with the Americans while in Washington were frustrated by the continuing inability of the State Department and the military to agree on a common programme. The death of Roosevelt created a further complication, although it did pave the way for an accommodation within the American government around the concept of 'strategic trusts'.[105]

San Francisco represented the final spurt in the Colonial Office's efforts to shape the diplomacy of post-war reconstruction. From the end of April for almost two months, Cranborne, who led the British delegation, and Poynton, as the Office representative who accompanied him, were immersed in the unrelenting grind of negotiation, consultation, and drafting. The full story of the negotiations is highly complex and cannot be given detailed treatment here.[106] In essence, the fact that the United States was prepared to give first priority to her strategic requirements opened the door for a working alliance with Britain for the achievement of specific and limited ends. Both sides had to make concessions, with Stanley being the chief objector in London to the American plan for strategic trusteeship over the Japanese islands in the Pacific.

Anglo-American cooperation in the Five Power Consultative Group acted as an effective counterweight to the Chinese and Russians, and allowed them some measure of control over the agenda and deliberations of the trusteeship committee (committee four) in Commission II. Britain's acceptance, after reference to Cabinet,[107] of the provision for 'strategic areas' in the section outlining the trusteeship system itself (Chapter XII), was reciprocated by American support, after some internal debate, for the British position over the framing of the general declaration of principles (Chapter XI). The exclusion of simple references to 'independence' (as opposed to 'self-government') was assured on the one hand, while the effective acquisition of the Japanese islands was achieved on the other.

Even so, the experience was a somewhat harrowing one for the British representatives. After a particularly bad day, Poynton confided to his department in London that he was feeling 'completely worn out and disheartened over the whole thing'. It was not always easy to know what was coming next. The question of the Palestine Mandate produced a considerable amount of heat among the Arab delegates. Nor did what was seen as Fraser's 'lamentable' chairmanship of the trusteeship committee make matters easier. It was necessary, too, to spend some time and energy in countering Evatt's proposals for the close supervision of trusteeship territories by the General Assembly. Although it was embarrassed by a leak in the *New York Times* of the details of the British plan of December 1944, the Colonial Office was relieved to find that no one seemed particularly interested in taking up regionalism during the conference. Even Gater's previous decision against sending a circular telegram to the colonies about the fate of this policy was breached only to the extent of a rather uninformative message explaining the contents of the leaked document to the West Indian Governors.[108]

On 14 June Cranborne reported on the final wording of the relevant chapters: 'We are satisfied that we shall not obtain anything better than this. I hope you will feel that it is acceptable.'[109] There was no sign that anyone in London thought otherwise. During the latter part of the year the Office became involved in the more routine tasks of the United Nations Preparatory Commission, notably in working out details of the Trusteeship Council and the specialised agencies.[110] In the autumn threads that had been severed by war were rejoined when a French delegation visited the Colonial Office to conclude an agreement on the exchange of information, the establishment of contacts over a wide range of subjects, and in due course the posting of colonial attachés to each other's embassies.[111]

Life was beginning to return to normal. But the definition of what was normal had changed all the same. By 1945 the Office was in regular touch with world opinion in a way which it had not been before the war. It could speak and conduct relations in a language with a currency extending well beyond the world of purely colonial affairs. The proposals it had developed during the war had ultimately been more important in what they revealed about the organisation's ability to adapt its doctrines than in shaping the post-war world. The Office's new-found responsibilities in the area of international affairs had not been accompanied by any equivalent increase in the weight it could wield in the making of Britain's foreign policy.

Yet, considering the prospects in 1942, there was some satisfaction to be taken from the Americans' willingness by the end of the war to refer to the virtues of 'interdependence' and preparation for 'self-government'.[112] Of course, there had been no intellectual conversion of the United States government in favour of the British colonial Empire; the softening of attitudes was mainly attributable to 'the growth of military influence in the determination of American post-war policy'.[113] If the Colonial Office's goals were not, however, in complete harmony with those of the post-war world as a whole, as the San Francisco conference made clear, the wartime experience of articulating doctrine had at least resulted in a much more conscious effort to relate internal purpose to external reality.

8

THE EFFECTS OF WAR

CONTEMPORARIES found different ways of describing the predicaments of managing the dependent Empire from London while a world war which was being waged looked like changing the basis of colonial sovereignty. As shown above, Hancock in 1942 thought that the developments he was studying might 'do a great deal to strengthen the will and enlarge the brain of the Colonial Office itself'.[1] *The Times* leader writer in 1945 wrote of 'the quiet revolution in concept and purpose'.[2] The conclusion to Shuckburgh's massive survey spoke in 1949 of 'the new angle of vision towards colonial problems as a whole'.[3] By then it was possible to regard the process of bringing the colonies to a point where they could stand on their own feet as 'a race against time'.[4] Even before that, the officials responsible could see the fragility of their position. The whole enterprise of colonial development rested upon bonds of trust and confidence which had been threatened by the sheer haste and anxiety of wartime administration, and by the changing expectations of each side. The more that was expected to be done, the less feasible it became to do it. Managed progress was seen as the keeping in step of three major lines of advance — social, economic, and political — in territories which lay at many different stages of development and therefore required 'an interval of political training and apprenticeship'.[5] As noted earlier, the commitment to a 'forward policy' called for the striking of a delicate balance between the dictates of central efficiency and of local initiative. The impact of war was not simple; it brought both welcome and unwelcome acquisitions. What the centre hoped — indeed, what it was forced to hope — was that it would be given the opportunity to take advantage of its increased capacity for effecting social and economic change. But this in turn depended, of course, on the extent to which there could be harmony between metropolitan and local expectations.

There is plenty of evidence to suggest that acceptance of fresh definitions of responsibility took place over a relatively short period of time — from the spring of 1940 to the summer of 1943. By the winter of 1943-44 the Office had grown accustomed to its new size and style. The crucial period in mobilising resources for the war effort was between the arrangements made to dispose of surplus produce in the autumn of 1940 and the campaign to extend colonial production in the spring and summer of 1942. The main phase of diplomatic activity in getting to grips with American criticism ran from the Atlantic Charter in August 1941 to the abortive discussions on a joint declaration in the spring of 1943. The Office's internalisation of the reconstruction debate ran from the examination of the role of research in the winter of 1941-42 to the greater participation in interdepartmental discussions in the autumn of 1943. The Secretary of State's speech in July 1943 was almost a catharsis which allowed the organisation to move forward in a confident manner. The content of official pronouncements reflected this process of conversion. In 1941 the Office's draft of a Cabinet paper on the Atlantic Charter explicitly stated that Britain should be careful not to commit itself to fully responsible government as the goal for the whole colonial Empire, and yet the July 1943 speech contained the specific pledge 'to guide colonial peoples along the road to self-government within the framework of the British Empire'.[6]

Macmillan's speech in the Commons on 24 June 1942, which had given Hailey's term, 'partnership', a wider circulation,[7] came at a critical time in the life of the Coalition government — between the fall of Tobruk and the attempted vote of censure on the Prime Minister. So many important factors which helped to determine the climate of political choice had reached a crucial stage in the summer of 1942. After America's entry into the war and the blow to the Allies effected by the Japanese capture of the Far East all the fundamental questions of colonial policy required examination in the light of the changing character of 'total war'. Argument about the future of the colonies ran in parallel with the 'transatlantic essay competition'[8] on strategy which centred on the possibility of a Second Front in Europe, but without the sharpness of definition which the military exchanges enjoyed. The Institute of Pacific Relations conference in December 1942 did not bring a clarity of purpose to colonial administration that could be compared to the achievement of direct negotiations between chiefs of staff at the Anglo-American 'summit' in Casablanca in January 1943 for the strategic management of the war. But similar forces of reconciliation were at work. The colonial participation in the system of supply and production had to be fitted into the 'mutual aid' arrangements and 'standard products' and supply budgeting; the British and American concepts of regional cooperation had to be reconciled, particularly in the Middle East and the West Indies; and the hopes placed in science and technology had to be put to the test in governmental schemes of mutual cooperation. All these different negotiations were conducted against the background of hard bargaining on the future constitution of India, demands from Jamaica and Ceylon, and requests from individual Governors to be allowed to make concessions to local opinion. There were many more 'agreements in principle' to proposed reforms during this period than could ever be brought to fruition when the intensity of the debate was lessened. Although proposals such as the Malayan Union Plan were eventually implemented, many others, such as Colonial Service reform, fell by the wayside.

The basic adjustments of Office life had been made before Oliver Stanley became Secretary of State in November 1942. The impact of the war was felt most strongly by his predecessors, and, at the official level, by Parkinson rather than by Gater. Both Parkinson and Hailey were absent from London during the crucial winter of 1942-43, the former in the West Indies on his first tour as a special representative and the latter in the United States after the Institute of Pacific Relations Conference. When they returned the debate on reconstruction had reached a point of general agreement. The increase in staff during 1942 and the promotions arranged for March 1943 set the seal on the Office's newly found position. It was not surprising that some of the greatest internal strains between subject and geographical departments, and between the latter and advisers, were experienced during 1942-43.

The drama of bureaucratic adaptation was staged in a setting dominated by two important changes of mood which the war had dictated. In the first place, there was a noticeable shift in the content and speed of official communication. The plethora of codes, cyphers, and telegraphese marked a debasement of the intimacy of colonial relationships. Messages were sent and received more quickly than ever before; aeroplanes carried people and goods to places previously remote. It was never precisely clear what claims would be made and met, but there was a general air of anticipation which encouraged a reexamination of basic principles. All the official pronouncements reflected an expectation of change in the tone and quality of political aspirations. In the second place, contemporary conceptualisation of world order was inimical to imperial systems which guarded the lines of communication between centre and periphery. It was fashionable to place greater faith in multilateral relationships, when the source of military strength lay in an alliance with America and Russia. However seductive the image of Empire, it was hardly feasible to pretend that whatever passed between the mother country and her dependencies could ignore the future shape of the system of alliances. All the elements in imperial relationships — settlement, trade, sources of production, sources of raw materials — were likely to be affected by the re-negotiations of the peace settlement. Both the changes in communication and the prospect of multilateralism required a re-appraisal of the concept of trusteeship.

The manner in which the Colonial Office absorbed these changes of mood while undertaking the unwelcome tasks of war administration has provided the principal centre of interest in this study. The process was less like the conscious formulation and application of lessons and more a matter of continuous cross-fertilisation between administering controls, defining war aims, and planning for reconstruction. The form of the absorption was a continuous reassertion of departmental identity and commitment to progress, sometimes with such vehemence that the actual degree of change had to be denied. Bureaucratic sources are full of myths about their own history. The requirements of the war effort, of the Allies, and of reconstruction planning met some initial resistance and complaint about the diversion of energy from the purposes of colonial administration, but they succeeded in accelerating organisational trends, and, as such, were perhaps a welcome confirmation that the values inherent in pre-war reforms had a broader validity.

The dilemmas of a central agency with supervision over local development were not removed by the new tasks, but presented in a light which offered fresh opportunities for initiative. The Secretary of State's position was still governed by the awkward combination of providing generalisations which could be applied to all territories, while representing the possibly conflicting interests of the metropolis and the colonies themselves. The war nevertheless brought to these traditional functions a set of meanings which combined confidence and scepticism. Colonial administration henceforth was handled from London with the knowledge that the central role had to be redefined in terms of both opportunity and danger. The task of describing what happened is to find ways of showing how particular kinds of experience altered the perception of those concerned. In all the different strands of departmental activity, there is evidence that the participants acquired — consciously or unconsciously according to sensitivity and rank — a number of habits which gave a further dimension to their appreciation of the machine they were running, even if the interplay of contemporary argument and appraisal remains necessarily elusive.

The explanation of their behaviour cannot be ascribed solely to a revolution in administrative technology. The changes in the official communication system were not so far-reaching that they required a thorough reconstruction of administrative relationships. The routine procedures were amazingly resilient under the pressure of expanded business. War administration was conducted with few formal modifications in the method of registering papers and the distribution of telegrams. In spite of the depletion of trained clerical staff and the abandonment of routine reporting, the Office followed the code of practice which had been determined before the war. Those who bent or broke the rules usually did so with impunity. The most obvious development was an expansion in the amount of 'executive' work which upset pre-war conceptions of grading and rank. The speed and volume of exchanges between London and the colonies underlined the fact that the traditional system of administrative guidance and control was likely to be called upon to perform new functions. Such improvements in administrative technology as were introduced — purchasing commissions, regional associations, supply centres — were all adaptable to colonial purposes, although they derived their authority from emergency regulations. What mattered in colonial affairs were the demonstration effects of the information available.

The expectations aroused by the prospect of multilateral alliances which would cut across imperial ties were influential in determining the status of colonial questions in public life. There was a great contrast between the impact of the First and that of the Second World War in this area of debate. Far from establishing a taste for multilateralism, the discussion of the peace settlement between 1916 and 1919 induced among those concerned with trade and shipping a form of neomercantilism which called for the development of 'empire resources' and promotion of 'empire industries'. Many of the interwar associations for imperial development drew their inspiration from economic doctrines which saw salvation for Britain in the 'undeveloped estates' of the colonies. Colonial Office officials found themselves at odds with their ministers on the dangers of fostering British trade at the expense of colonial producers, and thought it their duty to resist any schemes which appeared to expose the colonies to intolerable burdens of debt. Between 1942 and 1945, however, there was no comparable division of opinion. The majority of ministers did not feel favourably disposed to visions of Empire which would provide state assistance to work in partnership with private enterprise, although some objected strongly to the tactics which incurred the risk of submission to American commercial interests. L.S. Amery described the 'American offensive' as submission to a nineteenth-century concept of economic internationalism.[9] The first moves of the Board of Trade to engage the Americans in talks on commercial policy were all in accord with a model of interlocking multilateral agreements. Success was conceived in terms of the international commodity agreement, not the empire industries association or the colonial marketing board. The widespread abandonment of the theory that the British economy would benefit from imperial preference was in part the result of contemporary convictions that wars stem from imperial rivalry.

The bipartisan approach to colonial policy which was apparent in parliamentary debates throughout the war expressed this feeling. The responsibilities of the Colonial Office did not present important opportunities for ministerial initiative or arouse strong passions among the general public which could be exploited in domestic affairs. The broad mass of the people remained supremely indifferent to the colonial fate, but the leaders of the major parties were agreed on the need for a progressive colonial policy which would bring the individual territories along the road to self-government. Labour's 1943 pamphlet, *The Colonies*, impressed officials as displaying a greater grasp of realities.[10] If the Labour Party had a distinctive contribution to the debate, it lay in its ability to identify with the underprivileged. Bevin, in the Commons debate on the employment White Paper in June 1944, spoke of raising the standard of life of sixty-six million people in the colonies as 'a common effort achieving a common purpose'.[11]

The combined effects of a greater respect for communications and a faith in a negotiated world order had been to advance the particular specialisation which the Colonial Office was designated to embody in 1925 — the management of Britain's trusteeship over the dependent peoples — from a fairly narrow set of interests in native welfare to a major programme of reform on a par with the other items in any review of post-war reconstruction. The experience of war was essentially the means by which colonial questions had come to be seen as part of the wider picture of planned progress through public action. That is why the history of the Colonial Office during the war is just as important to an understanding of the enlightened posture which Britain wished to present after the war as any examination of Labour Party thinking. It was not the advent of Labour government in 1945 alone which offered the opportunity for a wholesale revision of the doctrine that colonies could attain independence, but the period of adjustment which preceded it. Shuckburgh, in concluding his history, allowed himself a mild criticism of Creech Jones for giving the impression in his Supply debate speech of July 1947 that the Labour government had started from a *tabula rasa*.[12]

The process of learning fresh conceptions of metropolitan responsibility was uncomfortable and uneven. The mobilisation of resources encouraged habits of generalisation and central direction beyond the normal circumstances of guidance and control to which the Office was accustomed. Even if it was widely appreciated that the emergency measures of wartime were dangerous precedents to consider when designing peace-time engagements, there remained nevertheless a firm conviction that specialist subject departments which had the capacity to examine problems common to several territories could alone supply the kind of expertise required in a 'forward policy'. In some spheres it was possible to measure the standards of attainment. The social services department in which so many hopes were placed in 1940 had been massively outpaced by a number of separate departments in the Economic Division. Not only was the basic responsibility for CDW shifted to Caine and the economic side, but the very act of doing this reflected and encouraged a much greater emphasis on long-range planning for economic growth, as opposed to the pre-war stress on social welfare. It was a shift that prepared the way for the 1945 Colonial Development and Welfare Act.

The Office also found ways of handling the language of diplomacy and public relations outside the normal run of its administrative responsibilities. The American alliance compelled a continuous redefinition of the purposes of colonial policy and dragged reluctant officials into the regular habit of making sense of war experience as it was then unfolding. Like the standard set in economic controls, the definition of war aims was a salutary discipline. Reconstruction planning was largely a series of paper exercises. But the obligation to plan had the undoubted merit of driving those responsible into the broader fields of the reconstruction debate where the needs of the colonies had to compete with those of other metropolitan interests. These needs had to be explained in ways which could be appreciated by a wider audience, and in the process the problems raised were examined in the context of disciplines which were not confined to 'colonial studies'. Reconstruction activities gave the Office a strong sense of the qualities which would attract talented people to consider its problems, and an eagerness to rebuild the system of central-local relationships in a manner which would admit a greater amount of basic research and planned action.

The Secretary of State's obligation to generalise for all colonies and to represent their interests as well as those of Britain was recast in accordance with the expectations of the time. The application of defence regulations showed the power of general rules, and the entry into arenas of diplomatic negotiation demonstrated the influence of an agreed form of words. At the same time, this very success in learning the value of bringing colonial administration on to a wider stage endangered the practice of representation. Colonial governments could well be confused by too aggressive a display of the generalising function. As in reconstruction planning, good instructions might always be misinterpreted. The war disturbed the pattern of reporting and the sense of mutual confidence between centre and periphery. Each side could appreciate while the war was being fought that when the time came to return to a peace-time footing there would be a rather different set of exchanges. The advisory committees' remoteness from day-to-day practice and the colonial lobbies' ignorance of world order negotiations were two sides of the same transformation. The organisation did not stand still while its energies were diverted from the normal practice of supervision; it absorbed the new elements of administrative practice into the traditional vocabulary and concepts of development policy.

The result was a central department which found fresh potential in its organisational roles. The division of labour between geographical departments, subject departments, and advisers was given an invigorating dose of intense activity which sharpened the appreciation of participants for tensions which had been latent in the 'forward policy' commitment. None of the many suggested reforms could be steered into providing a radical break with past tradition.[13] Those who stressed the need for stronger geographical departments to which subject and advisory functions would be subordinate found themselves contradicted by the palpable evidence of successful broad subject management across different regions; those who advocated a reduction in advisory committee activity and a limitation on the enterprise of advisers discovered a geographical demand for the expansion of common services.

But the articulation of the department's post-war identity was not sufficiently clear to warrant the use of any special metaphors or analogies in describing its status and function. L.S. Amery's characterisation of the department as a 'general staff'[14] was rarely taken up by his successors. They were not sufficiently sure of all the connotations of this vogue term in public administration to employ it with confidence. Their role in backing appropriate initiatives in the field and in encouraging the spread of knowledge about the best local practice did not seem to correspond to the discipline connection between strategic doctrine and military operations which the army could always effect. But they were interested in discovering whether there were any means of sending special 'shock troops' into action. Margery Perham wrote of the Adviser on Education that he needed to be 'chief of a general staff of able men and women who would go on a tour in order to collect the dispersed experience of our own and other Empires'.[15] All the discussions of Colonial Service reform were dominated by the seductive idea that the centre could find field officers who would be loyal to its own priorities. Those responsible for post-war recruitment kept as close as possible to War Office discussions on demobilisation, and even called for the early release of men committed to the Colonial Service. In November 1943 the suggestion was made in the Cabinet committee on demobilisation that the Colonial Office should open regional centres of recruitment in order to interest likely candidates from the armed services before they returned home. Renison was sent on a world tour of armies in the field between February and May 1945, and major centres were opened in West Africa, Cairo, and Delhi.[16] The Colonial Office was proud of the response it received. More than 2,800 expatriate officers were recruited to higher grade appointments between the end of the war and 1947 — figures which represented some seven years of normal pre-war intake.[17]

Any shift in central-local relationships seemed to call for some means by which the centre could by-pass the strict administrative hierarchy and make contact with projects on the ground. The short-term contract expatriates recruited as 'development officers' in Nigeria in 1944 were hardly a reliable means of getting suitable staff to 'chase' colonial governments into vigorous expansion programmes.[18] In 1948 only four liaison officer posts in economic investigation were created to cover the whole Empire.[19]

The role of expatriate Colonial Service officers was certainly important for the success of colonial development, but the whole enterprise ultimately depended on finding local collaborators among indigenous peoples. One of the paradoxes of increased confidence at the centre was an obligation to play down the importance of the 'lessons of war'. The bureaucratic achievements of wartime regulation and allied cooperation could not be presented to colonial governments as the model of partnership, because their special features were efficiency for metropolitan resources and accountability to allied purposes rather then voluntary cooperation for local development.

The July 1947 White Paper proclaimed the new climate of opinion, but not without betraying a trace of the doubt, scepticism, and incongruity which the subject of development conveyed. The White Paper was intended to revive the series of annual reports to Parliament for the Supply debate, discontinued in 1940, and to provide a summary of wartime experience drawn largely from Shuckburgh's official history. Apart from a section in the official history of medical services,[20] it constituted the only version of Shuckburgh's work to be presented in a published form. The text was peppered with phrases that acknowledged the impact of war. It declared that 'the war had a profound effect on political growth in the colonies', and that the expectations aroused 'found expression in new conceptions of the responsibilities and functions of government [and] more constructive approach to trusteeship . . .'.[21] The task facing the Colonial Office was 'to express the liberal spirit which the new conditions require and to work out policy and encourage development in bold and imaginative terms', because there was 'a new conception of relation-ships between London and the territories overseas'.[22] This official version of history emphasised that the war had introduced 'new ferments into the social system'[23] of the colonies, and implied that they were therefore calling for guidance and inspiration from London in a manner which had not previously been anticipated.

The same mood was apparent in the important enquiry into the organisation of the Office undertaken in 1948-49, although by then doubts about its effectiveness as an instrument of development policy had been overlain with anxieties about the consequences of any colonial investment for Britain's requirements in handling American dollars. Organisational questions were originally raised in fairly mundane terms. In 1945 Gater, as Permanent Under-Secretary, had rejected a request from the staff side of the departmental Whitley Council for a full-scale investigation, particularly into the grading system. He thought that any inquiry should await the implementation of plans then afoot to bring all staff under one roof from all the different scattered buildings in use.[24] The Treasury O & M team was also persuaded to delay its visitation for the same reason. Lloyd, on succeeding Gater in February 1947, agreed to arrange for an enquiry as soon as the removal of departmental staff from its old accommodation to Church House had been completed and there had been time to settle in. The Colonial Office staff left Downing Street and its other buildings and moved into Church House between June and September 1947, as the White Paper was published. But this move also coincided with the convertibility crisis of August 1947 when the government was forced to defend the pound sterling. Questions were then raised about the priorities to be given to colonial supplies and the place to be occupied by capital investment for the colonies within Britain's general economic strategy. By the time Lloyd had found three outsiders, including a retired Governor, to serve under his chairmanship as the Colonial Office Organisation Committee which began work in May 1948, colonial development had become a subject of sufficient interdepartmental interest to merit another enquiry, and the riots in Accra in the Gold Coast in February 1948 had touched off further speculation about the strength of feeling among colonial peoples. The Central Economic Planning Staff had welcomed a proposal to create a Colonial Development Working Party which, between November 1947 and February 1949, examined the value of the colonies to Britain.

The Office Organisation Committee confirmed that no fundamental changes of structure were necessary.[25] The shape which had developed in response to wartime demands was deemed appropriate for post-war needs. Perhaps this shape would have evolved in due course without a war, but it is hard to imagine either the scale or the speed of the process without the pressures and the working experience of a functional approach which war provided. After analysing the objectives and functions of the whole Office as well as the proper roles of its constituent parts, the committee reached the conclusion that there was no case for abolishing either geographical or subject departments, or for making one subordinate to the other. The only important modifications took place while the committee was sitting and with its approval: reorganisation of the Colonial Service and Economic Divisions, and the conversion of the legal advisory staff into a Legal Department. These changes, which included the addition of an Assistant Under-Secretary on the economic side, were the last notable adjustments in Office organisation before the transfer of power was completed. The subject and advisory sides of the Office provided the embryo of the Department of Technical Cooperation in 1961.

The report of the committee reaffirmed the importance of the geographical side of the Office which had tended to be neglected in the pressure of work on demobilisation and rehabilitation, and recommended that some papers on individual territories and regions should be transferred from subject to geographical files. This symbolic reinstatement of geographical responsibilities was part of an immediate post-war desire to rebuild the confidence of the colonies in central department activities. So much of the war effort in the sight of the field service appeared to have diverted central attention from the day-to-day practice of colonial administration.

The post-war Africa Division, which in February 1947 came under Cohen on his promotion to Assistant Under-Secretary, demonstrated that a number of geographical departments could create their own subject specialisations and advisory committees if allowed to build the necessary relationships for their own purposes. Cohen immediately released G. B. Cartland from routine activities to enable him to concentrate on long-term policy questions such as local government, land tenure, and law—the embryo of an African Studies Branch to which Ronald Robinson was recruited in July 1947—an arrangement which consolidated the previous year's work on native administration policy.[26] In the summer of 1946 the proposal was made that a despatch should be sent to African Governors on local government policy and the subject discussed at a special summer school in the following year. A little later preparations were set in train to hold a conference in London for African Governors in 1947, and for unofficial representatives in 1948.[27] By the time the Africa Division was moving to the Church House headquarters, it had set in motion a

254

series of enquiries, and after the 1947 summer school a panel on local government was created to join the existing panels on land tenure and law.

The conception of metropolitan responsibility for colonial peoples which was evident in the reconstruction of geographical department contacts came directly from the expression of confidence in central functions which the war had induced. The Colonial Office felt equipped to tackle the tasks which it envisaged, and competent to proclaim adequate doctrines for the changes anticipated in the post-war world. The idea of 'partnership' had acquired a number of fairly concrete expressions in central-local associations, and the prospect of further conferences for unofficial representatives seemed to overcome the constitutional handicap of a Parliament in which the colonies were not represented. Yet the confidence was tinged with a realistic approach to the dangers inherent in any enterprise which tried to manipulate the distribution of power at the local level.

The final irony was that the basic principles of colonial policy were always threatened by Britain's own economic weakness. The Secretary of State's despatch on African local government in February 1947 was issued just after the announcement of Britain's fuel crisis. The plans for the Colonial Development Corporation and the Overseas Food Corporation were brought to fruition when the whole economy was endangered by the convertibility of sterling. In August 1947 the Secretary of State was obliged to send a personal message to the colonies about Britain's economic difficulties, and one of his first ceremonial acts after moving to the Church House headquarters was to address the assembled staff on the government's dilemma. At the same time British public opinion was shocked by the actions of Jewish terrorists in Palestine on which a special committee of the United Nations was about to report; the Indian Independence Bill had just become law. The Colonial Office was clearly at the mercy of a new set of outside forces.

Any conscious recognition of the importance of wartime experiences was quickly overlaid by the need to consider the pressing problems of a country which could not easily pay its way. The obligation of wartime administration seemed in retrospect tedious and irrelevant to current interests. With the benefit of hindsight it was more promising to look back on the achievements of the 1930s than on the painful experiences of the war. Yet any fair account of the Colonial Office should not follow this natural inclination. All the evidence suggests that war work left traces on the formulation of colonial policy just as important as interwar discussions, because the war both increased the Office's capacities and sharpened its conception of its own potential. It was during the war that a comprehensive policy of 'progress', recognising social, economic, and political aspirations and relating them to one another, was spelled out for the first time. The confidence to expound such a policy of 'partnership', with its bias towards 'economics first', stemmed in large part from what had been experienced and acquired during the war, and from the assumption that those in the colonies would — or at least could be made to — recognise that these lessons of war had a direct bearing on the fulfilment of their expectations for change. Even if it is sometimes convenient to describe the process of policy-making as a conversion of input into output, it is unwise to ignore the organisational structure and procedures which contain it. The coming of peace, which brought a welcome end to the war's diversion of resources and effort, also found the Colonial Office much better equipped than it had been in 1939 to undertake a central development initiative.

NOTES

INTRODUCTION

1 Sir John Shuckburgh, 'The Colonial Civil History of the War' (four volumes, 1949, mimeo), is available in the libraries of the Royal Commonwealth Society and the Institute of Commonwealth Studies in London. Shuckburgh, in association with H. R. Cowell, was commissioned to write this official history by the Cabinet Office after his retirement as Deputy Under-Secretary of the Colonial Office in 1942. The work similarly commissioned from J. W. Davidson to cover the impact of the war on the colonies (see CSSRC [44] 5th meeting in CO 901/1) was never properly begun. It appears that Shuckburgh's volume did not merit publication in the Cabinet Office Civil Series. References in this book to 'Shuckburgh' are to the mimeographed text. References to 'Morgan' are to the first and fifth volumes of his *The Official History of Colonial Development* (five volumes, London, 1980), which belongs to the Cabinet Office Civil Series. The first volume, *The Origins of British Aid Policy, 1924-1945*, is cited as I, and the fifth, *Guidance Towards Self Government in British Colonies, 1941-1971*, as V, followed by the page reference.

2 CO 967/17: draft plan, 7 July 1942.

3 Sir Charles Jeffries, *Partners for Progress — the men and women of the Colonial Service* (London, 1949), pp. 181-9. Jeffries (1896-1972), Assistant Under-Secretary, 1939-1947, and Deputy Under-Secretary, 1947-1956, wrote a number of books on the Office and the Service, including *Whitehall and the Colonial Service: an administrative memoir, 1939-1956* (London, 1972).

4 For a summary of the debate, see Benson's minute of 22 February 1944 in CO 323/1877/9091/1944-5.

5 CO 733/407/75872/57/1939: minute, 3 February 1939.

1 PRE-WAR EXPERIENCE AND ASSUMPTIONS

1 W. K. Hancock, *Survey of British Commonwealth Affairs*, II, *Problems of Economic Policy, 1918-1929*, Part 2 (London, 1942), p. 270.

2 *Ibid.*, p. 323.

3 Prem. 1/247; the Office opposed the Foreign Office's proposed publication of details in 1943. See Prem. 4/6/13.

4 See pp. 38-9.

5 See the preface to the 1938 edition and F. Pedler, 'Lord Hailey' and 'Contribution of Lord Hailey to Africa' in *African Affairs*, lxviii (1969), p. 346, and lxix (1970), pp. 267-75, respectively.

6 No 3 in CO 859/68/12627/1943 gives the background to the nutritional surveys.

7 For the creation of the Economic Department, see CO 866/12/28543/1934.

8 CO 866/33/1327/1938.

9   Jeffries referred to this allocation as 'horizontal' rather than 'vertical' in CO 866/16/1015/1939; the 'secondary office' in Queen Anne's Gate (later Park Street) consisted of the Advisers, the Economic and Social Service Departments, the Main Registry, and the CSD typing pool.

10   Cmd 3149 (1928).

11   David Meredith, 'The British Government and Colonial Economic Policy, 1919-39', *Economic History Review*, xxviii (1975), pp. 484-99; Stephen Constantine, 'The Formulation of British Policy on Colonial Development, 1914-1929' (unpublished DPhil thesis, University of Oxford, 1974).

12   P. S. Gupta, *Imperialism and the British Labour Movement: 1914-64* (Cambridge, 1975), pp. 137-40; John Barnes and David Nicholson (eds), *The Leo Amery Diaries* (London, 1980), I, pp. 570-1; 597; Morgan, I, pp. 46 ff.

13   Misc. 382 and 391, Confidential Prints, 'Reports of the Committee on the organisation of the Colonial Office', in CO 885/29 and 30, discussed on CO 530/1926-8; see also Misc. 392, CO 885/30 (CO 885/48, Misc. 453, is missing).

14   Cmd 3554 (1930).

15   See p. 152.

16   See pp. 252-4.

17   G. B. Masefield, *A History of the Colonial Agricultural Service* (London, 1972), pp. 38-41; Amery records in his diary that the object of the conference was primarily to consider creating a pool for financing a research service, see *Diaries*, I, p. 506.

18   CO 866/30/1169/1942-6 and CO 866/40/1619/1944.

19   CO 866/35/1402/1939 and CO 1402/1/1940, 1941-2, 1942-3.

20   CO 866/2/28551/1934.

21   CO 866/12/25002/1935; the bulletin was on file 1027 and the schedule of work on file 1111.

22   There were thirteen 'beachcombers' on 25 May 1943, see CO 866/15/1007/1943; the Office had assumed full liability for their salaries with effect from the date of the expiry of their normal two-year secondment, see CO 866/15/1007/1/1941-2 and 1943-6.

23   CO 866/31/1212/1937.

24   Promotion difficulties are discussed in CO 866/15/1007/1938.

25   See A. J. T. Day, *Civil Service Guide* (London, 1935).

26   CO 852/190/15606/1938 Part 2; Morgan, I, p. 64.

27   Royal Commission report discussed in CO 318/433/71168/1938, CO 438/71168/1939 and CO 443/71168/1940 Part I. CO 950 contains the papers of the Commission, see CO 375/443 Part I.

28   No 51 in CO 318/443 Part 1/71168/1940.

29   CO 318/438/71168/3/1940.

30   Bourdillon wrote on 5 April 1939 (see CO 859/41/12901/1/1939 and CO 852/214/15201/1939) and attended the West African Governors' Conference in August, see CO 554/122/33629/1939; compare his 1943 discussions in CO 583/261/30453/1943.

31   CO 852/250/15606/1939 Part 2.

32   Calculations made for *The Crown Colonist* (June 1941) by Sir William

McLean in the summer of 1940 (see CO 859/39/12840/1/1940), and based on returns from the colonies requested in 1938 (see CO 859/39/12834/1/1939 and CO 859/39/12840/1940).

33 For the development of the idea of a 'fund', see Constantine, *op. cit.*

34 CO 847/15/47100 Part I/1939; register sheet for file CO 867/6/1426/1940 (destroyed).

35 CO 859/81/12905/9/1941-3.

36 Morgan, I, p. 73.

37 CO 318/433/71168/1938: No 5.

38 CO 859/40/12901/C/1940.

39 CO 859/41/12905/1/1940.

40 CO 866/36/1416/1939.

41 CO 852/190/15606/1938; Noel-Baker in the Commons on 20 November 1941 claimed that the House came very near to setting up a committee in July 1939, see *HC Debs.*, Vol. 376, cc. 509-10. (All parliamentary debates cited appear in the Fifth Series.)

42 Cmd 6023 (1939).

43 Cmd 6175 (1940); MacDonald's broadcast in February 1940 had been very optimistic, see *The Listener,*29 February 1940.

44 CO 859/19/7475/1939; letter, 5 January 1940.

45 *Ibid.*, minute, 14 January 1940.

2 THE ORGANISATION AT WAR

1 The Department's files are the 13076 series in CO 323 which became many sub-files by 1941 (see CO 968) after Lloyd took over; for the Congo Committee, see CO 323/1791 Part 2/13070/1940 Parts 1 and 2; the Treasury files on the Congo are in T160/1215-7/F17000/1-13, and on Equatorial Africa in T160/1218-21/F17006/1-18.

2 W3379/W7065/37/49 in FO371/28796 and 28800.

3 CO 866/35/1367/1939.

4 CO 866/16/1015/1940.

5 The committee papers have not been found, but they are frequently referred to.

6 CO 323/1753/7263/1940.

7 CAB 21/815.

8 CAB 21/876.

9 Shuckburgh, Vol. IV, Part 6, p. 210.

10 CO 866/37/1460/1940-3.

11 CO 866/36/1415/1940; Sir Cosmo Parkinson, *The Colonial Office from Within* (London, 1947), pp. 88-93, describes wartime living conditions.

12 Register sheet for file 1434/1940 (destroyed) in CO 876/6.

13 CO 866/16/1015/1940.

14 Shuckburgh, Vol. IV, Part 6, p. 209.

15 See pp. 97-100.

16 See pp. 101-3.

17 CO 859/39/12837/1940.

18 CO 859/39/12827/1940; minute, 11 Jan. 1939.

19 CO 859/125/12837/1944.

20 CAB 94/1-4.

21 CAB 21/1351-3; T 162/959/E 46009.

22 Africa Committee: CAB 95/10; Sir Ronald Wingate, *Lord Ismay: a biography* (London, 1970), p. 82.

23 The CO does not appear to have kept a card index to committees as the DO did.

24 CO 323/1858 Part 2/9057/1941.

25 The Ministry of Supply files tell something of the story, see AVIA 9/41 and AVIA 11/28.

26 K. C. Baglehole, *A Century of Service: a brief history of Cable & Wireless* (London, 1969), p. 24.

27 CO 850/195/20851/1943; letter, 3 June 1943.

28 CO 583/263/30554/1943.

29 *Imperial Calendar, 1941;* Parkinson, *op. cit.*, p. 87, refers to four 'key' principals who were prevented against their will from joining the forces.

30 See p. 37.

31 CO 866/16/1015/1940; EBN 182. Clauson, who pressed for the change as 'a useful economy of time and ink', also expressed his dislike for what he saw as 'a certain class distinction' in the 1925 ruling.

32 CO 318/452/71265/1942 Part 2.

33 See T 162/777/E 10258/10/1945.

34 CO 866/39/1593/1942.

35 The staff of the Dominions Office increased from 93 in 1938 to 278 in 1948 but these figures meant a rise in administrative officers of only 16, from 29 to 45.

36 Appointment made while the Colonial Office Organisation Committee was sitting, see pp. 253-4.

37 CO 866/40/1656/1943-5: No 12.

38 *Colonial Office Year Books.*

39 We wish to thank Michael Moynagh for helping in the compilation of the figures for the diagram.

40 A short description of the AEA organisation was prepared for South Africa, see DO 35/1226/WT 941/17; CAB 95/9; cf. CAB 21/1599 for SLA secretariat.

41 See pp. 201-4.

42 T 162/870/E 45491/09/1: letter, 15 May 1944.

43 The series of files dealing with the administrative officers are 1007, see for example CO 866/15/1007/1943 and 1944-7.

44 Lady Gater made available to us a few letters dealing with the appointment, but they do not indicate how the choice was made: Sir Horace Wilson to Gater, 10 July 1939, and Gater's reply, 11 July 1939. Newspapers announced the appointment on 19 July 1939.

45 Personal information from Sir Colin Thornley.

46 Not all the files on these journeys appear to have been preserved: for the West Indies, see CO 318/454/71299/1942 and 1943 and 11 sub-files.

47 Material from several different interviews. According to Dr K. E. Robinson, Gater was especially concerned to prevent departmental officers seeing Ministers except with the Permanent Under-Secretary, and he gave directions

about the handling of telegrams on the basis of meetings with Ministers and/or Under-Secretaries.

48   CO 822/12/46744/1943.
49   CO 850/194/20807/1941-2.
50   DO 121/10A/2.
51   Lord Lloyd's papers are in Churchill College, Cambridge.
52   Sir Alan Burns, *Colonial Civil Servant* (London, 1949), p. 170.
53   Personal information from Sir Colin Thornley.
54   Parkinson, *op. cit.*, pp. 87-8.
55   *Ibid.*
56   *Ibid.*
57   Harold Macmillan, *The Blast of War, 1939-45* (London, 1967), p. 161.
58   *HC Debs.*, Vol. 380, cc. 2002-124.
59   Lord Butler describes Stanley as 'a joyous master of the arts of opposition', who, when 'in office . . . too frequently exhibited an almost physical incapacity for making up his mind'. *The Art of the Possible* (London, 1971), pp. 144 5; cf. W. Roger Louis, *Imperialism at Bay: The United States and the Decolonization of the British Empire* (Oxford, 1977), pp. 35-6.

3   THE MOBILISATION OF RESOURCES

1   Some indication of the scope of this operation is given by the fact that between a half and a third of Shuckburgh's study is devoted to colonial economic policy.
2   Cmd 7167 (1947), *The Colonial Empire (1939-1947)*, para. 32, p. 8.
3   Shuckburgh, Vol. I, p. 119.
4   CO 866/15/1007/1943.
5   WM 129(43) in Cab 65/35 & WP(43)400 in Cab 66/40; WM 150(43) in Cab 65/36 and WP(43)488 in Cab 66/42.
6   Parkinson, *op. cit.*, p. 86.
7   CO 866/15/1007/1943.
8   Shuckburgh, Vol. I, p. 107.
9   See p. 42.
10   It was these two products which provided the first trial runs in surplus policy. Personal information from Sir Sydney Caine.
11   CO 852/346/18856/1940 and 18856/1/1940; CO 852/482/18842/A/1941.
12   Shuckburgh, Vol. I, p. 133.
13   CO 852/482/18836/1941.
14   CO 852/475/18495/1941.
15   CO 852/482/18836/1941.
16   The following account is based on CO 859/41/12905/4/1940.
17   See p. 42.
18   By the end of the war the total of monetary gifts made by colonial governments, native rulers, and other bodies and individuals to the British government amounted to £24,014,948. Cmd 7167 (1947), Appendix 11.
19   CO 859/41/12905/4/1941. This file serves as the basis for the account which follows.

20 See p. 42.
21 *HC Debs.* Vol. 357, cc. 322-23.
22 See, for example, the speech of Philip Noel-Baker during the general debate on colonial affairs in *HC Debs.* Vol. 376, cc. 516.
23 By this point the two streams had come together physically, and deliberations proceeded on CO 859/81/12905/4/1941.
24 It was published later in the year, with two minor changes, as Cmd 6299 (1941), *Colonial Policy in War Time.*
25 For the examples of marketing and local self-sufficiency see Sir William McLean's article 'Colonial Economy, Past, Present and Future' (published in 1942 by the British Library of Information in New York as part of the *Bulletins from Britain* series) at CO 875/18/9120/4/1942.
26 CO 859/81/12905/8/1941.
27 CO 852/496/18872/A/1941.
28 The following account is based on CO 852/506 Part 2/19051/1942; CO 852/496/18872/A/1941.
29 CO 852/496/18872/1942 and 1943.
30 For the manner in which war demanded a greater articulation of colonial policy see pp. 117-29.
31 CO 852/503 Part 3/19037/12/1942; CO 323/1859/9063/1942-43.
32 CO 852/475/18495/1941.
33 Shuckburgh, Vol. I, p. 192.
34 CO 852/510 Part 4/19400/1942 and 19403/1942.
35 CO 859/67/12603/1941 and 12601/10/1942-43.
36 CO 852/425/17505/1942 and 1943; CO 968/83/14702/1942 and 1943.
37 See above p. 78.
38 CO 852/482/18842/A1/1941 Parts 1 and 2; CO 852/506/19046/1942; see p. 190.
39 CAB 72/19; CO 852/502/19016/B/1942.
40 CO 852/430/18000/G/1941.
41 CO 852/430/18000/G1/1942.
42 See USE(42)23 in CAB 87/60.
43 CO 822/103/46523/1940.
44 The Eastern Group Supply Council, set up after the closing of the Mediterranean in the summer of 1940, represented an important model for later regional bodies. Personal information from Sir Sydney Caine.
45 Cmd 6175 (1940).
46 For the pre-war background see especially CO 968/159/14814/1C/&1G/ 1944; and Shuckburgh, Vol. III, pp. 83-4.
47 CO 822/103/46523/1940.
48 *Ibid.*; *HL Debs.*, Vol. 125, cc. 374-421.
49 CO 822/111/46701/1942-3.
50 CO 822/108/46523/1941-2.
51 CO 822/111/46709/1942-3.
52 *Ibid.*; Shuckburgh, Vol. III, p. 16.
53 CO 847/15/47100/1 Parts 1 & 2/1939.
54 CO 795/115/45104/17/1940; CO 968/159/14814/1G/1944.
55 CO 795/113/45007/1940.

56   CO 795/122 Part 1/45104/1941.
57   CO 795/113/45007/1940.
58   CO 795/120/45007/1941.
59   CO 795/122 Part 1/45104/1941.
60   CO 822/111/46701/1942.
61   CO 554/122/33642/1939; CO 554/124/33642/1940; CO 968/159/14814/1D/1944; see above pp. 97-101.
62   CO 554/124/33642/1940.
63   CO 554/129 Part 1/33662/1 & 2/1941; 33662/5/1941-2.
64   CO 554/133/33800/2/1942.
65   CO 852/506/19042/1942 Part 1; CO 968/159/14814/1D/1944.
66   CO 554/133/33800/2/1942; CAB 21/1370.
67   CAB 21/1371; see also Viscount Swinton, *I Remember* (London, 1948), p. 204.
68   CO 554/133/33823/1942.
69   CO 554/133/33824/1942-3.
70   Swinton, *op. cit.*, p. 203; see also p. 224.
71   Shuckburgh, Vol. III p. 91.
72   See above p. 50.
73   CAB 21/1370 (Eden to Churchill, 3 June 1942).
74   CAB 95/12.
75   Shuckburgh, Vol. III, pp. 111-12.
76   CAB 21/1599; CAB 95/9; CAB 115/696.
77   Report by Swinton's office quoted in Shuckburgh, Vol. III, p. 91.
78   CO 968/46/13601/19/41; Prem. 3/502/1.
79   See below, pp. 223-4.
80   *HC Debs.*, Vol. 364, c. 1171.
81   CO 971/1/72001/1941.
82   CO 318/452/71265/1941: A3316, A3376 and A5324 in FO 371/26175.
83   CO 852/506 Part 2/19055/1943. Also CO 866/38/1540/1941-3, and Shuckburgh, Vol. III, p. 74.
84   CO 318/452/71265/1941; CO 318/453/71275/1941. Also see W. Roger Louis, *op. cit.*, pp. 180-1, 484.
85   CO 971/20/72058/1941; CO 318/452/71275/1941.
86   CO 318/452/71265/1941.
87   A10691/67/45 in FO 371/26175; A431/431/45 in FO 371/30673; CO 318/452/71265/1941.
88   CO 968/159/14814/1E/1944; cf. Morgan, I, p. 157.
89   CO 318/452/71265/1942 Part 1; FO 371/30673.
90   CO 866/38/1540/1941-43; CO 852/506 Part 2/19055/1943; CO 318/452/71265/1942 Part 1.
91   CO 318/452/71265/1942 Part 2.
92   A4740/431/45 in FO 371/30673; A5137 & A5367/431/45 in FO 371/30674.
93   See especially Downie's minute of 11 June and Caine's of 12 June on CO 318/452/71265/1942 Part 2.
94   Minute of 17 June on CO 318/452/71265/1942 Part 2; Downie was transferred to be Third Crown Agent with effect from 1 August, see CO 866/3/1195/1942-3.

95 *Ibid.*, A6429 and A6807/431/45 in FO 371/30674.

96 CO 852/506 Part 2/19055/3/1942 and 19055/1943; CO 866/38/1540/ 1941-43; the link with the Crown Agents is even more visible in the light of the fact that the two members of the Colonial Supply Liaison next senior to Melville were seconded from the Crown Agents' London Office at the Colonial Office's request. Personal information from Sir Sydney Caine.

97 CO 318/455/71311/1942; CO 875/18/9120/1942.

98 CO 318/452/71265/4/1943.

99 CO 318/452/71265/1943/Part 1.

100 CO 968/159/14814/1E/(1944).

101 For an example from Nassau in the Bahamas see CO 971/1/72002/ 1942-43.

4 WAR AIMS AND PUBLIC RELATIONS

1 See pp. 193-9.

2 For a detailed account of British and American exchanges and planning on colonial questions during the period 1941-43 see Louis, *op. cit.*, pp. 121-286. What follows here concentrates on those aspects which provide evidence of organisational adaptation and innovation within the Colonial Office.

3 Sir Cosmo Parkinson, *op. cit.*, p. 66; CO 875/19/9137/1943. Elspeth Huxley's appointment occurred shortly after her husband, Gervas, had taken up the post of Director of the Ministry of Information's Empire Division. See Gervas Huxley, *Both Hands* (London, 1970), pp. 207-8.

4 U3152/14/70 in FO 371/35311.

5 CO 323/1698/7450/1939 Part 1.

6 See pp. 50,104-5.

7 A.J.P. Taylor, *English History, 1914-1945* (London, Pelican edition, 1970), pp. 649-50. Also see Louis, *op. cit.*, Chapter 6, and Morgan, V. p. 1.

8 CO 733/426/75872/85/1940.

9 CO 323/1858/9057/1941 Part 2.

10 K. E. Robinson, *The Dilemmas of Trusteeship* (London, 1965), p. 89. For a typical example of the pre-war treatment of this topic, see the excerpt from MacDonald's speech of 1938 quoted in *ibid.*, p. 91.

11 CO 323/1858/9057/1941 Part 2.

12 These lectures were published as *The Position of the Colonies in a British Commonwealth of Nations* (Oxford, 1941).

13 WP(G)(41)89 in CO 67/9.

14 War Cabinet Minutes WM(41) 89 in CAB 65/19.

15 *HC Debs.*, Vol. 374, c. 69; Morgan, V, pp. 4-5.

16 *Empire*, January 1942.

17 Parkinson, *op. cit.*, p. 87.

18 *The Times*, 14 March 1942. Most of Miss Perham's contributions to *The Times* in 1942 were later reproduced in her *Colonial Sequence, 1930-49* (London, 1967). For the British reaction to anti-colonial criticism at this time see Louis, *op. cit.*, Chapter II, Christopher Thorne, *Allies of a Kind: the United States, Britain and the war against Japan* (London, 1978), pp. 209-10.

19 *The Times*, 14 March 1942.
20 Leland M. Goodrich (ed), *Documents on American Foreign Relations*, IV (Boston, 1942).
21 See, for example, *Empire*, June 1938.
22 J.M. Lee, *Colonial Development and Good Government* (London, 1967), pp. 4-5.
23 See pp. 30,43-4, 129-30, 139.
24 Members of the Fabian Society and its Colonial Bureau were given free tickets to see a showing of these films in London, and *Empire* commented favourably on them in its November 1941 issue. For a more detailed picture of the Public Relations Officer's activities, see the register sheets CO 978/1-13.
25 CO 875/18/9120/1942.
26 CO 875/18/9120/4/1942.
27 CO 875/19/9121/1942 and 9121/1/1943.
28 *The Times*, 4 April 1942.
29 CO 875/18/3120/1942.
30 Both minutes were written on 17 June 1942 by G.E.J. Gent. The first appeared on the Public Relations file CO 875/18/9120/1942; the second in the Eastern Department file CO 825/35/55104/1942.
31 The following account of Far Eastern discussions is based on CO 825/35/55104/1942, unless otherwise indicated. Also see Louis, Chapter 2, and A.J. Stockwell, 'Colonial Planning during World War II: The Case of Malaya', *Journal of Imperial and Commonwealth History*, ii (1973-4), pp. 333-51.
32 The note, entitled 'Note on Future Policy in the Far East' is number 16 in CO 825/35/55104/1942.
33 R.I. Campbell to Foreign Office, 14 July 1942, in CO 875/18/9120/1942.
34 'British Far Eastern Policy', number 27 in CO 825/1942/55104/1942.
35 CO 877/25/27265/7/1944.
36 CO 875/18/9120/3/1942; FO 371/31801.
37 Hailey referred to 'partnership' in a speech delivered to the Lords on 20 May, *HL Debs.*, Vol. 122, c. 1095, and in his address to the annual meeting of the Anti Slavery and Aborigines Protection Society of 28 May (later published under the title A Colonial Charter).
38 *The Times*, 23 June 1942.
39 *HC Debs.*, Vol. 380, cc. 2015-16.
40 *Empire*, July 1942.
41 *Ibid.*
42 *HC Debs.*, Vol. 381, cc. 199.
43 The following account is based on CO 323/1848/7322/1942.
44 For this committee, see pp. 152-3, 194-5.
45 U1062/27/70 in FO 371/31415.
46 See p. 174.
47 *The Times*, 1 August 1942; U512/27/70 in FO 371/31513. For Roosevelt's attitude and State Department activity on the colonial question during the first part of 1942, see Louis, *op. cit.*, Chapters 8, 9, and 10; Thorne, *op. cit.*, pp. 214 ff.
48 Department of State, *Postwar Foreign Policy Preparation 1939-45*

(Washington, 1949), pp. 109-10; CO 875/18/9120/1942.

49   CO 323/1858 Part 2/9057/B/1942.

50   U719/27/70 in FO 371/31514; CO 323/1848/7322/1942.

51   A record of the meeting can be found in CO 825/35/55104/1942. For 'high policy' discussions in London, also see Louis, *op. cit.*, Chapter 11, and Thorne, *op. ci.*, pp. 222-4.

52   CO 323/1858 Part 2/9057/B/1942; U828/828/70 in FO 371/31526. For the exchanges between Colonial and Foreign Office ministers in the autumn of 1942 about American involvement in the West Indies, see p. 113. cf. Morgan, V, pp. 5-8.

53   See Anthony Eden, *The Reckoning* (London, 1965), p. 32.

54   U828 and U1138/828/70 in FO 371/31526; CO 323/1858 Part 2/9057/B/1942.

55   U1138/828/70 in FO 371/31526; CO 323/1858 Part 2/9057/B/1942.

56   CO 323/1858 Part 2/9057/B/1942; U1080/828/70 in FO 371/31526.

57   U1292/828/70 in FO 371/31526.

58   U1598/828/70 in FO 371/31527.

59   CO 323/1858 Part 2/9057/B/1942; U1660/828/70 in FO 371/31527.

60   WP(42)544 in CAB 66/31. The paper, entitled 'Colonial Policy' was originally to be submitted by the Foreign Secretary only, but was given a wider sponsorship at the request of the Prime Minister. U1660/828/70 in FO 371/31527.

61   WM(42)166 in CAB 65/28.

62   The leading critics were Wendell Wilkie and Henry Luce, the editor of *Life* magazine. See CO 875/18/9120/1942; *The Times*, 28 October 1942; Robert E. Sherwood, *Roosevelt and Hopkins: an intimate history* (New York, 1948), pp. 672-3; Louis, *op. cit.*, Chapter 12.

63   CO 875/18/9120/1942-43 (Secret).

64   *The Times*, 11 and 21 November 1942.

65   CO 875/18/9120/1942-43 (Secret).

66   A9422/1684/45 in FO 371/30685. Law was a logical choice for this post in view of his very active role in Anglo-American discussions about international economic reconstruction. He had visited Washington in the late summer of 1942, and before leaving had discussed current American criticism and British propaganda needs with Cranborne: CO 825/35/55104/1942. See also R.F. Harrod, *The Life of John Maynard Keynes* (London, 1951), p. 557.

67   A9423/1684/45 in FO 371/30685.

68   A9422, A9423 and A10559/1684/45 in FO 371/30685; WM(42)154 in CAB 65/28; *HL Debs.*, Vol. 125, cc. 401-16.

69   A10559, A11763/1684/45 in FO 371/30685; A78/3/45 in FO 371/34086. Other departments represented on the Law Committee, besides the Colonial and Foreign Offices and the Ministry of Information, were the India, Dominions, and War Offices. Early in 1943 an informal committee under Sir George Sansom was set up in Washington to act as a kind of 'local Law Committee': U3332/3332/70 in FO 371/35457; CO 875/19/9120/9/1943 Part 1.

70   See pp. 107 ff.

71 CO 875/18/9120/1942-43 (Secret).
72 For accounts of the conference see CO 875/18/9120/3/1943 and the folder on the IPR Conference in the Creech Jones Papers, Box 12, Rhodes House Library, Oxford. For accounts of the Conference, see Louis, *op. cit.*, pp. 205-9, and Thorne, *op. cit.*, pp. 212-4.
73 For the growth of the bi-partisan approach to colonial affairs, see pp. 158-60. Regionalism was given a further boost by the endorsement given to it by Smuts in an article which appeared in *Life*, 28 December 1942.
74 A1502/3/45 in FO 371/34086.
75 See Louis, *op. cit.*, pp. 211 ff.
76 WP(43)8 in CAB 66/33; WM(43)4 in CAB 65/33.
77 For the background to the exchange of drafts see Louis, *op. cit.*, Chapter 14 (esp. pp. 231 ff).
78 CO 323/1858 Part 2/9057/B/1943.
79 *Ibid.*
80 U2026, U2381/14/70 in FO 371/35311; CO 323/1858 Part 2/9057/B/1943. Also see Louis, *op. cit.*, Chapter 13.
81 CO 875/18/9120/1943.
82 CO 323/1831/ Part 2/4407/1943.
83 CO 875/18/9120/6/1942-3; CO 875/19/9131/1942-43; Parkinson, *op. cit.*, p. 68.
84 CO 323/1831 Part 2/4407/1943; CO 875/18/9120/1943.
85 The original wording read: 'with your permission, I should like to deal with the subject'. This was changed to: 'I do not intend to raise the subject myself, but if I am pressed on it, I should like your permission to deal with it.' The alterations were made in Stanley's own hand. CO 323/1858 Part 2/9057/B/1943.
86 Louis, *op. cit.*, pp. 255-6; cf. Morgan, V, p. 9.
87 *HC Debs.*, Vol. 391, cc. 47-151.
88 U3153/14/70 in FO 371/35311.
89 A8483/3/45 in FO 371/34093.
90 U3152/14/70 in FO 371/35311.
91 A9434/3/45 in FO 371/34094; A11033/3/45 in FO 371/34095.
92 CO 875/18/9120/1943; CO 875/19/9120/19 & 9120/20/1943. An additional reason for not placing an adviser in New York was the opposition this was likely to produce from the Ministry of Information.

5 FROM MOBILISATION TO RECONSTRUCTION

1 Arthur Marwick, *Britain in a Century of Total War* (London, Pelican edition, 1953), pp. 315-23.
2 Paul Addison, *The Road to 1945: British Politics and the Second World War* (London, 1975), p. 223.
3 See p. 17.
4 CO 852/503 Part 1/19037/33/1941 Part 5.
5 CO 859/78/12820/1943.
6 CO 554/132/33718/1943.
7 Albert O. Hirschman, *The Passions and the Interests* (Princeton, 1977), p. 177.

8 CO 323/1859/9063/1942-3; CO 554/132/33718/1943.
9 See Addison, *op. cit.*, Chapter 4 ('New Deal at Dunkirk').
10 *Ibid.*, p. 167.
11 CO 859/80/12841/1/1941.
12 Addison, *op. cit.*, p. 181; CO 323/1850/7740/1941.
13 See p. 183.
14 CO 323/1858/9051/1941.
15 CO 850/194/20804/1941-2.
16 *HL Debs.*, Vol. 119, cc. 715-16; *HC Debs.*, Vol. 373, c. 593.
17 CO 323/1858/9051/1941 (minute of 14 July 1941).
18 The minutes of only the first four meetings of the Post War Problems Committee have survived in CO 967/13; the committee papers are filed (1-80) in CO 852/503 Part 1/19037/33/1941, (81-128) in CO 852/504, and (129-163) in CO 852/505.
19 CO 323/1859/9063/1942-43.
20 CO 323/1859/9068/1942.
21 See pp. 166-7.
22 See Chapter 3.
23 *HC Debs.*, Vol. 380, c. 2015; also see p.
24 See pp. 59 ff.
25 CO 866/38/1546/1941-42.
26 See, for example, *The Position of the Colonies in a British Commonwealth of Nations* (1941), pp. 13-14; *Britain and her Dependencies* (1943), p. 29; *The Future of Colonial Peoples* (1944), p. 61.
27 *Britain and her Dependencies*, pp. 16-47; *Future of Colonial Peoples*, p. 52.
28 Sir Keith Hancock, *Argument of Empire* (London, 1943), pp. 106-7.
29 *Ibid.*, p. 111.
30 *Ibid.*, p. 120.
31 *Ibid.*, p. 99.
32 *Ibid.*, p. 136.
33 *Ibid.*, p. 159.
34 See pp. 157ff and CO 875/19/9120/19/1943.
35 Hancock, *op. cit.*, p. 156.
36 P. S. Gupta, *Imperialism and the British Labour Movement, 1914-1964* (London 1975), p. 275 ff; David Goldsworthy, *Colonial Issues in British Politics, 1945-1961* (Oxford, 1971), p. 121.
37 Goldsworthy, *op. cit.*, p. 121.
38 CO 323/1858 Part 1/9050/3/1943.
39 Gupta, *op. cit.*, pp. 275-84; Goldsworthy, *op. cit.*, p. 122.
40 As Clauson noted, in reference to *The Colonies*, Labour's 'closer contact with colonial realities has brought about a more realistic tone . . .'. CO 323/1858 Part 1/9050/3/1943.
41 The relevant file is CO 323/1831/4407/1943, on which the following account is based.
42 See pp. 140-1.
43 *HC Debs.*, Vol. 391, cc. 47-151. The points of emphasis in Stanley's speech were repeated in a booklet prepared by Sabine in conjunction with the Ministry of Information which appeared in October 1943 under the title *50 Facts about*

the Colonies; attention was drawn, for example, to the policy of education for self-government, and the shift from 'trusteeship' to 'partnership': CO 875/19/9120/8/1942-43.

44 *The Times*, 14 July 1943.
45 *Empire*, September 1943.
46 See p. 120.
47 This remark came at the end of the Commons speech of 13 July 1943.

6 THE DIMENSIONS OF PLANNING

1 CO/554/132/33718/1943.
2 In the period 1940-43 Benson worked on the staff of Major Desmond Morton, Churchill's Personal Assistant, whose chief function was to produce a daily selection of Ultra intercepts for the Prime Minister. Ronald Lewin, *Ultra goes to war: the secret story* (London, 1978), pp. 186-9.
3 EBN 97/43 discussed in CO 323/1859/9072/1943.
4 Furse asked for Benson's help for four to six weeks in the Appointments Department 'before he had got dug into his new work!' See CO 877/25/27253/4/1942-4.
5 CO 323/1859/8072/1943.
6 *Ibid.*
7 Schedule of work in CO 323/1858/9050/4/1943.
8 For this memorandum, with a covering note dated 16 August 1943, see CO 852/588/19260/1944; see also Morgan, I, p. 183.
9 See p. 78.
10 CO 852/503 Part 1/19037/33/1941 Part 5.
11 Italics added.
12 Benson's minute of 19 August 1943 in CO 852/588/1920/1944.
13 See No 3 on CO 852/588/19260/1944.
14 Clauson's special responsibility was for long-term commodity planning. Personal information from Sir G. Clauson; see also CO 323/1859/9072/1943.
15 CO 554/132/33718/1943.
16 CO 323/1859/9072/1943; minute, 29 June 1943.
17 See, for example, CO 852/587/19250/12/2/1944.
18 CO 866/30/1169/1942-6.
19 CO 866/39/1562/1942-5 and 1574/1943-7.
20 CO 866/31/1219/1943-5 and CO 866/39/1420/1939, 1941.
21 See p. 216.
22 CO 860/39/1580/1942-5.
23 From time to time officials toyed with the idea of setting up a 'colonial' Chatham House; see CO 323/1831 Part 2/4431/1943 on efforts to see whether officials might benefit from corporate subscriptions.
24 CO 866/30/1619/1942-6.
25 CO 967/16.
26 See pp. 40-2.
27 12905/1C/1943, 12905/9/1941-3 and 12905/14/1942 in CO 859/81. The CDWAC met seven times in the year following June 1942, but only four times in that following June 1943.

28   CO 859/75/12810/5/1941; the minutes of the meetings could not be found in 1948 when the Colonial Office Organisation Committee asked for them.

29   Personal information. Queen Anne's Gate and Palace Chambers are close to the Houses of Parliament, while Park Street is some distance away in Mayfair.

30   CO 859/75/12810/5/1943.

31   *HC Debs.*, Vol. 376, cc. 507-71; *HL Debs.*, Vol. 121, cc. 3-26, 107-36.

32   CO 859/59/12281/1941-2.

33   Shuckburgh, Vol. IV, Part 6, pp. 120-1, says that CLAC was introduced at the end of 1941.

34   CO 859/75/12810/10/1942-3.

35   CO 859/77/12818/1943.

36   Personal information.

37   CO 866/33/1327/1/1943-8.

38   Sir Kenneth Blackburne, *Lasting Legacy* (London, 1976), pp. 67-75.

39   See *ibid.*, pp. 76-91 and below p. 220.

40   For the accommodation of 'science', see especially pp. 205, 207-8.

41   See pp. 157-8.

42   CO 852/503 Part 1/19037/20/1943.

43   CO 852/543/15483/3/1944.

44   CO 852/555/16601/1944 Parts 1 and 2; CRC(44)132.

45   CO 852/543/15583/3/1944: CRC(44)105.

46   *HL Debs.*, Vol. 128, cc. 557-8.

47   Cmd 6486 (1943); see CO 859/79/12831/3/1943.

48   CO 859/79/12830/1/1942.

49   See p. 88.

50   See pp. 19, 42-3.

51   CSC 5/305 and 308.

52   See CO 967/14 and CO 866/40/1678/4/1941: minute, 18 December 1941.

53   No 3 on CO 859/68/12627/1943 summarises the nutrition organisation.

54   Personal information from Dr Meyer.

55   CO 852/592/19350/9/1945 and 19350/1944.

56   See diagram CRC(45)135 in CO 900/2.

57   CO 859/79/12830/8/1943; the law group's report was discussed in CO 323/1878/9317/1944; a housing group was also formed in 1944-45, see CO 859/125/12830/23/1944, and CO 927/7/28046/1/1945 and 2/1945.

58   CO 901/1: CSSRC minutes.

59   See p. 189.

60   CO 899/1: minutes of the Council.

61   CO 323/1851 Part 2/4413/1942.

62   CO 859/84/12003/9/1944-46.

63   See pp. 215-6.

64   F.S.V. Donnison, *Civil Affairs and Military Government: central organisation and planning* (London, 1966), p. 42, describes the British organisation, settled largely after the July 1943 meeting of ministers; see GEN 6/3rd in CAB 78/5.

65   For an historical survey of the Anglo-American discussions under Article VII see BT 11/2403.

66 For a summary of negotiation, see the Dominions Office confidential prints, DO 114/79 and 102. The main Colonial Office files are 13716/1942-3 Parts 1-5 in CO 968/53 continued on 22934/1944 in CO 937/32.

67 CO 859/81/12862/1/1943.

68 Even the Resident Minister's office in West Africa could, in London's view, become excessive in its demands for information. See, for example, CO 554/133/33824/1942-43.

69 CO 967/10: minutes 10 and 13 June 1940.

70 See pp. 127-8.

71 Surveys of constitutional studies: CPP 27 (21 August 1941) and CPP 110 (28 January 1942), see CO 852/503 Part 1/19037/33/1941.

72 Martin Wight, *The Development of the Legislative Council, 1606-1945* (London, 1946), p. 7.

73 Goldsworthy, *op. cit.*, p. 124.

74 The Colonial Office Organisation Committee (1948-49) considered these possibilities; see pp. 253-4.

75 Shuckburgh, Vol. IV, Part 6, pp. 103-17.

76 Prem. 4/43A/4: the Southern Rhodesia Armoured Car Regiment moved in on 5 October 1942.

77 For example, see CO 583/263/30554/1943.

78 CO 866/15/1007/1944-47. The official eventually appointed to work with Poynton was K.E. Robinson.

79 See pp. 125-6.

80 See Eastwood's comment about 'having our finger in all the post-war pies'. quoted above p. 161.

7 THE WORK OF RECONSTRUCTION

1 CO 847/18/47029/1940; CO 859/45/12041/1941 and 1943.

2 CO 847/21/47029/1942-43.

3 CO 859/45/12041/1941-43.

4 Cmd 6647 (1945), *Report of the Committee on Higher Education in the Colonies*.

5 *Ibid.*

6 Jeffries, *Whitehall and the Colonial Service*, p. 33.

7 *Ibid.*, p. 29.

8 For replies to the circular, see CO 850/195/20807/3/1943.

9 Jeffries, *Whitehall and the Colonial Service*, pp. 29-31.

10 CO 850/215/20807/1944-45.

11 Jeffries, *Whitehall and the Colonial Service*, pp. 32-3.

12 CO 877/24/27576/2/1943.

13 Col No 198 (1946), *Post-War Training for the Colonial Service*.

14 Jeffries, *Whitehall and the Colonial Service*, p. 39.

15 CO 927/37/28047/Part 1/45-7; CO 795/125/45355/2/43.

16 CSSRC (44) 23 and (45) 30 in CO 901/2; and CO 927/2/28021/1/1944.

17 Harold Laski, *Reflections on the Revolutions of Our Time* (London, 1943), p. 37.

18 See pp. 168 ff.

19   CO 554/132/33718/1/1943.

20   See above p. 174.

21   See Susan Howson and Donald Winch, *The Economic Advisory Council, 1930-39* (Cambridge, 1977); Anthea Bennett, 'Advising the Cabinet — the Committee of Civil Research and Economic Advisory Council: A Brief Comparison', *Public Administration*, liv (1978), pp. 51-71; and Morgan, I, pp. 181-96.

22   CO 852/587/19250/7/1944 and CO 852/586/19250/2/1944.

23   Lewis was appointed as a Temporary Administration Officer attached to the Financial Adviser's Department. See EBN 110 (28 September 1943) in CO 878/27.

24   CO 852/510 Part 4/19250/1943; CO 852/588/19260/1944.

25   The following discussion of the CEAC's deliberations is based on 19260/1944 and 19260/66/1944 in CO 852/588; 19250/1943 Parts 1 and 2, 19250/3/1943 and 19250/5/1943 in CO 852/510 Part 4; 19250/1944 and 19250/2/1944 in CO 852/586.

26   See CO 852/1003/19934/1947; minute by Caine, 23 April 1946.

27   The memorandum is No 28 on CO 852/588/19260/1944; Morgan, I, pp. 191-3, provides a verbatim list of the questions and answers.

28   The Office had in fact been interested in conducting a systematic survey of native land tenure in Africa since 1939, and from late 1943 the General Department, in conjunction with the Africa Division, began to give serious consideration to the question. A special land tenure committee established under Lord Hailey produced a report in 1944 outlining the general principles and problems involved, and advocating improved machinery for the gathering of information. Significantly enough, it was decided that the report should only be referred to the CEAC after it had been sent to the African Governors: CO 847/19/47084/1940; CO 847/21/47084/1941 and 47084/1943; CO 847/24/47084/1944 and 47084/1944-46.

29   See CO 852/588/19260/1944.

30   Disagreements between Durbin and Lewis on the one hand, and Caine on the other, were beginning to surface as early as 1943. See CO 323/1859/9092/1943; and CO 852/510 Part 4 and 19250/1943 Part 2.

31   CO 852/588/19260/1944.

32   *Ibid.*; minute of 13 November 1944.

33   Lewis' resignation minute appears on CO 852/586/19250/2/1944.

34   See p. 171.

35   CO 852/586/19250/1945.

36   CO 323/1858/9050/4/1943.

37   Cmd 6422 (1943); CO 859/81/12905/1941-43. During the first four years of the CDW Act's operation, only £4 million out of a possible £20 million had actually been spent: CO 852/588/19260/1944. See especially Morgan, I, pp. 198 ff.

38   See p. 179.

39   CO 859/126/12905/1/1944 and 12905/1C/1944.

40   CO 852/588/19275/1944; Louis, *op. cit.*, pp. 102-3.

41   CO 852/588/19260/1944; minutes of 9th CEAC meeting.

42   CO 852/588/19275/1944.

43 Blackburne, *op. cit.*, p. 80.
44 Louis, *op. cit.*, p. 101.
45 CO 852/588/19260/1944: minutes 9th CEAC meeting.
46 *Ibid.*
47 *Ibid.*
48 CO 323/1831 Part 2/4433/1942-43.
49 CO 323/1831 Part 2/4436/1943-44.
50 CO 318/449/71251; CO 318/471/71357/1944-45.
51 Sir Robert Stanley, *King George's Keys* (London, 1975), p. 122; Blackburne, *op. cit.*, p. 78.
52 CO 318/449/71238/1943.
53 CO 318/499/71238/17/1941.
54 CO 554/132/33718/4/1943.
55 CO 795/125/45355/2/1943.
56 The following account is based on the files in CO 825/35, 42B, 42C; CO 273/677; CO 865/1-5; and WO 32/10200. See especially 55104/1/1943 and 55104/6/1943 in CO 825/35; 55104/1/1944 and 55104/1C/1944 in CO 825/42B; CO 55104/15/1944 and 1945 in CO 825/42C. See also Thorne, *op. cit.*, pp. 459, 606-7 and Stockwell, *op. cit.*
57 See. 121, 124-5, and CO 825/35/55104/1942 and 55104/1A/1942.
58 See p. 67.
59 CO 318/447/71015/1942.
60 CO 318/453/71295/1/1942-43.
61 Col No 187 (1944).
62 CO 318/466/71295/1945.
63 See pp. 99 ff. Prem. 3/502/7 describes the difference of opinion between the Resident Minister and the Secretary of State on post-war organisation.
64. CO 554/139/33768/1944-45: the Secretary of State saw the four Governors in October 1945, see CO 554/140/33780/1945.
65 See p. 93.
66 CO 822/114/46523/1944.
67 See p. 96.
68 Wight, *op. cit.*, pp. 136-7, 170-2.
69 CO 866/35/1367/1/43/1943-44.
70 CO 96/782/31499/1945; minute 16 July 1945.
71 Goldsworthy, *op. cit.*, pp. 124-5 shows that the Fabian Colonial Bureau gave priority to West Africa.
72 CO 584/131/33702/1942.
73 CO 554/132/33712/1/1943.
74 CO 584/132/33727/1943.
75 CO 554/133/33732/1943.
76 See note 74: telegram 15 September 1943.
77 For Jamaica, see CO 137/849/68714/1941, 1942, 1943; for Ceylon, see CO 54/980 Part 1/55541/1941.
78 For a detailed account of British and American deliberations during this phase see Louis *op. cit.*, pp. 274-573. Also see Thorne, *op. cit.*, pp. 592-604.
79 CO 323/1877/9057/B/1944; *Post-War Foreign Policy Preparation*, p. 201; Louis, *op. cit.*, Chapter 17.

80   Louis, *op. cit.*, p. 286.
81   CO 323/1859 Part 2/9057/B/1943; CO 323/1877/9086/1944; CO 968/ 157/14811/10/1944; U910/910/70 in FO 371/40749. For the role of regionalism in organising world affairs, see the FO Research Department paper 'Regional Organisation' on CO 323/1877/9086/1944; for the Australia-New Zealand Agreement over the South Seas Regional Council see Louis, *op. cit.*, Chapter 18.
82   See the files 14814/1B-1H covering the Western Pacific, East Africa, West Africa, the Caribbean, the Middle East, Central Africa, and South East Asia in CO 969/158 and 159. For the Office's regional planning in early 1944, see also Louis, *op. cit*, Chapter 19.
83   CO 323/1877/9086/1944.
84   *Ibid.*
85   U2238/210 in FO 371/40749; CO 323/1877/9057/B/1944; Louis, *op. cit.*, Chapter 20.
86   U3408, U3444, U3587, U3625/190/180 in FO 371/40749; Ruth B. Russell, *A History of the United Nations Charter* (Washington, 1958), pp. 175-7; Louis *op. cit.*, pp. 327-34.
87   DPM(44) 3rd meeting in CAB 99/27; GEN 32 series in CAB 78/20; WP(44) 211 in CAB 66/49; WM(44)58 in CAB 65/42; U3625/190/180 in FO 371/40749; CO 968/158/14814/1/1944-45; Louis, *op. cit.*, Chapter 21.
88   WP(44) 211 in CAB 66/49.
89   See p. 197.
90   CO 968/156/1411A Part 1/1944; U6683, U6731/180/70 in FO 371/ 40703.
91   See Louis, *op. cit.*, Chapters 4,22, and 23; Cordell Hull. *The Memoris of Cordell Hull* (London, 1948), II, p. 1599.
92   Louis, *op. cit.*, Chapter 24.
93   CO 968/160/14814/11/1944.
94   *Ibid.*
95   The following account is based on CO 968/160/14814/11/1944; also see Louis, *op. cit.*, Chapter 25.
96   Louis, *op. cit.*, p. 463.
97   WP(44)738 in CAB 66/59.
98   *Ibid.*; WM(44)172 in CAB 65/44; see Morgan, V, pp. 10-13.
99   Louis, *op. cit.*, Chapter 29; W.H. McNeill, *America, Britain and Russia: their cooperation and conflict* (London, 1953), p. 554; Russell, *op. cit.*, pp. 540-41; Sherwood, *op. cit.*, p. 865.
100   CO 968/161/14814/11 Part 1/1945; Louis, *op. cit.*, Chapters 28 and 30.
101   CO 968/161/14814/11 Part I/1945, WM(45) 200 in CAB 66/64; WM(45) 38 in CAB 65/50. The colonies, unlike the Dominions, had always been excluded from deliberations on the international order.
102   14817/1/1944 and 1945 in CO 968/165 and 166.
103   CO 733/444 Part 1/75872/A/1943; CO 733/461 Part 1/75872 Parts 1 and 2; CO 733/461 Part 2/75872/1945 Part 1; CO 968/164/14814/21/ 1945. For Palestine policy see Michael J. Cohen, 'The British White Paper on Palestine, May 1939; Part II: The Testing of a Policy', *The Historical Journal*, xix (1976), pp. 727-58, and *Palestine: Retreat from Mandate, the*

making of British Policy, 1936-1945 (London, 1978).

104 WP(45)228 in CAB 66/64; WM(45)42 in CAB 65/50; for this conference and the background to the Australia-New Zealand views on trusteeship, see Louis, *op. cit.*, Chapters 26 and 32.

105 CO 968/161/14814/11/1945 Part 1; Russell, *op. cit.*, 586-9; Louis, *op. cit.*, Chapter 31.

106 The following account is based on CO 968/161/14814/11 Parts 2 and 3/ 1945. See also Russell, *op. cit.*, pp. 808-42; Louis, *op. cit.*, Chapters 33 and 34, and Thorne, *op. cit.*, pp. 602-4.

107 WP(45)300 in CAB 66/65; WM(45)61 in CAB 65/50.

108 CO 968/161/14814/11 Part 3/1945. The assessment of Fraser's chairmanship was Poynton's.

109 *Ibid.*

110 CO 968/157/14811F/1/1945; CO 968/164/14814/11/12 and 13/1945.

111 CO 968/164/14814/12/1944-45.

112 Louis, *op. cit.*, p. 535.

113 McNeill, *op. cit.*, p. 597.

8 THE EFFECTS OF WAR

1 See p. 17.

2 *The Times*, 10 January 1945.

3 Shuckburgh, Vol. IV, Part 9, p. 113.

4 *Ibid.*, p. 120.

5 *Ibid.*, p. 117.

6 See p. 163.

7 *HC Debs.*, Vol 380, cc. 2002-124.

8 Ronald Lewin, *Churchill as Warlord* (London, 1973), p. 171.

9 L.S. Amery, *The Awakening* (London, 1948), especially pp. 82-93, 175-6.

10 See p. 159.

11 *HC Debs.*, Vol. 401, c. 223.

12 Shuckburgh, Vol. IV, Part 9, p. 116.

13 For examples of reforms proposed, see Private Office file CO 967/10.

14 L.S. Amery, *The Forward View* (London, 1935), p. 236.

15 *The Times*, 13 March 1942; Margery Perham *op. cit.*, pp. 223-31.

16 CO 877/26/27265/23D and 26A/1945.

17 Cmd 7167 (1947), para. 93.

18 CO 877/28/27311/1945.

19 The subject was investigated by the Select Committee on Estimates, see HC 181 — I (1947-8), p. 10, Q. 90.

20 Sir A. S. MacNalty (ed), *The Civilian Health and Medical Services,* II (London, 1955).

21 Cmd 7167 (1947), para. 59.

22 *Ibid.*, para. 77.

23 *Ibid.*, para. 80.

24 CO 866/2/1045/1945-6: No 1.

25 The report of the Colonial Office Organisation Committee is confidential print No 516, see CO 885/118. The files on the committee are in CO 866/ 49 and 50.

26 CO 847/25/47234/1946.

27 CO 847/36/47238/1947.

INDEX

285